Death Valley
and the
Northern Mojave

A VISITOR'S GUIDE

William C. Tweed and Lauren Davis

Cachuma Press
Los Olivos, California

Writers: William C. Tweed and Lauren Davis
Editors: John Evarts and Marjorie Popper
Graphic Production: Katey O'Neill
Cartographer: Suzi Kuromiya
Printed in Singapore

Library of Congress Cataloging-in-Publication Data

Tweed, William C.
   Death Valley and the Northern Mojave: a visitor's guide / William C. Tweed and Lauren Davis.
     p. cm
   Includes bibliographical references (p.) and index.
   ISBN 0-9628505-7-8 (pb. : alk. paper)
    1. Death Valley (Calif. and Nev.)--Guidebooks. 2. Mojave Desert (Calif.)--Guidebooks.
   I. Davis, Lauren, 1955- II. Title.

F868.D2T88 2003
917.94'870454--dc21

                               2003055159

We appreciate the contribution of many individuals who read portions of the manuscript and offered technical corrections, clarified important details, and provided invaluable advice. For their multiple reviews of the text, we would like to extend a special thanks to biologist Janet Westbrook of Ridgecrest and to the interpretive staff at Death Valley National Park led by Coralee Hays and Terry Baldino. We also wish to thank the following reviewers for their comments and assistance: Dave Barajas, Marta Beckett, Brian Brown, Pat Brown-Berry, Lloyd Brubaker, Margaret Brush, Michael J. Conner, Chip Cramer, Blair Davenport, Marty Dickes, Chris Fairclough, Mark Faull, Marydith Haughton, Stephen Ingram, Cliff Lawson, Bill Michaels, James Morefield, Robert Norris, Beth Porter, Bruce M. Pavlik, Denyse Racine, Myrt Railey, Patrick Shields, Steve Smith, Beth and David St. George, Doug Treloff, Elva Younkin, Darrell Wong, and Lauren Wright.

Front Cover: *Death Valley Sand Dunes.* LEWIS KEMPER
Back Cover: *Amargosa River and the Black Mountains.* FRED HIRSCHMANN
Title Page: *Badwater and the Panamint Range.* CHUCK PLACE

Contents

Red Rock Canyon is one of the desert jewels of California's State Park System. The park's 28,000 acres encompass a diverse flora, including the Mojave's signature plant—the Joshua tree. WILLIAM SMITHEY

Death Valley National Park and the Northern Mojave contain many historic mining sites, such as this tunnel in Wildrose Canyon. Most mineshafts are too dangerous to enter, and they should serve only as reminders of the risks and hardships encountered by early-day prospectors who scoured the region in search of mineral wealth.
MARC SOLOMON

Contents

Contents

The wetlands of Grimshaw Lake Natural Area near Tecopa are recognized for their sensitive biological resources by the Bureau of Land Management, which administers large areas of the Northern Mojave. DAVID LANNER

Introduction

A century ago, in a tiny, isolated town at the eastern base of California's great Sierra Nevada, there lived a woman driven to write. A congenital rebel against Victorian sensibilities, she did not write about schooled urban people or civilization's lush, well-tended gardens; instead, she wrote about the harsh empty land and solitary people who shared her life. In 1903 she penned what would become the best remembered of her books. Turning to the great arid country to the east of her home she wrote:

You may come into the borders of it from the south by a stage journey that has the effect of involving a great lapse of time, or from the north by rail, dropping out of the overland route at Reno. The best way of all is over the Sierra passes by pack and trail, seeing and believing. But the real heart and core of the country are not to be come at in a month's vacation. One must summer and winter with the land and wait its occasions. Pine woods that take two and three seasons to the ripening of cones, roots that lie by in the sand seven years awaiting a growing rain, firs that grow fifty years before flowering—these do not scrape acquaintance.

—Mary Austin, *Land of Little Rain*

Mary Austin's "land of little rain" embraces a huge desert area where there are no cities, no lush fields of corn, and no railways. Austin was looking beyond the well-watered Owens Valley corridor to the arid wildlands of the Northern Mojave—a land with no lakes or large flowing rivers, no towering forests, and no green pastures.

Once, not so long ago, there were cities here, and the desert still bears their remains; there were railways, too, and their linear, overgrown scars still connect ghost towns. Lakes and large rivers, too, once existed here, but the ancient watercourses have stood mostly mute and empty for several millennia now. And scattered forests and pastures do exist, only

Above: Death Valley and its vast, salt-encrusted playa was regarded as a landscape of utter desolation by the first pioneers and explorers to enter the region. WILLARD CLAY
Opposite: This famous vista point in the Panamint Range is named after Pete Aguereberry, an early-day prospector who appreciated the austere beauty of the Northern Mojave. SCOTT T. SMITH

Like many other scenic destinations in the Northern Mojave, the Ibex Dunes are isolated yet relatively accessible. STEPHEN INGRAM

they are remote and hidden, invisible to all but the patient and determined.

What there is, more than anything else, is spaciousness. Here there are mountains—almost the whole landscape, it seems, consists of mountains—ridge after ridge, each rising thousands of feet into the dry desert air, and each framed by deep, often narrow basins. The mountains, at least the larger ones, have powerful, evocative names—Slate, Argus, Panamint, Last Chance, Cottonwood, Black, Funeral, Inyo, Grapevine, Greenwater, Owlshead—and the names tantalize those who love remote places. Between the ranges, the valleys are sparsely populated too. All are arid now, but many once held

lakes. Where there once was water, now there are white-crusted salt pans. Where Native Americans once hunted along rocky beaches, now the wind wears on desert gravel.

Like the landscape, the climate runs to extremes. In summer, the desert valleys are some of the hottest places on earth, with temperatures sometimes peaking 20° to 30°F above the century mark. In winter, arctic winds drift snow on the high ranges, in the process slowly wearing away the long-fallen logs of ancient pines. Almost always it is dry. The lowest valleys are among the driest places on the continent. But occasionally, especially at the hottest time of the year, violent, unpredictable, localized

storms drench the desert, releasing short-lived floods to scour the land.

And yet, if this land is empty by human terms, and undeniably hostile, it is occupied by its own unique assemblage of flora and fauna. Here, in this harsh hostility, live thousands of species of carefully adapted organisms—bushes and trees that live for thousands of years, animals that never drink water, wildflowers whose seed can remain viable for decades in the baked desert gravels waiting for the right moment to germinate and rush into ephemeral life.

Ultimately, it is a land that fascinates and captures. Again, Mary Austin said it well so long ago: "A land of lost rivers, with little in it to love; yet a land that once visited must be come back to inevitably. If it were not so there would be little told of it."

As Austin knew, there is much to tell, and this book attempts to tell some of it. The following pages strive to give the reader an understanding of what makes the region unique—its dynamic geology, its fine-tuned biology, its boom and bust human history—and then to share some special places, places where an informed traveler might gain insights into the desert's stony heart.

This book embraces a region that provokes diverging addresses from practitioners of different human disciplines. To biologists, it is the borderland where the Mojave Desert meets the Great Basin Desert, and where their distinctive life forms intermix. To geographers, this area lies within the Great Basin, a part of the American West where all drainage is internal. To geologists, it belongs to the huge Basin and Range Province that extends from Oregon to Mexico. To political scientists, it comprises much of Inyo County, California, and small portions of neighboring Kern and San Bernardino counties. To historians, it takes in well-known places like Death Valley, Randsburg, and Skidoo, and much lesser known surrounding country like the Saline, Eureka, and Panamint valleys. For the purposes of this book, this region will be called simply the "Northern Mojave."

As complex and vast as the Northern Mojave seems, it has a strong unity of character. A series of tall desert mountain ranges and deep intervening basins dominate the landscape, all of them trending north-south. The mountain ranges are high—the Inyos and Panamints have summits that exceed 10,000 feet. Between the mountains, the desert valleys are deep and low; the lowest, Death Valley, actually drops to 282 feet below sea level. The result is a strikingly consistent yet endlessly varied landscape.

Historically, there also is unity. Before the mid-nineteenth century, Native Americans of the Western

Shoshone, Paiute, and Kawaiisu cultures lived undisturbed across the entire region. Then, after initial cursory exploration by fur trappers, traders, and lost '49ers, determined prospectors and miners assumed the lead. For half a century, mining enthusiasm broke across the country periodically like oceanic tsunami, scattering miners, teamsters, shopkeepers, and other entrepreneurs into remote, short-lived towns. In most areas, ranching was the only industry that endured after the mines played out. Later, as the Northern Mojave's mining booms faded, the transportation network that was left behind allowed the beginnings of tourism into the remote and largely empty region. Ultimately, tourism led to a totally different view of the landscape and its significance.

What are the boundaries of the Northern Mojave region? The area forms a rough triangle. Its western boundary follows the Indian Wells and Rose valleys—much like the modern route of Highways 14 and 395—and then runs north to Owens Valley and the Inyo Mountains. The eastern edge approximates the California/Nevada state line as it takes its long southeasterly tangent towards the Colorado River. The Garlock fault, a major east-west trending fault zone, marks the southern edge of the region. The fault is a feature better known to geologists than travelers. It

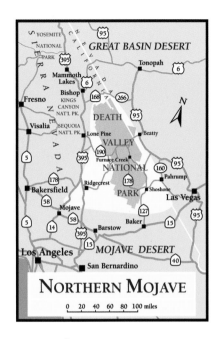

NORTHERN MOJAVE

0 20 40 60 80 100 miles

runs east from Interstate 5 near Gorman, passes north of Mojave, California, crosses Highway 395 just north of Randsburg, and slashes south of the Trona area to its junction with the Death Valley fault zone near the Avawatz Mountains. (For a complete regional map, see inside back cover.)

Most of the book's focus lies within this huge triangle. It is a land Mary Austin described as beginning south of Yosemite and east of the Sierra Nevada and continuing "east and south over a very great assemblage of broken ranges beyond Death Valley, and on illimitably into the Mojave Desert."

—William C. Tweed

Desert Travel Advice

An enjoyable trip to Death Valley and the Northern Mojave begins with advance planning. Traveling safely in this region of temperature extremes and great aridity requires assembling more than road maps and personal gear. You will also need to carry adequate water supplies and adhere to basic desert safety rules. Temperatures vary widely throughout the year (see "Northern Mojave Temperature and Precipitation Averages" on back flap), and your travel preparations need to take into account the season and the elevations of your destinations.

Desert travel in warm-weather months presents the clearest challenge because humans lack the special adaptive features possessed by desert flora and fauna. We can, however, emulate the behavior of desert animals by avoiding activity during the heat of the day. Midday temperatures registering 110°F are common during the summer, and even if you are resting in the shade, you may lose one quart of water per hour through perspiration. If this water is not replenished, you will become dehydrated. Estimates of a person's daily water needs in the desert vary from one to six gallons per day depending on temperature and level of activity.

Exposure to high temperatures also poses the risk of heat exhaustion and heat stroke. Heat exhaustion is less serious than heat stroke, but both conditions require immediate attention to avoid injury or, in the case of heat stroke, even death. Protecting yourself from direct sun and wearing appropriate clothing are important ways to minimize these risks.

Here are some recommendations from experienced desert travelers that should help you enjoy a safe desert trip:

1. If possible, travel with another party. This is especially important when exploring more isolated parts of the region. Inform a reliable person about your travel itinerary and be sure to tell them when you return.
2. Dress appropriately. Lightweight layers of natural-fiber clothing help keep you cool; wide-brimmed hats reduce sun exposure. Don't forget sunglasses and plenty of sunscreen.

This lightly traveled dirt road in Death Valley National Park is typical of many routes in the region. A safe desert trip begins with proper preparation and planning. JIM STIMSON

Bring warm-weather clothing for travel to higher elevations where desert nights are cool, even in summer, and cold in winter.

3. Carry plenty of water. Absolute minimum recommendations are one gallon per person per day with an extra five gallons for the vehicle you are driving.

4. Be watchful for signs of heat exhaustion or heat stroke. Both conditions require treatment. A person with heat exhaustion will experience weakness, nausea, headaches, and clammy skin. If you experience heat exhaustion, rest in a cool place, drink water, and get medical help as soon as you can. Heat stroke occurs when the body's temperature-regulating mechanism ceases to function properly. A person with heat stroke has a very high body temperature. He may either sweat profusely or stop sweating entirely. Soak down a heat stroke victim with water and fan him to cool him off. Seek medical attention immediately for sufferers of heat stroke.

5. Stay out of mine shafts. Cave-ins are a real risk due to rotting timbers and unstable rock formations. Concentrations of methane, carbon monoxide, carbon dioxide, or hydrogen sulfide gas can accumulate inside the underground passages. Vegetation or decaying boards may conceal vertical shafts hundreds of feet deep.

6. Make sure your vehicle is in good working order. Check fluid levels and have plenty of fuel. Take an additional quart or two of oil as a safety precaution, and bring a one-foot square, one-inch thick piece of plywood or a piece of carpet to use beneath your tire jack in sandy conditions. It is advisable to bring an extra spare tire or fix-a-flat materials when traveling to isolated areas. Carry spare keys, flares, some basic tools, a flashlight, extra batteries and a cell phone; there is no guarantee that a cell phone will get reception in remote basins of the Northern Mojave.

7. Beware of flash floods and keep watch for thunderclouds over the mountains. A mountain thunderstorm can release large quantities of water. The word "flash" is a good adjective to describe just how fast floodwaters may reach dry washes several miles away.

8. Be sure to acquire the necessary backcountry permits for camping where applicable.

Leave No Trace

Travelers in the desert need to be aware not only of their own safety but of the fragility of the land they are passing through. An arid climate that preserves fossils and artifacts of past cultures can also retain tracks and trash left behind by humans for tens, even hundreds of years.

Visitors can help protect the desert environment by following simple "Leave no Trace" ethics that are designed to help them tread lightly. Here are some of the key guidelines: Drive vehicles only on established roads and jeep trails. Do not drive through riparian areas or on mud hills that are easily scarred by churning wheels. Use established campgrounds, and if none are available, choose an area free from vegetation with a durable surface such as sand. Avoid locations with desert pavement to prevent damage to the varnish on the pavement's surface rocks, and be sure to camp at least 200 feet away from desert water sources. Wildlife depends heavily on natural seeps, springs, and streams for survival, and keeping your distance helps protect them from human waste and other pollutants.

The National Antiquities Act of 1906 and the Archeological Resource Protection Act of 1979 prohibit disturbance or collection of artifacts. Consider yourself lucky if you encounter an arrowhead or a potsherd, but leave them in place. Observe and photograph petroglyphs and pictographs but leave them untouched for future generations to study and admire. (For more sources of information on desert travel, see "Visitor Resources in the Northern Mojave" on page 192.)

Northern Mojave Geology and Landforms

East away from the Sierras, south from Panamint and Amargosa, east and south many an uncounted mile, is the Country of Lost Borders. . . . There are hills, rounded, blunt, burned, squeezed up out of chaos, chrome and vermilion painted, aspiring to the snowline. Between the hills lie high level-looking plains full of intolerable sun glare, or narrow valleys drowned in a blue haze. The hill surface is streaked with ash drift and black, unweathered lava flows. After rains water accumulates in the hollows of small closed valleys, and, evaporating, leaves hard dry levels of pure desertness that get the local name of dry lakes. Where the mountains are steep and the rains heavy, the pool is never quite dry, but dark and bitter, rimmed about with the effloresence of alkaline deposits. . . .

Here you find the hot sink of Death Valley, or high rolling districts where the air has always a tang of frost. Here are the long heavy winds and breathless calms on the tilted mesas where dust devils dance, whirling up into a wide pale sky. Here you have no rain when all the earth cries for it, or quick downpours called cloud-bursts for violence. A land of lost rivers, with little in it to love; yet a land that once visited must be come back to inevitably. If it were not so there would be little told of it.

—Mary Austin,
The Land of Little Rain, *1903*

Opposite: The badlands of Death Valley's Twenty Mule Team Canyon are a good place to contemplate the dynamic processes of deposition and erosion. JEFF GNASS

At the Continent's Edge

To even the most casually curious of travelers, the landforms of the Northern Mojave region demand explanation. Why are there so many mountain ranges, all trending in the same direction? Why is the physical relief—the difference in elevation between the mountains and valleys—so extreme? What is the origin of the area's many dry lakes? Why in just a few places in the landscape are there huge sand dunes and elsewhere miles of boulders? What made the region a center for mining enterprises that extracted gold, silver, salt, borax, and even talc? For more than a century, scientists have sought answers to these questions and many others, attempting in the process to understand this stark and rugged land.

The imposing mountains, deep basins, and extreme aridity that now characterize the Northern Mojave are fairly recent developments in geologic time. Many of the rocks within the region, however, are relatively ancient. For decades, geologists have studied the region's rocks, and the local, successive stratas they comprise, known as formations. From this research they have assembled a history of this fascinating American landscape.

Although it may be hard to imagine, the land that is now the Northern Mojave bordered the western edge of a continent for several hundred million

The banded western face of the Panamint Range offers a sequential record of geologic history that spans several hundred million years. WILLIAM SMITHEY

years. During this time, a variety of marine sediments were laid down in shallow coastal waters and eventually became the building blocks for future mountains. Some of the region's oldest sedimentary formations date to the late Precambrian Era, which ended about 570 million years ago. A few are visible today, such as the 700-million-year-old marine deposits known as the Noonday dolomite found in Mosaic Canyon in the Panamint Range. There is still older rock in the Northern Mojave, however. It is found in the steep western face of the Black Mountains above Badwater, where intense faulting and

erosion has exposed metamorphic rock that is 1.8 billion years old. Rock of this age is usually covered by more recent layers, and exposures of it are rare.

At the beginning of the Paleozoic Era (570 to 245 million years ago), much of the Northern Mojave consisted of vast tidal flats along the edge of a fluctuating coastline. Great deposits of sand washed down from eroding mountains, and along with layers of mud, formed sedimentary deposits. Some of these early Paleozoic formations are seen on the road to Aguereberry Point, including the light-colored band of Eureka quartzite that is prominent at the overlook.

Starting about 550 million years ago, and continuing for another 300 million years, the Northern Mojave began to witness a slow accumulation of carbonate sediments. During much of this time the North American plate, which was the precursor to the modern continent of the same name, drifted near the equator and experienced a tropical climate. Over an immense span of time, sediments originating primarily from coral reefs and tropical lagoons and containing large amounts of carbonates accumulated in the marine basins that would later be part of the Northern Mojave landmass. As a result, carbonate-based rocks such as limestone and dolomite are relatively widespread in the region, with concentrations in the Panamints, Grapevine Mountains, and Kingston Range. These rocks weather very slowly in the dry desert climate and today are exposed in some spectacular gorges and mountain faces like Titus Canyon and the Last Chance Range above Eureka Valley.

Most of the Paleozoic Era was characterized by a quiet accumulation of horizontally deposited sedimentary beds in shallow waters along the continental margin. Radical changes in the tectonic character of the region began about 250 million years ago, and a long period of relative geologic stability came to an end.

Much of today's Northern Mojave was once beneath a shallow sea along the western edge of the continent. Some of the region's oldest sedimentary rocks are marine deposits that date from this time, including the 700 million-year-old Noonday dolomite seen in Mosaic Canyon. ERIC WUNROW

Plate Tectonics and the Northern Mojave

The Northern Mojave is one of the premiere zones of dynamic tectonic activity, or tectonism, on the North American continent. The region's geologic history and current landforms are better appreciated with some understanding of plate tectonics.

The concept of plate tectonics was developed in the twentieth century and is now universally accepted. It proposes that earth's outer, rigid shell, which is known as the lithosphere and is composed of the crust and upper mantle, floats above a semi-fluid molten layer that underlies it. This lower mantle layer is in continuous motion, with the hotter mantle

Striped Butte's contorted and folded layers are the result of the tectonic forces that have—and continue to—shape the Northern Mojave. DAN SUZIO

rising then sinking as it cools, creating giant circular currents. Sections of the lithosphere, known as plates, shift slowly in response to the currents below. Sometimes these plates collide, forming huge mountain chains such as the Himalayas or the Alps. In other areas the plates spread apart, and magma rises from the fluid zone below to form new rock near or on the earth's surface in "spreading zones." The overall effect is similar to the action of ice floes on slowly moving water. Where ice floes collide, pressure ridges of ice are pushed up; where they diverge, cracks form and water rises from below and then freezes, forming new ice. And like ice floes, tectonic plates are capable of more complex movements, including one plate being forced beneath another.

The movements of earth's plates are very subtle and would go unnoticed in a human time-scale were it not for reminders like earthquakes. It takes millions of years to create or erode major landforms, and it is hard to imagine that the landscape we see today is entirely different from what existed thousands or millions of years ago.

Colliding Plates and Magma Plumes

During the Mesozoic era (245 to 65 million years ago), the westward-moving North American plate and the eastward-creeping oceanic Pacific plate pressed against each other with increasing force. Eventually, the North American plate rode up and over the heavier Pacific plate, while the latter plunged as much as 50 miles beneath it, often at a steep angle. This process of subduction, in which one plate is forced or dragged (subducted) beneath another, occurs because plates often differ in their relative densities; some are lighter than others, with the heaviest plates usually being those originating beneath the sea.

As the Pacific plate was subducted beneath the North American plate, resulting friction generated an enormous amount of heat. The heat was augmented as the oceanic plate sank into progressively hotter parts of the mantle, melting some of the rock that was being subducted. This newly molten material (magma) began a slow rise toward the surface, and some of it ultimately breached the crust, emerging in a chain of volcanoes paralleling the subduction zone along the continent's edge. Lava flows, some thousands of feet thick, combined with the uplift of coastal mountains, eventually pushed the ocean more than 200 miles to the west. The Northern Mojave was no longer at the continent's edge.

Most of the magma plumes generated by this plate subduction never reached the surface. Instead, they intruded deep into the overlying crust, deforming and metamorphosing the surface rock; they gradually cooled—over millions of years—and congealed into crystallized formations known as plutons. The largest plutons, called batholiths, measured nearly 40 square miles in size and remained beneath the surface until subsequent episodes of uplift and erosion later exposed them.

Granite, the hard, crystalline, "salt and pepper" rock seen in mountains from Baja California northward through California to Alaska is a plutonic rock most travelers easily recognize. Large areas of granite can be seen in the western part of the Northern Mojave, particularly in the Inyo, Cottonwood, and Argus mountains. Granite is also exposed along Wildrose Road in Emigrant Canyon. The region's youngest granites are visible in the Panamints near Telescope Peak and in the Funeral and Greenwater ranges. The most dramatic Mesozoic batholith, however, is the granite massif of the Sierra Nevada, which juts two miles above Owens Valley to cast a long rain shadow over the Northern Mojave.

The rising magma that congealed into granite had another important effect: it heated ground water and

The Northern Mojave's granite, such as this outcrop in Butte Valley, formed as magma intruded into the earth's crust during tectonic plate subductions. FRED HIRSCHMANN

A body of igneous rock created this dark dike that slices through Surprise Canyon, an area of the Panamints that teemed with miners in the nineteenth century. FRED HIRSCHMANN

formed hot solutions that invaded joints, fractures, and cavities in overlying rock. Minerals that precipitated from these hot solutions reacted with surrounding rock and eventually cooled to form what are known as hydrothermal veins. Some of the veins held concentrations of gold, silver, zinc, and lead. Much later, rock formations containing these veins were uplifted and eroded. Some would become centers of intense mining interest.

The Modern Landscape Takes Shape

In comparison to the intense geologic activity of the late Mesozoic, much of the Cenozoic era (65 million years ago to present) that followed was relatively quiet, dominated by slow weathering of the landscape. About 30 million years ago the Pacific and North American plates changed the relative direction of their motion. Subduction along the California coast gave way to diagonal shear as the two plates began to slide past each other. The result was modern California, where the land to the west of the San Andreas fault zone is moving north in relation to the remainder of the continent.

As recently as 14 million years ago, however, the Northern Mojave still bore no physical resemblance to the modern landscape. The major building blocks were present at that time, but there was no hint of the current structure. Beneath the surface were masses of Mesozoic granites, as well as even larger complexes of Paleozoic marine sediments, many of them severely cooked and deformed by the granites that had invaded them. What was missing was the topography we today associate with the region—the dominant pattern of deep basins and high ranges.

It would take additional major tectonic activity to create the immense Basin and Range province, which extends from southeastern Oregon to northwestern Mexico and includes the Northern Mojave. The Basin and Range took shape as the Pacific plate began sliding north in relation to the North American plate while also pulling away from it, causing the region to stretch in an east-west direction. As a result of this extension, the earth's crust in the area was uplifted and elongated, causing it to break into parallel blocks that run north-south, or at right angles to the axis of elongation. These blocks were tilted and pulled apart in response to the elongation, creating a distinct landscape pattern of parallel mountains and valleys. (The Basin and Range geologic province also encompasses the smaller physiographic region known as the Great Basin.)

The striking modern landforms of the Northern Mojave—the tall, fault-bounded ranges and deep basins—are thus the direct result of tectonic

The distinctive Basin and Range topography—steep, narrow ranges separated by deep basins—is evident in this eastward view from Wildrose Peak in the Panamints. Death Valley's playa, the Amargosa Range, and distant mountains of Nevada are all visible. GEORGE WUERTHNER

action. In geologic time, they have come into being rather quickly, and the process of crustal extension is still very active. The Northern Mojave remains a dynamic landscape where mountains are rising and valleys are sinking. Studies conducted by the United States Geological Survey indicate that portions of the Death Valley area may be rising or falling at rates exceeding a foot every 500 years. Indeed, the tectonic uplift and stretching of the earth's crust in the vicinity of Death Valley make it one of

Top: Volcanism has played a central role in the region's geologic history and produced dramatic landforms such as this lava flow in Rose Valley south of Olancha. MARC SOLOMON
Bottom: Tectonic stresses cause crustal fractures, such as the Furnace Creek fault, which runs along the western base of the Grapevine Mountains. This aerial view shows how lower portions of the stream channels have shifted northward along the west side of the fault. STEPHEN INGRAM

the most deformed landscapes on earth. Death Valley, Panamint Valley, Saline Valley, and the Owens Valley have all dropped amazing vertical distances in relation to their surrounding ranges.

Tectonic forces that extended the earth's crust in the Northern Mojave region also facilitated a second major phenomenon—volcanism. Due to the movement of tectonic plates huge amounts of molten rock were formed deep beneath the surface. As the crust began to crack, and resulting faults developed, molten rock surged up along the faults to the surface. Some of the volcanism that is now evident in the region first occurred in the southwestern Nevada volcanic field about 16 million years ago and in the central Death Valley field about 11 million years ago, and there have been many subsequent eruptions. Today, volcanic rocks are widespread along Highway 190 where it crosses the Darwin Plateau west of Panamint Springs and at Towne Pass in the Panamint Range. Other good examples of volcanism are visible on the road to Dante's View, at Shoreline Butte in southern Death Valley, and along Highway 395 near Fossil Falls and Red Hill in Rose Valley northwest of Ridgecrest.

Much heat remains in the earth beneath the Northern Mojave, and volcanism continues to influence local geology. In northern Death Valley, volcanic heat beneath the surface generated steam explosions at Ubehebe Crater a few thousand years ago. Along the region's western edge, in the Coso Range and Rose Valley areas, volcanic eruptions and lava flows have occurred within the last 10,000 to 20,000 years. In this same locale, near the former resort of Coso Hot Springs, the Navy has drilled deep into the earth to tap geothermal energy to power generators that can produce enough electricity for up to one million people. In 2001 "swarms" of small earthquakes near Rose Valley were attributed to the movement of magma. A team of geologists has concluded that the magma chamber beneath the Coso Geothermal Field is steadily rising toward the surface at the rate of one-half inch per year.

Evidence of past volcanic eruptions is widespread in the Northern Mojave, such as this basaltic debris scattered over the floor of Eureka Valley. FRED HIRSCHMANN

DESERT VARNISH

Desert varnish is a dark patina that coats many rock surfaces in the Northern Mojave. Some people prefer the term rock varnish rather than desert varnish because rock coatings

Petroglyphs were often created by pecking or scrapping through desert varnish, the thin, dark veneer which coats many desert rocks. FRED HIRSCHMANN

occur in many environments, not just the desert. It is in desert regions, however, where these very thin black- or reddish-brown-colored layers are most notable.

Scientists used to think that the materials for desert varnish emanated from the rock below it. The problem with this hypothesis was that desert varnish overlies rocks that contain no iron or manganese. More current research identifies wind-borne clay particles as the main source of desert varnish. Infrared spectroscopy analysis of samples from a wide variety of locations shows that clay constitutes about 70% of the varnish; the other 30% is composed mainly of manganese and iron oxides as well as trace elements and some organic materials.

Not all rock surfaces in the desert carry a coat of varnish. Soluble rocks like limestone, or rocks subject to rapid decomposition such as granular fragments of quartzite, bear no varnish. Stable rocks with rough, porous surfaces make a good substrate for its formation because dust and moisture from dew collect on the rock's rough exterior. When the dew evaporates, it leaves behind a thin film of clay and oxides.

In the Colorado Desert region of southeastern California, varnish on the rocks is reddish brown in color and contains a high iron oxide content while the Northern Mojave rock coatings are darker due to concentrations of manganese oxides. Manganese is not abundant in the earth's crust and geologists attribute its accumulation in desert varnish to bacteria that live on the rock surfaces whose biochemical activity precipitates manganese oxides.

Desert varnish helps both geologists and archeologists in their research. The rock coatings darken over time, and their color aids geologists when they are attempting to assess relative ages of rock formations or deposits. In Copper Canyon, south of Badwater in Death Valley National Park, for example, geologists who examine desert varnish can identify four separate periods of deposition on the alluvial fan spilling out of the canyon's mouth. The darkest colored varnish covers the oldest deposits, and successively lighter-colored varnish marks the earlier deposits. Archeologists use radiocarbon dating on the small amount of organic materials in desert varnish to help date petroglyphs and artifacts.

A Desert Land of Fossil Lakes

While the Northern Mojave's rocks reveal a complex geologic story extending back more than one billion years, its dusty lakebeds are the link to an intriguing and more recent chapter in the evolution of this landscape. Not so long ago, this was a land with lakes.

Like elsewhere in the Great Basin, all of the drainage in the Northern Mojave is internal; its streams and rivers have no outlet to the sea, and many do not even drain into neighboring basins. The lack of external drainage results mostly from the rapidity with which the mountains and basins have been formed; there has simply not yet been time to wear the landscape down into more normal drainage patterns. The result is that many basins collect all their own floodwaters and develop natural evaporation ponds at their low points. These sites, known as "playas" (Spanish for beach or shore), collect water-borne silts, clays, and minerals and develop large, open, nearly level surfaces that are usually free of all plant life.

Although today's playas only capture ephemeral desert runoff, most of them occupy basins that once held much larger amounts of water. When scientists first entered the Great Basin in the mid-nineteenth century, one surprising fact struck them almost

immediately: within recent geologic time, vast, low-lying areas of the Great Basin had been under water. Early geologists knew what they were seeing, even if they could not explain why. From the eastern base of the Sierra Nevada to the Great Salt Lake area of western Utah, large tracts of the desert had been inundated beneath giant lakes.

Eventually, as geologists studied them, the ancient lake systems began to come into focus, and as they did, each received a name. The largest one, known as Bonneville, covered much of western Utah, while the other, named Lahontan, inundated

Top: The region's dry lakebeds, such as the playa at Racetrack Valley, capture ephemeral runoff during wet years. RANDI HIRSCHMANN
Bottom: This aerial view shows the Saline Valley playa and its adjacent wetland at the foot of the Inyo Mountains. STEPHEN INGRAM

Top: The massive tufa towers known as Trona Pinnacles formed at the bottom of ancient Searles Lake, which existed when an ice-age river flooded this basin to depths of over 600 feet. MARC SOLOMON
Bottom: The Amargosa River is usually a small stream, although it is sometimes swelled by storm runoff, as seen here in southern Death Valley. An ice-age Amargosa River filled ancient Lake Tecopa and may have been a major water source for Lake Manly. JOHN DITTLI

many basins in western Nevada and eastern California. Scientists eventually described another major system of ancient lakes that filled a chain of basins between Owens Valley and Death Valley. The shimmering, salt-crusted playa at Badwater is a dramatic lake remnant, but other Northern Mojave basins also contain lakebeds that were part of ice-age river systems.

During the latter part of the Pleistocene epoch (1.8 million to 10,000 years ago), the southwestern United States, including the Northern Mojave, experienced a climate that was both wetter and cooler by perhaps 9° to 13°F. One theory proposes that this pattern resulted from a more southerly polar jet stream track during periods when much of the north-central and northeastern United States was covered with glacial ice. If this is true, then the polar jet stream brought to California a climate similar to modern British Columbia. As a result, the Sierra Nevada, like the modern ranges of British Columbia, developed an extensive glacial ice cap, and considerably more rain reached the mountains' eastern (desert) side. It is likely that the frequent presence of the polar jet stream also greatly increased cloudiness in the region, and thus reduced evaporation. As a result, large amounts of water entered the Northern Mojave, both as precipitation and as runoff. Since evaporation was slower than at present, the water tended to accumulate in the down-dropped valleys of the Basin and Range country east of the Sierra Nevada.

In the wettest periods, ancient Owens River began on the eastern escarpment of the Sierra Nevada, perhaps as far north as Mono Lake, and flowed through Owens Valley along the path of modern Owens River into Owens Lake. From there, the river continued south through Rose Valley and entered Indian Wells Valley where it swung east to reach China Lake (near modern Ridgecrest). Outflow from China Lake drained into deep Searles Lake (at modern Trona) via a prominent river-cut gorge. Geologists have long believed that this river system then spilled east from Searles Valley to Panamint Valley and from there flowed through Wingate Wash into Death Valley to terminate in Lake Manly, which at its largest was 600 feet deep and more than 75 miles long. Some new research, however, challenges this theory by claiming there is insufficient evidence that Panamint Valley's lake overflowed to Death Valley via Wingate Wash.

Lake Manly's major water source may have been the Amargosa River, which originates in mountains to the northeast of Death Valley; today it still carries a largely subterranean flow into southern Death Valley. Until at least 150,000 years ago, however, the

A key piece of evidence that helped geologists confirm the existence of past lakes in the Great Basin was the presence of ancient beach lines. This photo of lower slopes in the western Panamints shows a series of beach lines (most evident in the upper right) that correspond to different lake levels. JOHN S. SHELTON

Amargosa was impounded in vast Lake Tecopa. It eventually breached the Tecopa basin and carved a new channel to Death Valley, following the path of the modern Amargosa River. Another possible contributor to Lake Manly was the ice-age Mojave River. This desert river today begins high in the San Bernardino Mountains and flows about 125 miles to the northeast before finally disappearing underground at Soda Dry Lake. During several periods of high glacial runoff, the Mojave apparently overflowed its terminus at ancient Lake Mojave (where the Silver and Soda lake playas are found today, near Baker) and ran north to join the Amargosa River just south of Death Valley.

The major Pleistocene lakes in the Northern Mojave system clearly show multiple beach lines, thus

Death Valley once held 600-foot-deep Lake Manly and subsequent smaller lakes. As the ice-age lakes evaporated, each Northern Mojave lakebed accumulated a different mix of residual minerals, including salts that would later be mined, such as borax and trona. LARRY ULRICH

demonstrating that water stood at different levels at different times. Ancient beach lines, typically located on slopes above the lakebed, provide vivid evidence of just how large and deep some of the lakes were. Research at Searles Lake near Trona and elsewhere in the Great Basin has disclosed that the lakes rose and fell numerous times. Glacial records for the Sierra Nevada also show sometimes rapid and erratic fluctuations in the extent of glacial ice. The wave-cut shorelines from prehistoric lakes are easy to see in portions of Death Valley, especially at Shoreline Butte. Searles Lake, Panamint Valley, and the Owens Lake area also display similar examples.

One last major surge of water into the Northern Mojave occurred about 10,500 to 11,000 years ago. These dates correlate closely with a period of rapid glacial retreat in the Sierra Nevada at the end of the Pleistocene. In the ensuing millennia, the climate gradually became warmer and more arid, the lakes' inflow was reduced, and evaporation rates increased. The Pleistocene lakes eventually dried up, although much smaller water bodies sometimes formed in some basins during wetter periods; Death Valley, for example, contained a 30-foot-deep lake that may have existed between 2,000 to 5,000 years ago.

The evaporating Pleistocene lakes all developed a unique mix of trapped minerals. The distinctive chemical composition of each lakebed resulted from the fact that the once-connected chain of lakes had served to settle out and concentrate different minerals at different locations within the watershed. Searles Lake and the Death Valley basin received the strongest residual doses of minerals, setting the stage for later mining activity on both playas. The early borax mining that put Death Valley on the map took place on the evaporated remains of Lake Manly.

Similar events occurred elsewhere in the region, as mineralized playas developed at the bottoms of many desert basins. The only major lake in the region to retain water into modern times was Owens Lake, which still received direct runoff from the east side of the Sierra Nevada via Owens River. Owens Lake survived until the early 1920s, when the Los Angeles Department of Water and Power diverted its remaining inflow for domestic use by the City of Los Angeles. This water diversion led to evaporation of the lake's surface waters and exposed yet another intensely mineralized desert playa. To help curtail excessive levels of particulate-dust air pollution generated during windy conditions at Owens Lake, about 16 square miles of the playa have been flooded with a shallow layer of water or replanted with salt grass.

Water and Wind, Twin Forces of Erosion

The tectonic pressures that are lifting up the Northern Mojave's mountains are far less evident than the forces of erosion that are wearing them down. Any desert visitor who has experienced a summer cloudburst or blowing dust storm has witnessed two of the great sculptors of arid landscapes: water and wind. The Northern Mojave's generally sparse cover of vegetation gives little protection to the soil, making it highly susceptible to erosion.

Nearly every square inch of this land has been shaped by one of the desert's least common elements—

At the same time that tectonic forces are lifting the Northern Mojave's mountain ranges, the inexorable process of erosion is wearing them down. These alluvial-fan boulders have been steadily transported downhill from the Black Mountains toward the floor of Death Valley. JIM STIMSON

Top: When strong winds scour sand and dirt particles from the desert's surface, they contribute to the formation of dunes and desert pavement, and generate dust storms such as this one in Panamint Valley. LARRY ULRICH
Bottom: Runoff from a heavy winter rain transports alluvium out of a canyon and onto an alluvial fan near the base of Tucki Mountain in Death Valley. JOHN DITTLI

This broad alluvial fan, braided with small washes and arroyos, spills out from the mouth of Red Wall Canyon in the Grapevine Mountains south of Scotty's Castle. Northern Mojave ranges are rimmed by such fans, which often merge together to form bajadas. STEPHEN INGRAM

running water. Two factors tend to amplify the role of water as an agent of erosion in the Northern Mojave: the region can experience very intense, localized downpours, and its steep topography concentrates and increases the velocity of runoff from rain events. The erosion power of flowing water is perhaps best exemplified by the immense deposits of gravel, sand, and boulders that fan out from mountain canyons and rim the base of most Northern Mojave ranges. Following cloudbursts, flooded canyons carry enormous loads of gravel and sand (alluvium) toward the valleys. As long as a flood is confined within a steep, narrow canyon, the materials continue to move downslope, but once the floodwaters exit a canyon, the water spreads and slows, and the debris load is abruptly dumped.

These canyon-mouth deposits are known as alluvial fans, and they constitute one of the region's most

dominant and recognizable landforms. In many areas the fans come
close enough together to merge,
forming a continuous gravel slope
along the foot of the mountains. The
English language does not have a spe-
cific term for this landform, but
Spanish-speaking explorers, whose
experience in Mexico and the arid
southwest taught them much about
desert landscapes, called these com-
pound alluvial fans "bajadas."

The larger mountains of the
Northern Mojave often are flanked by
bajadas that measure several thousand feet thick. In many basins, the
total area of bajada slope exceeds that
of the valley floor itself. Saline Valley,
the northern part of the Panamint
Valley, the west face of the Grapevine
Mountains, and the west side of
Death Valley all have prominent
bajadas. Generally, the size of the
bajada is determined by the relative
size and steepness of its contributing
canyons and by the relative subsidence rate of the valley floor it rests
on. When valley floors are dropping
rapidly, accumulating alluvium may
be incorporated into the level valley
floor rather than displayed as a slop-
ing bajada. The relative disparity in
the size of the bajadas on either side
of Death Valley is mostly due to the
fact that the valley floor is sinking
unevenly. In some places on the east
side, the valley floor is dropping so
rapidly that the alluvial fans have not

*This view in the Zabriskie Point area sweeps across the spectacularly eroded Furnace Creek
Formation. These soft, sedimentary deposits of mud, silt, sand, gravel, and volcanic ash settled at
the bottom of a long-vanished lake and were later uplifted and tilted.* LARRY ULRICH

This expanse of desert pavement is near Death Valley Buttes, northeast of Stovepipe Wells. Geologists theorize that the "pavement" forms where winds have scoured away lighter soil particles, leaving behind a compact surface layer of small, but heavier rocks and pebbles. MARC SOLOMON

been able to build a bajada. On the west side, where subsidence is slower, the fans have accumulated to form a massive bajada.

Flowing water is also the principal architect of one of the desert's most photogenic features: badlands. Desert vegetation that can protect and hold soil has a difficult time getting established on badlands since they often erode so rapidly. The deeply dissected hills near Zabriskie Point and Furnace Creek Wash are primarily composed of mudstones and siltstones that formed in an ancient lake.

Now exposed to the dry desert air, these soft sediments are easily, if infrequently, sculpted by rain and runoff. The sedimentary lakebeds of ancient Lake Tecopa near Shoshone offer another example of water-carved badlands.

Compared to water, wind exerts a far more subtle impact in arid landscapes. Whereas running water shapes desert topography by carving canyons and transporting large volumes of alluvium, wind influences the face of the land by constantly scouring sand and silt from its sur-

face. To appreciate the work of wind in the Northern Mojave, examine an arroyo bank or a road cut. These and other disturbed sites provide an informative soil "profile." Typically, the profile contains a surface crust that consists largely of gravel or broken rock; beneath it lays a deeper soil layer that comprises particles of silt, clay, and sand. With little vegetation to help anchor them in place, small surface particles of desert soil are whisked away by the wind. Left behind is the surface layer of more wind-resistant, heavier, and flatter

rocks that form what is known as "desert pavement." (Some geologists disagree with this explanation of desert pavement formation. They propose that small rocks work their way upward through expansive silt and clay soils, during alternating wetting and drying, to form the pavement.) As long as the desert pavement stays in place, the fine particles beneath it are protected from the wind. World-class expanses of desert pavement are especially abundant in parts of Panamint Valley, such as at the base of the Slate Range on the Trona-Wildrose Road.

Soil particles that are swept up and carried by winds are eventually transported out of the region or are deposited in one of the desert's most exotic landforms: sand dunes. The dunes usually form where local topography interrupts the prevailing wind pattern and forces the wind to slow and drop its particle load. Significant sand dunes are present in Death Valley, Panamint Valley, Eureka Valley, and the Amargosa River drainage, but they cover only a tiny percentage of the land surface in these basins. Some dune areas are quite concentrated and the resulting dunes are relatively high. In Eureka Valley they rise nearly 700 feet to form one of North America's highest dunes. Elsewhere, the dune fields are much lower, accumulating in sand "sheets" such as those seen in Saline Valley.

The Death Valley Sand Dunes, like others in the Northern Mojave, came into existence primarily because of two things: a pre-existing source of sand—such as a dry lakeshore or riverbed—and the transport and deposit of this sand by prevailing winds. CRAIG BLACKLOCK/ULRICH STOCK PHOTO

Northern Mojave Climate and Life

The desert floras shame us with their cheerful adaptations to the seasonal limitations. Their whole duty is to flower and fruit, and they do it hardly, or with tropical luxuriance, as the rain admits. . . .Very fertile are the desert plants in expedients to prevent evaporation, turning their foliage edgewise toward the sun, growing silky hairs, exuding viscid gum. . . .

. . . Go as far as you dare in the heart of a lonely land, you cannot go so far that life and death are not before you. Painted lizards slip in and out of rock crevices, and pant on the white hot sands. Birds, hummingbirds even, nest in the cactus scrub; woodpeckers befriend the demoniac yuccas; out of the stark, treeless waste rings the music of the night-singing mockingbird. If it be summer and the sun well down, there will be a burrowing owl to call. Strange, furry, tricksy things dart across the open places, or sit motionless in the conning towers of the creosote. The poet may have "named all the birds without a gun," but not the fairy-footed, ground-inhabiting, furtive, small folk of the rainless regions. They are too many and too swift; how many you would not believe without seeing the footprint tracings in the sand. They are nearly all night workers, finding the days too hot and white.

—Mary Austin,
The Land of Little Rain, 1903

In a rare year, blooms of desert gold cover an entire bajada at the western base of Death Valley's Black Mountains. RANDI HIRSCHMANN

An Arid Climate

Only a few North American landscapes are justifiably famous because of the dramatic environmental contrasts they display within a small area. One of these places is found in the Northern Mojave, where the below-sea-level basin of Death Valley and the 11,049-foot-high summit of Telescope Peak are located less than 15 miles apart. Within clear view of each other are the salt flats of the valley floor, too mineralized and too hot for any flowering plants, and the sub-alpine slopes of the peak, studded with bristlecone and limber pines. These two topographic extremes, and the various natural communities found in between, reflect much of the diversity that makes the region unique.

The Northern Mojave supports a surprising array of plants and animals. They must, however, contend with a climate that is among the most severe on earth. Amazing temperature swings and extreme aridity pose challenges to many species. Their different strategies for survival are among the more intriguing aspects of desert ecology.

During most of the past 10,000 years, prevailing weather patterns have not brought wet storms to the region with any frequency or certainty. When such storms do come off the Pacific, they first must pass over tall ranges to the west—particularly the Sierra Nevada—that wring moisture out of the clouds as they ascend and cross the mountains.

Comparing annual rainfall averages along a transect from west to east tells the story. Beginning at the western foothills of the southern Sierra Nevada, annual precipitation averages about 15 inches. Farther upslope this total increases significantly, with as much as 60 inches of annual precipitation occurring at an elevation of 9,000 feet. Immediately east of the Sierra Nevada crest, annual rainfall totals abruptly taper off. The floor of Owens Valley usually receives no more than six inches, while Indian Wells Valley garners a mere four inches. As storms

In a remarkable juxtaposition of different environments, the arid salt flats of Death Valley are located just miles from the snow-dusted woodlands of Telescope Peak. JOHN DITTLI

Death Valley receives scant precipitation because of a rainshadow effect. Pacific storms shed their moisture in the Sierra Nevada before reaching the area, and desert mountains such the Inyo, Argus (foreground) and Panamint ranges (background), capture most of what is left. MARC SOLOMON

continue east into the Northern Mojave, the higher desert ranges, particularly the Inyos and Panamints, force even more water from the clouds. East of the Panamints, at Furnace Creek on the floor of Death Valley, annual precipitation averages less than two inches, or barely 3% of the average recorded just 100 miles to the west in the high Sierra. The Northern Mojave also receives occasional summer rain when subtropical moisture flows north from Mexico, but accumulations from this "monsoon" precipitation are usually quite localized.

Death Valley is not only one of the driest spots in the Western Hemisphere, but also one of the hottest. The average July maximum temperature at Furnace Creek is 115°F; a record high of 134°F for this location was set in July 1913. Many factors combine to create this great heat: the region is far enough south to be subject to intense summer sun;

the summers are mostly cloudless, which allows the sun's heat to reach the surface most of the time; Death Valley's deep basin and steep mountain walls trap heat; the desert is without the modifying effects of moisture from humidity or nearby bodies of water; and the Northern Mojave is not regularly subject to moderating air movements from cooler regions in summer. These conditions are similar in all the valleys of the Northern Mojave. Death Valley is the hottest simply because it is the lowest. Other relatively low basins, including Searles, Panamint, and Saline valleys, also frequently see extreme summer temperatures.

Dry, searing heat exerts a powerful influence on desert life by dramatically boosting rates of evaporation. During a 12-month sample period from 1958 to 1959, more than 155 inches of water evaporated from a test site at Furnace Creek. Plants and animals in Death Valley must adapt to an

environment where only two inches of precipitation falls annually from the atmosphere and where almost 13 feet of water can evaporate during the same period!

Many of the same factors that intensify summer heat produce cold nights in winter. The combination of minimal cloud cover, low surface humidity, and the lack of moderating bodies of water allow temperatures to plummet during the winter, even in the lowest valleys. In the same year that Furnace Creek recorded its all-time high temperature of 134°F, its weather station also recorded a January low of 15°F. The average low temperature for January is 39°F at Furnace Creek. This pattern of winter cold is far more severe at higher elevations. During the coldest months of winter, Pacific cold fronts enter the region, bringing strong winds and intense cold to the higher mountains; temperatures well below 0°F are often recorded.

VEGETATION HISTORY AND PACKRAT MIDDENS

The scientists who unraveled the story of the Northern Mojave's Pleistocene-Era lakes made clear that the region's climate has changed dramatically during the last 15,000 years. One of the ways in which they came to understand and document earlier climates was through the

By studying preserved plant remains in desert packrat middens, scientists found that creosote bush was not yet in the region 10,000 years ago. WILLARD CLAY

study of prehistoric vegetation patterns. At first hampered by the tendency of plant materials to rot away within a few decades, researchers eventually discovered that the preserved ancient nests of desert packrats, or woodrats, are a major source of information about plant communities of the past.

The desert packrat is found throughout the southern half of California, including the Northern Mojave, where it often inhabits pinyon-juniper woodlands. This nocturnal rodent builds large nests of sticks and other plant materials in dry, protected caves, under thick bushes, or in other sheltered places. A packrat collects and stores large amounts of material from plants that grow within 75 to 100 feet of the nest. It frequently urinates just outside the nest, and the nest materials become saturated with uronic acid. The acid crystallizes into a long-lived substance that somewhat resembles asphalt and is called amberat. The preserved nest materials as a whole are called packrat middens.

Had modern scientists sat down to design a way for preserving vegetative samples, they probably would not have created a better vehicle for preservation than the urine-saturated

packrat middens. The middens are assembled in layers, with the oldest materials forming the base. Scientists examine the fruits, spines, and twigs imbedded in the old layers and carbon date these organic materials to gather clues about past vegetation and climate. In the Northern Mojave, packrat middens can contain layers dating back nearly 20,000 years.

Research into packrat middens and analysis of ancient pollen samples taken from old lakebed sediments and shorelines provide an intriguing window on the past. They document dramatic climate changes between the current period and the late Pleistocene. A sample from a packrat midden dated 19,500 years old clearly indicates that juniper trees were growing on the low bajadas surrounding Death Valley; today, the average elevation at which junipers are found begins almost 5,000 feet higher. Just as striking is what was not collected by the packrats at that time—creosote bush. Creosote bush invaded the Northern Mojave from the south at the end of the Pleistocene about 10,000 years ago and reached its current distribution barely 5,000 years ago. Today it is the most common lowland shrub in the Northern Mojave.

Vegetation Patterns in the Northern Mojave

One of the great joys of learning about the natural world is observing its patterns. Some patterns are intricate or reveal interrelationships between species and the environment. True randomness of pattern is rare, especially in the distribution of desert plants. Each species has a preferred habitat where the environmental conditions allow it to function physiologically and compete effectively with other species in the same community.

The primary factors that influence plant distribution in the desert are water availability and temperature. The underlying rock, or substrate, can also influence vegetation in more localized patterns. In addition, the direction the land faces, known as slope aspect, can create microclimates within a small area. For example, the mixture of plants on a hot, south-facing canyon wall will be different from that on its cooler, shady north side.

Each of these key factors is affected by elevation. Even on the hottest summer days, high mountains are much cooler than desert valleys; after winter storms, a mantle of snow descends as low as 3,000 feet but slopes and basins below remain snow-free. It is cooler at high elevations because atmospheric pressure decreases inversely with elevation gain. When rising air encounters lower air pressure it expands and cools. A rough rule of thumb for dry air is that temperatures drop 3°F to 4°F for each 1,000 feet of increased altitude. This rule, which generally applies in summer and winter, day and night, explains why the summits of the Inyos and Panamints are usually more than 30°F cooler than the valleys below.

Cooler temperatures at high elevations also provoke increased precipitation. Clouds must rise to cross the higher mountains, causing cooling and an increased chance of precipitation. As a result, higher mountain areas in the Northern Mojave receive 3 to 10 times as much precipitation as the surrounding basins. Reduced temperatures at high elevations also decrease rates of evaporation, which further increases water availability for living things, especially plants. These factors combine to produce broad patterns of plant life that are relatively easy to discern.

One obvious vegetation pattern in the Northern Mojave is the treeline that generally occurs at an elevation between 6,000 and 7,000 feet. Woodlands and scattered forests often cover the landscape above this line, while below it shrubs predominate. Northern Mojave lowlands are dominated by shrubs because the climate is too dry for trees except near localized water sources such as springs and streams. The treeline is a major landmark and occurs on Northern

Top: Like these specimens on Lee Flat, the region's Joshua trees tend to be concentrated at elevations of 3,500 to 5,000 feet, where there is more precipitation than in the lowland basins. FRED HIRSCHMANN
Bottom: Vegetation in this area of Red Rock Canyon State Park is dominated by woody, drought-tolerant shrubs, which are widespread in the Northern Mojave. STEPHEN INGRAM

Top: Botanists have recorded more than 1,000 plant species in Death Valley National Park, including endemics such as the rare Death Valley monkeyflower, seen here in Echo Canyon in the Funeral Mountains. STEPHEN INGRAM
Bottom: Mojave mound cactus is found above 3,500 feet elevation and grows mostly on limestone. DENNIS FLAHERTY

Mojave ranges that are high enough to support populations of pinyon and juniper trees. The Inyos claim the distinction of having two treelines. This range shows a lower-elevation desert treeline, but it is also sufficiently tall to display a conventional high-elevation timberline. Above its alpine timberline, shrubs and herbs prevail because the climate is too cold and dry and the growing season too short to support most trees.

The Northern Mojave straddles two great North American deserts, the Mojave Desert and the Great Basin Desert. The Great Basin Desert, distinguished from all other North American deserts by its intense winter cold, is the Northern Mojave's neighbor to the east and north, spreading out in a seemingly endless succession of valleys and ranges. The Panamint and Inyo mountain uplands are the southwestern-most ranges of this cold, high-elevation desert. The hot and relatively low-lying Mojave Desert sprawls to the south and east; low-elevation basins, such as Eureka, Saline, Panamint, and Death valleys are the Mojave Desert's northern frontiers. The transition from shrublands and Joshua tree woodlands to pinyon-juniper woodlands indicates the broad dividing line between lowland vegetation, dominated by Mojave Desert species, and upland vegetation, largely composed of Great Basin Desert species.

With contributions from the floras of both the Mojave and Great Basin deserts, the Northern Mojave claims a rich mixture of species, including a number of plants that are common in Nevada but uncommon in California. In Death Valley National Park botanists have recorded more than 1,000 plant species, including 17 that are endemic to the immediate park area. The updated *Flora of the Northern Mojave Desert, California* describes about 1,250 plants; author Mary Dedecker wrote in her introduction: "The Northern Mojave provides a rich field for studying the needs and tolerances of unusual species."

The abundance of limestone formations in the Northern Mojave supports another distinctive feature of the area's flora: a large number of calcium-loving plants. Limestone typically weathers into thin soils that are nutrient-poor, alkaline, and high in calcium. Plants that are widespread elsewhere in the Northern Mojave may be entirely absent from limestone outcrops, but calcium-loving plants—including many endemics—often grow in great profusion and diversity on these sites. Some of the region's limestone-associated species are relatively common, such as hedgehog cactus and Newberry's locoweed; others are rare, such as Death Valley monkeyflower and rock lady, a plant found in only two canyons of the Grapevine Mountains.

Plants of Lowland Basins and Slopes

The lowlands of the Northern Mojave contain some of the most severe desert environments in North America. The three lowest basins—Saline Valley, Panamint Valley, and Death Valley—are famous not only for their intense summer heat, but also for their stark, barren beauty. Although each of these basins has a large, mineralized playa where plants cannot grow, there are also better-drained areas on the valley floors and surrounding slopes where plant life flourishes.

Along the edges of many desert playas, scattered springs and seeps may support some plant life if the emerging water is not too high in mineral content. The dominant plants of playa margins and the lowest valley floors are adapted to the amount of salt in the immediate environment. One of the most salt-tolerant species is pickleweed, or picklebush, which can tolerate water containing up to 6% salt, nearly twice as salty as the sea. A low-growing succulent shrub, picklebush borders the barren salt flats on the floor of Death Valley; a good place to see it is along Salt Creek or near the edges of the salt pan on the west side of the valley. Picklebush occupies similar environments in Panamint and Saline valleys.

As one moves away from the playa, salt concentrations usually decline and the vegetation changes accordingly. Lowland areas with less salty groundwater often support arrowweed or mesquite. Arrowweed tolerates lightly saline water and grows in tall, well-spaced clumps on fine, silty soils. (A famous patch of wind-pruned arrowweed is the "Devils Corn Field" on Highway 190 east of Stovepipe Wells.) The presence of honey and screwbean mesquite trees signals a further reduction in groundwater salinity. These spreading, deciduous trees grow on the

Top: Picklebush (also called pickleweed) is the desert's most salt-tolerant shrub. Its segmented, fleshy stems, which resemble tiny pickles or beads, store salt in their tissues, allowing the plant to grow where groundwater has high levels of salinity, such as along Salt Creek. STEPHEN INGRAM
Bottom: Arroweed grows in alkaline soils at Death Valley's "Devil's Corn Field." FRED HIRSCHMANN

desert floor, often among low sand dunes. Potable water usually exists relatively close to the surface where mesquite trees grow, but their roots may extend down 50 feet or more to reach groundwater, allowing them to survive in environments where no other trees are present.

Mesquite can tolerate about 0.5% salt content in water, a level that is similar to the upper limit of human salinity tolerance in drinking water. Since it is an indicator of subsurface potable water—usually found along faults—desert wells are often located near large thickets of mesquite, sometimes called "bosques," the Spanish word for forests. There are few trees on the desert floor, so honey and screwbean mesquite play a critical role in lowland desert ecology. They provide shelter for small mammals and birds, and many animals consume their bean-like seeds. Native peoples made extensive use of mesquite as a food source, fuel, and building material. Mesquite is common in the lowland valleys of the Northern Mojave wherever there is sufficient groundwater. It is prevalent in the northern part of Death Valley, where local place names include Mesquite Flat and Mesquite Springs. Extensive mesquite thickets grow in Panamint Valley near Ballarat and in Saline Valley north of the playa.

Perhaps the most unexpected habitat in the lowland desert valleys

is marshland. At several Northern Mojave locales fresh water rises from springs in such volume that brackish marshes, or even open water, occur. Two good examples are Saratoga Springs in southern Death Valley and the spectacular marsh complex near the base of the Inyo Mountains in Saline Valley. Both wetlands provide critical resting and feeding sites for migratory birds. Saratoga Springs also

Top: Mesquite is the most common tree of low elevations in the Northern Mojave. Its deep taproot reaches subsurface water and helps anchor it in dunes, such as these in Death Valley. DAVID LANNER
Bottom: Visitors to the Northern Mojave are sometimes surprised to learn that the region contains a number of wetlands, such as this freshwater marsh at Saratoga Springs. STEPHEN INGRAM

has its own native fish species, a desert pupfish whose ancestors were marooned when Death Valley's ancient Lake Manly dried up.

One of the largest marsh complexes in the Northern Mojave is found in the Ash Meadows National Wildlife Refuge. Located just east of Death Valley in Nevada's Amargosa Desert, Ash Meadows comprises a large complex of pools and springs. These wetlands are a result of the underlying geology: water-soluble limestone, riddled with caves and fault lines, channels ancient groundwater to the surface and creates a habitat that is amazingly different from surrounding terrain. This oasis supports a rich assortment of plants and animals and harbors one of the nation's highest concentrations of endemic species. Evaporation around the springs produces heavily mineralized soils that are home to 11 rare plants, including the Ash Meadows ivesia and Ash Meadows blazing star. The refuge is also home to rare fish, along with springsnails and other invertebrates.

Above the playas, vegetation on the bajadas and slopes faces new challenges. The problem is no longer too much salt in the water but simply too little water; the groundwater here is usually too far below the surface for most roots to reach. Rather than relying on deep, water-seeking roots, the plants that succeed in this environment are effective collectors of seasonal moisture, tolerators of dehydration, and extremely efficient users of water.

Successful water-conserving strategies are evident in two of the region's most widespread lowland shrubs, desert holly and creosote bush. Often called the "toughest" plant in Death Valley, desert holly meets the demands of its environment through a number of adaptations. Easily recognized by its low clumps of white, holly-like leaves, this shrub is so successful at conserving moisture that it can survive a year or more without measurable rainfall. Its pale foliage reflects light, reduces heat load, and minimizes water loss. Desert holly is also salt tolerant. It has an affinity for limestone bajadas and grows on some of the lowest and driest valley slopes that surround the salt pans.

Creosote bush, the other characteristic shrub of the Northern Mojave, occurs nearly everywhere, from non-saline valley bottoms to steep mountain slopes up to 4,000 feet. It is a four- to eight-foot-tall shrub with numerous stems and tiny, waxy, dark-green leaves that resist water loss. Creosote survives heat, cold, drought, and even flooding. It is so drought-resistant that its leaves can continue photosynthesis after 30 months without rain. When sufficient rain follows a dry spell, this shrub will "change leaves" by dropping the old ones and growing a new set, sometimes within five days.

During summer, the leaves of desert holly become shriveled and brittle, which reduces the plant's rate of photosynthesis and its need for moisture; they also become more silver-colored to reflect light and heat. This resilient shrub may form nearly pure stands, like this one in Saline Valley. FRED HIRSCHMANN

CREOSOTE BUSH, LONG-LIVED PLANT OF THE DESERT

Based on data collected from packrat middens, we now know that creosote bush, a shrub considered to be characteristic of the Northern Mojave plant community, is a relatively recent arrival. Only 20,000 years ago creosote grew no closer to Death Valley than southwestern Arizona; then, as the Pleistocene glaciers receded about 12,000 years ago, weather patterns gradually became drier and creosote bush began to disperse northward. It had arrived in the Amargosa Desert just east of Death Valley by 9,000 years ago, but did not reach the mountains north of Death Valley until approximately 5,000 years ago. Today, the northern edge of the creosote bush's range falls outside of Death Valley National Park and marks the boundary of the biological Mojave Desert.

Creosote bush is found not only in the warm deserts of North America, but also in the deserts of Chile and Argentina. More than 7,000 miles separate these closely related species, which share the same common name. Most botanists who have pondered this unusual distribution pattern believe that the North American creosote is descended from its South American cousins. There is speculation that creosote seeds were carried to North America in the digestive tracts of long-distance migratory birds. This hypothesis would help explain the vast equatorial gap in its distribution.

In addition to its intriguing distribution, creosote is distinguished by its amazing longevity. Although a creosote bush can germinate from seed, the plant can also spread when adventitious roots emanating from the root crown of an established shrub send up new shoots that are clones of the parent plant. One spreading specimen on the southwestern edge of the Mojave Desert is estimated to have lived for 11,700 years. If this is true, a creosote bush can be one of the longest-lived plants on earth, and some of the first creosote bushes ever to grow in the Mojave Desert may still be alive.

This view across Eureka Valley to the Last Chance Range depicts a classic creosote bush scrub community. It covers the entire basin except the playa and dunes. JEFF GNASS

As elevation increases, annual precipitation also increases, and plant life begins to proliferate. The upper bajadas and slopes support a surprising variety of well-adapted species; among these are burrobush, brittlebush, and several types of cactus. These plants range down toward the valley floors but are more widespread in the Northern Mojave's middle elevations.

Burrobush is a low shrub with small, deeply lobed, pale gray-green leaves and tiny, inconspicuous flowers. A tough and resilient desert plant, burrobush is drought-deciduous: it can drop its leaves and go dormant for long periods of time when moisture is unavailable. Its frequent neighbor, brittlebush, is generally more eye-catching—at least during winter and spring. At home on rocky slopes and in dry washes, this small shrub often displays broad, gray-green leaves. With sufficient rainfall, it blooms with dozens or even hundreds of two-inch yellow sunflowers at the tips of brittle, foot-long stalks. By late spring, the plant scatters its seed to the hot wind and drops its leaves; nothing remains above ground to face the summer but short, seemingly lifeless white stems. It remains dormant until the rains of late fall and winter return.

Joining the shrubs across most bajadas, slopes, and washes are the cacti—leafless plants that for many

The yellow flowers of brittlebush envelop a rocky slope in the Amargosa Range; by summer, the brittlebush will shed its leaves to conserve moisture. SCOTT T. SMITH

visitors are the epitome of desert vegetation. The Northern Mojave supports about 20 species of cacti, and they occur from hot, lowland valleys near 1,000 feet elevation up to 9,500 feet in pinyon-juniper woodlands. Some are relatively widespread, such as beavertail cactus, known for its showy magenta flowers and skin-irritating, tiny spines called glochids. Others are uncommon, such as the

Above: The Mojave fishhook cactus, known for showy flowers atop its 8- to 12-inch stem, is one of about 20 cacti species in the Northern Mojave. DENNIS FLAHERTY
Right: Sand verbena, desert gold, and dune evening primrose create vibrant color in sandy terrain near the Dumont Dunes. JOHN DITTLI

little fishhook cactus (also called corkseed cactus), which rarely exceeds 10 inches in height and is associated with areas of limestone.

The spines on cacti deter animals from eating the plants' succulent tissue. They also help conserve water by acting as a reflective coating, similar to dense "hairs" on leaves. By reflecting light, spines and leaf hairs lower temperatures on plant surfaces, thereby decreasing evaporative loss. Some cacti also have ribs, and similar to the fins on a car radiator, the ribs serve to dissipate heat. Many cacti have another adaptation for life in hot, arid climates: their stomates can open at night when temperatures drop and humidity increases. By opening their stomates to take up carbon dioxide at night rather than in the day, cacti reduce water loss. The carbon dioxide is stored as a weak acid in plant tissue until daytime, when it is converted into food using the sun's energy in the process of photosynthesis.

The Ephemeral Annuals

Hidden in the seemingly poor soil of arid slopes and flats is one the desert's grandest treasures—a supply of long-lived wildflower seed. Perhaps once or twice in a decade Pacific storms deliver ample rains at ideal intervals between late fall and early spring. If sufficient warmth and not too much desiccating wind accompany this well-timed moisture, the lowlands

may burst forth with annual wild-flowers in totally unexpected numbers. As the season progresses and wildflower fields in basins and on bajadas dry out, the bloom often moves upslope, eventually extending to lower mountain areas and producing more scattered displays of annuals.

The Northern Mojave's periodic wildflower shows astound even the most experienced desert visitor. Some years the desert comes alive with intense color. The palette of desert wildflowers is expansive: purple flowers of several species of phacelia contrast vibrantly with the bright yellow sunflower called "desert gold;" coreopsis, desert dandelion, and golden evening primrose add more hues of yellow; other members of the fragrant evening primrose family contribute white blossoms; and desert five spot and Indian paintbrush supply tones of red and pink.

Desert annuals have their own strategy for surviving the lowland heat and drought. Rather than hardening permanent leaves and stems for summer, like creosote, or dropping their leaves in summer, like brittle-bush, these plants rely on dormant seeds to take them through the tougher parts of the year. They sprout only when conditions are favorable and then rush through their lives to produce seeds again. The seeds may lay dormant for years, waiting for the right conditions for germination.

The seeds of desert annuals, such as this notch-leaved phacelia in Death Valley, can remain in the soil for years, waiting until ample, well-spaced winter rains and mild temperatures create good conditions for plant germination, growth, and flowering.
WILLIAM SMITHEY

DUNES OF THE NORTHERN MOJAVE

Desert dunes are islands in a dry sea. Their origin, structure, and basic functions differ so much from the surrounding landscape that only certain plants and animals inhabit the sandswept slopes. Such "castaways" can become isolated from plants on other dunes and, over time, evolve into unique forms that are endemic to a particular dune system.

A systematic survey of major dune systems in California and Nevada documented more than 160 plants that live on sand dunes but only 52 of these were truly sand-restricted. In the Northern Mojave, these can include sand verbenas,

The Eureka Dunes evening primrose grows only in sandy areas of Eureka Valley.
JOHN DITTLI

naked cleome, desert dicorias, and birdcage primrose. All of these are annuals, the most common growth form on desert dunes. Dune perennials tend to be species that can resist sand movement and abrasion, and include milk vetch, dune broom, and sandpaper plant. Slow-growing shrubs and cacti typical of the surrounding regional vegetation, such as creosote bush and silver cholla, are excluded from unstable dune slopes.

Unusual distributions of dune plants in the Northern Mojave reflect the long dynamic history of this desert landscape. Some dune plants have populations that lie far to the south or far to the north of their central geographic range, suggesting migratory redistribution during climatic fluctuations of the Pleistocene. One species, the Eureka Valley dune grass, is an ancient relict from an extinct subtropical ecosystem. Found only on the dunes in Eureka Valley, it persists in an arid region due to moisture storage in dune sands.

Dunes of the Northern Mojave vary greatly in their size and age. The tallest and most extensive dune system is found in Eureka Valley and has probably been around in one form or another for almost 500,000

Short Canyon near Indian Wells Valley contains low dunes. JOHN EVARTS

years. Smaller and younger, but still impressive, are the dunes of Panamint and Saline valleys, created as Pleistocene lakes receded during the last 20,000 years. A few dunes and sand sheets are very young, perhaps formed within the last 6,000 years, and include those of Death Valley and Indian Wells Valley.

At least seven significant dune systems lie within the Northern Mojave. A traveler to this region can visit Big Dune, Death Valley, Dumont, Eureka, Ibex, Panamint, and Saline Valley dunes. Taken together, these and other smaller dunes represent the greatest concentration of desert dune systems in the western United States.

—Bruce M. Pavlik

Plants of Upland Slopes and Mountains

At about a mile above sea level, the Mojave Desert-dominated lowland vegetation gradually gives way to the Great Basin-influenced upland vegetation. Scattered below this vegetative transition line are woodlands of Joshua trees. These tall, evergreen, tree-sized yuccas have fibrous trunks and sharp, dagger-like leaves. In spring they bear large, cream-white flowers that are pollinated by a species-specific moth. The branches and trunks of live and dead Joshua trees provide critical nesting habitat for a variety of birds.

What usually first attracts attention to Joshua trees is their size. While most Mojave Desert plants are small, Joshua trees sometimes reach more than 30 feet in height, and 20-foot-tall specimens are common. Joshua trees do not preserve growth rings in their fibrous trunks and branches, so it is difficult to estimate the age of the largest specimens. Their slow growth rate suggests that some of the bigger trees are at least several centuries old. In addition to their size, Joshua trees' angular and often contorted limbs and shaggy appearance make them one of the more distinctive plants of the North American deserts.

The Joshua tree is almost entirely confined to the Mojave, which is why it is sometimes called an "indicator"

The slender green stems of ephedra, along with silver cholla and sagebrush, grow among Joshua trees in the Last Chance Range where Mojave and Great Basin species overlap. FRED HIRSCHMANN

species for this desert. Within the Northern Mojave its distribution is somewhat patchy. Absent from the lowest basins and bajadas, Joshua trees are concentrated at elevations from 3,500 to 5,000 feet, particularly on plateaus and in upland basins that are subject to winter snowfall. These areas provide the small amounts of

The Joshua tree is a yucca that can attain heights of over 30 feet and may live for 200 years. This typical specimen grows in the Santa Rosa Hills. FRED HIRSCHMANN

groundwater and deeper soil that support Joshua trees. Since much of the upland Northern Mojave is steep and rocky, the region's potential habitat for Joshua trees is relatively limited. Some of the largest stands are found near Highway 190 where it crosses the rolling uplands that connect the southern end of the Inyo Mountains with the Coso and Argus ranges. The Darwin area, south of Highway 190, and Lee Flat, north of Highway 190, both claim extensive Joshua tree woodlands. The appropriately named Joshua Flats, found along Big Pine-Death Valley Road where it descends toward Eureka Valley, contains another fine stand. The southwestern edge of the region embraces additional dense stands in the Kelso Valley and along Highway 178 as it approaches Walker Pass.

At an elevation of about 4,000 to 5,000 feet, two new plants begin to dominate the shrublands: sagebrush and rabbitbrush. Both plants are somewhat less drought tolerant than lower-elevation neighbors like creosote bush and burrobush. By living higher on the slopes, sagebrush, Great Basin sagebrush, and rabbitbrush are able to obtain enough water from the soil to retain their small, soft, gray-green leaves throughout the dry season. Most growth occurs in spring and summer and is limited more by winter cold than summer heat.

Above the scattered Joshua tree

woodlands and sagebrush scrub, real trees begin to dominate. Utah junipers first appear on the higher mountain ranges around 6,000 or 7,000 feet. Seldom more than 20 feet high, these compact, evergreen conifers are descendants of ancestors that grew on the lowest slopes of Mojave valleys during Pleistocene ice ages. Now, after enduring thousands of years of a relatively arid climate, the junipers persist in mountains where precipitation, often in the form of snow, is more plentiful and summer heat less extreme than at lower elevations.

A little farther upslope, single-leaf pinyon makes its debut. A true pine, with large, highly nutritious seeds, the pinyon is another diagnostic Great Basin plant. Before the end of the Pleistocene, pinyon was common in the low valleys of the Mojave but absent from the Great Basin. Today it occurs throughout the Great Basin and in all the major ranges of the Northern Mojave.

Single-leaf pinyon and Utah juniper usually grow together in what is called pinyon-juniper woodland. This widespread plant community is draped across much of the mountainous Northern Mojave between about 6,000 and 9,000 feet and somewhat lower on north-facing slopes. The term "woodland" describes a tree-dominated landscape where the trees do not grow close enough together to form a true forest canopy. At first glance pinyon-juniper woodland may appear to be little more than a scrub forest of stunted evergreen trees growing on what seems to be gravel or bedrock. But such a view misses the importance of pinyon-juniper woodland to the Northern Mojave: its presence indicates a departure from the low-desert extremes of aridity and heat.

Pinyon-juniper woodland can develop in areas that receive a minimum of 9 or 10 inches of annual precipitation. This is a great deal of water in the Northern Mojave, and that water, combined with the lower evaporation rates found at these higher elevations, allows more plant life to flourish. In addition to the two dominant conifers, numerous species of shrubs, sub-shrubs, and perennial grasses grow here. Visitors to the pinyon-juniper woodland often notice shrubs such as mountain mahogany, with its distinctive, feathery seeds, and ephedra, recognizable by its jointed, bright green, seemingly leafless stems.

Pinyon-juniper woodland is particularly attractive to animals because when pinyon pine cones mature, they enclose a bounty of large and highly nutritious seeds. Throughout much of the American West, "pine nut" means the seed of the pinyon pine. Pine nuts are consumed by everything from insects, birds, and small rodents to bears, coyotes, and humans. Pinyon

seeds were one of the most important food sources for indigenous people in the Northern Mojave. There is more to eat in a pinyon-juniper woodland than just pine nuts, however, particularly for animals. Flocks of birds feast on juniper berries in the winter. In spring and early summer, deer, rabbits, and even bighorn sheep may graze the grasses and shrubs that grow in the openings between trees. Coyotes, foxes, and mountain lions prey on the browsing herbivores and the abundant rodent population. Compared to the slopes below, this world teems with animal life.

Within the Northern Mojave, only the Inyo, Panamint, and Kingston

Top: With their gnarled limbs and trunks, Utah junipers dominate this woodland at the northern end of the Inyos. STEPHEN INGRAM
Bottom: Pinyon-juniper woodland covers the Panamint's eastern slopes near Mahogany Flat, elevation 8,100 feet. STEPHEN INGRAM

ranges and a small part of the Grapevine Mountains actually rise above the pinyon-juniper belt. Mountain habitats that are quite distinct from the rest of the region begin at about 9,000 feet in the Inyos and Panamints. Although life-enhancing precipitation continues to increase at these elevations, a new limiting factor has entered the equation—cold. Two closely related species, limber pine and bristlecone pine, grow near summits of the Inyo and Panamint ranges. Both pines are well adapted to the cold, aridity, and nutrient-poor soils that are characteristic of their mountain habitat.

Limber pine first appears at about 9,000 feet, overlapping with a few pinyons. Named for its highly flexible small branches, limber pine is a hardy subalpine tree distributed throughout the Rocky Mountain cordillera and west to the ranges of California. It seldom attains a height greater than 35 feet but may live as long as 2,000 years. Limber pines often grow in clumps, their trunks twisted by the wind.

Great Basin bristlecone pine grows in the Panamint and Inyo ranges beginning at elevations near 10,000 feet. Bristlecone pine is not a big tree. Although its trunk may achieve substantial basal mass—up to 8 to 10 feet across in some cases—the tree is never very tall. It usually grows to about 25 feet and rarely exceeds 40

feet. Bristlecone pine can live several thousand years, and the oldest ring count for this species approaches 5,000 years. No other tree on earth reaches this age.

The amazing longevity of limber and bristlecone pines may be enhanced by the severity of the environment they grow in. Most of the agents that commonly kill trees are severely limited by the dry, cold conditions on these summits. Fungi and insects are both discouraged, and

Top: The north slope of Telescope Peak supports extensive stands of limber and Great Basin bristlecone pine, with bristlecone extending all the way to the mountain's 11,000-foot summit. STEPHEN INGRAM
Bottom: The Northern Mojave is home to two of the world's longest-lived organisms, creosote bush and Great Basin bristlecone pine. Bristlecones, such as these in the Panamints, grow very slowly, producing a dense and decay-resistant wood that contributes to their astounding longevity. STEPHEN INGRAM

tree mortality is thus reduced. Lightning-ignited fires rarely inflict major damage in these sparse forests because there is little accumulation of ground fuels and fires can't easily spread from tree to tree. An additional factor, which may be particularly true for bristlecones, is that they grow so slowly that their wood is uncommonly dense and decay resistant. The same conditions that promote longevity in the pines seem to limit their ability to reproduce. Individual trees may grow for centuries, producing seed annually, and yet see no significant success in creating offspring. However, to regenerate they need only one seedling to survive in their several thousand years of life. Even in death bristlecone and limber pines prove to be amazingly durable. Dead standing trees and fallen logs can persist for centuries or even millennia.

Mountain Biological Islands

Surrounded by lowland desert, each discrete high-mountain area of the Northern Mojave functions as a biological island—a habitat that is isolated from its neighbors by a sea of other habitats. As recently as 12,000 years ago, many of today's mountain species of flora and fauna were prospering in areas that are now lowland desert. As the Pleistocene ended and the climate began to get warmer and drier, the plants and animals that

required cooler, wetter climates gradually migrated to higher elevations.

Since most plants and many animals had no easy way of getting from one range to another, some species became isolated and marooned on a few of the highest mountains. For example, the summits of the Panamint and Kingston ranges harbor a few stands of white fir in shady, north-facing canyons. Although common in

the Sierra Nevada, white fir is a fading ice-age relict in the Northern Mojave where it is confined to a tiny habitat and is at risk of extirpation. From fossil records and other evidence, scientists determined that marmots and Jeffrey pine—widespread in the Sierra Nevada—were once found in the Northern Mojave. Today they are gone from the region, vanquished by gradual natural environmental change.

These perennials and small shrubs found at high elevations in the Panamints are better adapted to the mountains' harsh winters and short, cool growing seasons than annuals. STEPHEN INGRAM

DESERT STREAMS

Riparian habitat is rare in the desert since the primary location where it occurs is along the banks of running streams. Water-dependent vegetation such as willows, cottonwoods, and cattails may flourish in these few favored places. In the Northern Mojave, streams are mostly limited to canyons below higher mountains where springs and runoff produce enough water to form small surface flows. Some of the best riparian corridors follow drainages in the Panamints, including Wildrose, Surprise, Pleasant, and Johnson canyons; in the Inyo Mountains above Saline Valley; and in Darwin Canyon in the Argus Range. Although small in area, both ephemeral and permanent water-courses have played a big role in supporting wildlife and human endeavors in the Northern Mojave. Since sensitive animal and plant species are often concentrated along desert streams, a number of riparian areas have been given added protection through road closures in recent years.

Above: Pacific tree frogs, such as this mating pair in Surprise Canyon, are among a handful of amphibian species that live in the Northern Mojave's moist habitats. MORGAN BALL / PLACE PHOTOGRAPHY
Left: This creek in the Panamint's Surprise Canyon provides enough water to support riparian vegetation that will become more dense over time, since the jeep road up the streambed was closed to vehicles in order to protect sensitive species. FRED HIRSCHMANN

Considered one of the desert's most heat-tolerant lizards, the desert iguana is also an excellent climber. It is seen here near the Ibex Dunes seeking out the flowers of creosote bush, one of its favorite foods. DAN SUZIO *Bottom: This roadrunner in Death Valley may attain speeds up to 18 mph when pursuing its prey.* MICHAEL SEWEL

Wildlife of the Northern Mojave

The climate of the Northern Mojave is every bit as challenging for animals as it is for plants. Fauna face the same difficulties as flora: aridity and extremes of heat and cold. But animals utilize different survival strategies than plants to meet the challenge of a desert climate. Their great advantage is that, unlike plants, they can move: from sun to shade, between food and water, or, in some cases, from the desert to some distant landscape. Animals, however, cannot make their own food as plants do; instead they must forage or hunt for it. Desert animals spend much of their lives avoiding climatic extremes and searching for food.

The amount of wildlife in the Northern Mojave tends to surprise visitors. Despite its harsh conditions, this region is inhabited by an amazing variety of creatures. About 380 species of birds have been recorded within Death Valley National Park. Other animal life within the national park is equally diverse, including 51 species of mammals and 41 species of reptiles and amphibians. The Northern Mojave even boasts six species of fish that are found nowhere else.

The area's many habitats are the key to its wildlife diversity. Living conditions in the area's lowland basins and slopes are not the same as on the upland slopes and mountaintops.

These different environments, in turn, comprise additional habitats, such as riparian corridors, sand dunes, or coniferous woodlands. Each habitat offers its own set of foraging, hunting, breeding, and nesting opportunities for animals.

Animals of Lowland Basins and Slopes

At times, the Northern Mojave lowlands may seem nearly devoid of animal life. One may walk for hours through creosote bush scrub and encounter little more than a few birds, lizards, or jackrabbits. Even when wildlife is not readily visible, there may be ample evidence of its presence, such as the tracks of reptiles and beetles, scat piles left by mammals, the buzz of unseen insects, or the rustle of birds in the brush.

During much of the year, lowland wildlife is difficult to see because many desert mammals and reptiles are nocturnal or confine their daylight activity to the cooler twilight hours at dawn or dusk. The night's cooler temperatures and higher humidity help animals conserve water and thus extend the available range over which they can forage. Darkness also provides protection from predators, although some animals are well adapted for nighttime hunting. Rattlesnakes, for example, can precisely locate warm-blooded animals in complete darkness because they have

Above: The desert spiny lizard, seen here in the Coso Range, helps regulate its body heat by changing color while basking on rocks. In the cool hours of morning, it is darker in order to absorb heat; it changes to a lighter color by mid-day as temperatures increase. FRED HIRSCHMANN
Right: Desert-dwelling coyotes are smaller and lighter-colored than other coyotes. MARK DOLYAK

highly sensitive receptors on either side of their snouts that allow them to detect heat given off by their prey. In winter most of the Northern Mojave's cold-blooded animals hibernate: snakes, lizards, tortoises, and other reptiles are inactive during this time.

Desert wildlife has additional ways of contending with the Northern Mojave's extremes of temperature.

Many animals, such as snakes or coyotes, retreat to the protection of shade or underground dens during the hot days of summer. The temperature at midday in an animal's burrow can be as much as 100°F cooler than the above-ground soil surface temperature. Some creatures, such as roadrunners and antelope ground squirrels, engage in evaporative cooling activities

like panting or licking. Jackrabbits and kit foxes can dissipate body heat through their large ears. Migratory birds escape the summer heat altogether; some species move into nearby mountains or milder coastal areas, while others only pass through the desert lowlands in fall and spring during long-distance migrations. Since reptiles have thin skins and cannot generate their own body heat, they spend much of their time engaged in behavior known as thermoregulation. Depending on the season, weather, and time of day, diurnal reptiles adjust their temperature through a variety of activities including basking, changing orientation to the sun, shuttling between sun and shade, and resting on different surfaces. Nocturnal reptiles regulate body temperatures by their contact with the air or different surfaces. It is not unusual to spot snakes on roads at night soaking up radiant warmth from asphalt surfaces that were heated up during the day.

Some Northern Mojave animals cope with the harsh summer by entering a period of dormancy known as estivation. One of the mammals that estivates is the Mojave ground squirrel. This small, brown denizen of the Northern Mojave's western lowlands is listed as threatened under the California Endangered Species Act. The Mojave ground squirrel fattens up in spring and early summer when its favored foods—fresh leaves and seeds from native shrubs and annuals—are relatively plentiful. By midsummer, when forage has become scarce, the Mojave ground squirrel is ensconced in its underground nest. The animal's heart rate, metabolism, and body temperature drop dramatically, allowing it to live on stored body fat until it emerges in late fall or winter after rain has stimulated the growth of new vegetation. In response to drought, when there is little green forage, the ground squirrel may begin estivating as early as April and may not mate or bear young until the following year.

Aridity poses another formidable challenge to wildlife. Many of the most common desert animals live almost entirely without easy access to fresh water. They typically rehydrate their bodies not by drinking but by deriving water from the food they consume. Insects and small rodents gather, concentrate, and retain water in their bodies from plant sources; this water is taken up by snakes, bats, roadrunners, coyotes, and other animals that prey on them. Some animals obtain water in unique ways. Doves, unusual among birds because they can swallow with their head down, can drink dew. The western blind snake burrows into sand where it drinks capillary water suspended between the sand particles. The chuckwalla, a large lizard that is often seen basking on rocky slopes, stores extra water in the fatty tissues of its stout tail. No matter how they get it, nearly all desert creatures conserve water in every possible way. Some mammals, reptiles, birds, and insects have even evolved methods of body waste elimination that use almost no water.

The desert tortoise is perhaps the most emblematic species of the Mojave Desert. This long-lived (60 to 100 years) reptile occupies a number of different habitats ranging from rocky bajadas to sandy washes where it can find suitable sites for its burrows. In the western part of the Mojave, the tortoise constructs several 3- to 10-foot-long underground burrows where it spends much of its life, since it hibernates during winter and estivates in summer. It is most active in spring and early fall when it forages heavily on annual wildflowers and grasses. The tortoise can endure

Top: A Mojave ground squirrel feasts on green vegetation. These squirrels cope with the heat of summer by estivating in underground burrows. B. MOOSE PETERSON/WRP
Bottom: Western chuckwallas favor habitat with rocky outcrops, such as this site in the Panamint Range. Adult chuckwallas subsist entirely on plant material. DAN SUZIO

ong periods without drinking because it obtains most of its water from the plants it eats; it can also store a quart of water in its urinary bladder. In late spring, as the temperatures climb and annual plants dry out, the tortoise spends more time underground,

Top: *Desert tortoise burrows in the western part of the Mojave feature tunnels 3 to 10 feet long where the tortoise spends much of its time.* DENNIS FLAHERTY
Bottom: *Rapidly declining desert tortoise populations helped prompt the establishment of the protected Desert Tortoise Natural Area, where this animal lives.* MARK DOLYAK

emerging only in the cool hours of early morning or late afternoon. By July the tortoise generally keeps to its burrow and only ventures out to drink and forage in the immediate aftermath of a summer rain.

As recently as the 1950s, desert tortoises were one of the most commonly seen native animals in the Mojave; they are now increasingly rare. Habitat destruction caused by land development, livestock grazing, and off-highway motor vehicle recreation appears to be the primary agent in the rapid decline of tortoise populations. Grazing cattle and sheep, as well as feral burros, compete with tortoises for sparse vegetation while cars, motorcycles, and dune buggies cave in their burrows and sometimes crush them. Ravens also contribute to plummeting tortoise numbers because they prey heavily on the thin-shelled baby and juvenile tortoises. Although ravens have long been a part of the Mojave Desert ecosystem, in recent years their numbers have grown 15-fold in response to increased food supplies provided by garbage dumps and trash, and new perching and nesting sites such as power poles and buildings. Finally, the tortoises have had to face epidemics of often-fatal diseases including upper respiratory tract disease. Researchers believe that habitat destruction may increase susceptibility to infection, and the rapid spread of highly contagious diseases

may have been exacerbated by the release of infected captive or relocated wild tortoises. The desert tortoise became a federally listed threatened species in 1990, only 20 years after it was designated as the California State Reptile.

While the tortoise often builds its burrows in gravel soils, other lowland desert animals make their homes in sand. Loose sand is a special habitat for wildlife, and a number of desert creatures have adapted to its demands. The Mojave fringe-toed lizard has scale patterns on its rear feet that facilitate traction and digging. Its ability to quickly excavate is critical to its survival, allowing the lizard to burrow into the sand and escape its predators or excess heat.

The Mojave fringe-toed lizard is well adapted to dune habitats where it burrows into sand to avoid predators or excess heat. DAN SUZIO

The sidewinder is another creature of sandy country. Two small, horn-shaped protrusions on the sidewinder's face help keep sand out of its eyes and also dissipate heat. A quick, efficient hunter, the sidewinder often awaits its prey while submerged in the sand with only its eyes and nostrils exposed. This small rattlesnake is named for its distinctive method of locomotion. To move ahead, it throws a loop of its body forward and then pulls itself up on the loop. As it sidewinds, the snake presses into the surface at only two points and thereby holds much of its body off the hot desert sand. Sidewinders leave J-shaped tracks.

Sharing sandy habitats with the sidewinder are several species of desert kangaroo rat, which are the sidewinder's main source of food. This small rodent uses strong rear legs to propel itself forward in a kangaroo-like hopping motion, and can spend its entire life without drinking a drop of water. Active almost entirely at night, the kangaroo rat moves quickly across the sand, seeking plant stems, seeds, and fleshy fungi. It derives nearly all of the water it needs from these foods. During the heat of the day it rests in a burrow with the entrance plugged; this causes the humidity in the chamber to increase, allowing the kangaroo rat to absorb water vapor through its nasal membranes. Kangaroo rats also eat their

own feces to reclaim some moisture.

One of the primary predators of kangaroo rats is the desert kit fox. Like its prey, this small fox is well adapted to arid climates because the food it consumes supplies the water it requires. The desert kit fox is about the size of a house cat and is easily distinguished by its black-tipped tail, big eyes, and very large ears. It frequently hunts in sandy areas and is unique among canines in using dens year-round. Known as an especially curious mammal, the kit fox often approaches desert campsites at night.

The Northern Mojave has some lowland habitats where water is relatively plentiful and aquatic species

Top: A desert kit fox rests at the entrance to its den in the Eureka Valley. The surfaces of this fox's large ears help it dissipate body heat. JOHN DITTLI
Bottom: A sidewinder leaves behind J-shaped tracks as it crosses the sand in the Ibex Dunes. This form of locomotion reduces body contact with hot sand surfaces. DAN SUZIO

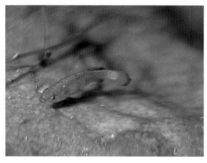

Top: *The Amargosa vole is on California's endangered species list and is found only in a small area of salt marsh at Grimshaw Lake near Tecopa.* B. MOOSE PETERSON/WRP
Bottom: *A male Ash Meadows pupfish defends his territory at Point of Rocks Springs in the Ash Meadows National Wildlife Refuge.* STEPHEN INGRAM

can prosper. The region's widely scattered desert wetlands function as biological islands. While most desert wildlife can mingle and breed widely across the landscape, species whose survival is tied to seasonal or year-round water or water-loving vegetation often have a very limited range. The Amargosa vole, which relies on a thick cover of salt marsh rushes to conceal it from predators, is confined to less than a square mile of wetland habitat near ancient Lake Tecopa. In Death Valley the Badwater snail is limited to a handful of salty pools. But of all the examples of relict or "stranded" species, the most intriguing story is that of the Northern Mojave's pupfish. During the Pleistocene, pupfish occupied the freshwater lakes and streams that once connected and filled many basins of the Northern Mojave. As the ice age ended and aridity set in, the pupfish managed to survive—but only in increasingly shrinking and isolated aquatic areas. Today, these one- to two-inch-long fish are confined to widely scattered sites where year-round desert streams, wetlands, and springs support the aquatic habitat they require.

Over millennia separate pupfish populations have evolved in response to localized conditions and have gradually diverged into separate species or subspecies. Most biologists now recognize 4 species and 10 subspecies of

pupfish in the Northern Mojave. In the Amargosa Valley east of Death Valley, three different pupfish survive within the confines of Ash Meadows National Wildlife Refuge: one is a very rare species, the Devil's Hole pupfish; the other two, the Warm Springs pupfish and Ash Meadows pupfish, are subspecies belonging to a second species. The Devil's Hole pupfish survives only in the mouth of a water-filled limestone cavern; its entire world consists of this one tiny pool of water. All three pupfish are on the U.S. Fish and Wildlife Service's endangered species list. The Amargosa River pupfish is found at two locales where the Amargosa River has some year-round surface flow. A closely related but distinct and isolated pupfish subspecies, the Saratoga pupfish, occurs only at Saratoga Springs in the extreme southern end of Death Valley.

More specialized yet are two pupfish found in northern Death Valley: the Salt Creek and Cottonball Marsh pupfish. Salt Creek is a permanent but largely underground stream that rises to the surface about 10 miles northwest of Furnace Creek; the above-ground portion of the creek is approximately 2 miles long. During spring, spawning Salt Creek pupfish are common in the downstream portion of the creek. Cottonball Basin is south of the Salt Creek interpretive trail and contains some shallow,

Salt Creek flows above ground for about two miles; the downstream portion supports spawning Salt Creek pupfish in spring. MARC SOLOMON

year-round pools. The creek's salinity is nearly equivalent to ocean water, while Cottonball Marsh can be five times saltier than the sea. These two subspecies belong to the same species of pupfish. They survive in their respective habitats despite the high salinity and warm temperatures of the water. The State of California lists the Cottonball Marsh pupfish as a threatened species.

A group of gastropods known as springsnails have an even more restricted distribution than the Northern Mojave's pupfish. These tiny mollusks live at some of the region's smallest and most mineralized seeps and springs; a single pool that measures no more than three feet across and one inch deep may harbor the entire population of one species. In recent years biologists have described at least 20 new springsnails within the Great Basin and Mojave deserts, and at least eight species are now documented in the Death Valley region.

If fish, snails, and other aquatic life can survive in the Northern Mojave's arid basins, it should come as no surprise that the region is also home to small crustaceans known as fairy shrimps. These primitive creatures have a fringe of gills, or "gill feet," protruding from their underside that they use for breathing, gathering food, and locomotion. They move through water by swimming on their backs, paddling with their upturned gills. Unlike desert pupfish and springsnails, fairy shrimp commonly reside in ephemeral pools and puddles. Along with their fellow branchiopods, which include the tadpole and clam shrimps, fairy shrimp females produce extremely durable cysts, or "resting eggs." Cysts withstand freezing and passage through digestive tracks and resist desiccation. They can remain dormant in dry clay—for 15 or more years—until the right combination of moisture, temperature, and other stimuli induce

them to hatch. Large populations of fairy shrimp and tadpole shrimp periodically erupt during wet years in the Northern Mojave when normally dry depressions, potholes, and playas are flooded. The shrimp reach maturity and reproduce within a matter of weeks—before their watery home dries out.

In stark contrast with the desert's aquatic animals, whose movements are usually confined to tiny territories, the birds that populate the Northern Mojave travel great distances. Although some species such as ravens and roadrunners are year-round residents, most birds in the region are migratory. From November until March the lowland basins and slopes provide a winter refuge for many bird species. During these months large numbers of birds congregate at the Northern Mojave's few oases, including Furnace Creek Ranch and the freshwater marsh in Saline Valley. The ephemeral lakes that form

An American avocet wades in Saline Valley's flooded playa. JOHN DITTLI

in dry playas during wet years, such as Panamint Lake, are also very important as breeding and nesting areas for inland populations of shorebirds.

During spring and fall, long-distance migrants such as warblers, swallows, and tanagers pass through on their way to distant northern summer breeding grounds or southern wintering areas. Some bird species have a more local migration. The verdin, for example, nests in mesquite thickets where it stays through spring until its young have fledged; during summer it moves out of the lowlands to cooler areas at higher elevations. One songbird that remains in the same part of the Northern Mojave year-round is the Inyo California towhee. It lives only in dense riparian thickets that occur at scattered springs and seeps in the southern Argus Range. The State of California lists this brown, robin-sized towhee as an endangered species, and wildlife biologists are working to minimize impacts to its habitat from activities such as water diversion, stock grazing, and mining.

Almost in a class by themselves are the desert's ravens. Ravens manage to make a successful living year-round in the Northern Mojave's lowland valleys. These intelligent and resourceful birds are highly adaptable. In fact, their adaptability makes them among the most versatile of animals. Only two species of vertebrates survive year-round in both the hottest parts of Death Valley and in the extreme northern Arctic: ravens and human beings.

The greatest abundance and diversity of lowland Northern Mojave wildlife are found among the arthropods, a group that includes animals such as insects, spiders, and scorpions. Arthropods are a vital part of the desert's food chain and the primary source of nourishment for many birds, mammals, and reptiles. Some, notably insects, play an important role as pollinators, especially during the short-duration blooming period of desert annuals. Arthropods are also the desert's most common recyclers, and their ranks include millipedes that eat detritus, beetles that consume dung, and red ants that feed on carrion. The numbers and concentration of arthropods can be astonishing; at one study area in the Northern Mojave, a single species of the tiny darkling beetle was calculated at more than two pounds of biomass per acre.

Bats are common predators of arthropods. They use echolocation to navigate, and rely on vision and prey-produced sounds while foraging. Some bat species can consume up to 600 mosquito-sized insects in an hour. The region's thousands of abandoned mines provide shelter for at least 10 species of resident bats, which utilize mine shafts for day and night roosts, rearing young in summer, and hibernation in winter. Throughout the world, including the California deserts, bats have—for a variety of reasons—lost the use of many traditional roosting and foraging areas, and their populations are in decline. Since inactive mine shafts provide the darkness and protection that roosting bats need, they are a good replacement for lost habitat. Wildlife biologists are working with property owners, including the federal government, to close the entrances of abandoned mines by using metal grates with horizontal bars rather than earthen fill; this technique allows bats to enter, but excludes people from these often unstable and dangerous caverns. While historic mining used deep shafts that created bat habitat, renewed mining in many districts employs open-pit methods that displace resident bats.

VENOMOUS ANIMALS OF THE NORTHERN MOJAVE

The prospect of seeing a venomous animal in the desert stirs anxiety in some people and eager anticipation in others. The Northern Mojave's most common venomous creatures are nocturnal invertebrates such as the desert tarantula, giant desert hairy scorpion, and desert centipede. These animals produce toxins in volumes sufficient to immobilize only small prey species. For humans, the bite of a desert tarantula or the sting of a giant desert hairy scorpion is often compared to the sting of a bee in terms of its severity.

Three species of rattlesnake are found in the Northern Mojave, and their bites can be dangerous. A rattlesnake uses its fangs to puncture its victim and, in most cases, simultaneously injects a dose of venom. Since its toxins are potent enough to kill much larger animals—including humans on rare occasions—it is essential to get immediate treatment for a rattlesnake bite at the nearest hospital emergency room.

Rattlesnakes take their name from interlocking segments on the ends of their tails. A new rattle is added each time the snake sheds its skin, which can occur more than once per year. Rattlesnakes use their tails to make a rattling buzz if disturbed. If you hear that sound consider it a warning: stop moving and slowly back away from the snake or from where the buzz is emanating.

The Mojave rattlesnake (also called Mojave green rattlesnake) is especially feared because its venom is considered the most deadly among the North American rattlesnake species; not only does it cause breakdown of body tissue as with other rattlesnake venoms, but it also has neurotoxic properties that can lead to serious respiratory distress. The Mojave rattlesnake typically hunts at night; it is associated with rocky areas and open vegetation such as creosote bush scrub and Joshua tree woodland.

The other two rattlesnakes in the region tend to occupy different habitats. The Panamint rattlesnake, which is the Northern Mojave's own subspecies of the speckled rattlesnake, is more likely to live on rocky slopes in the mountain areas. Sidewinders generally inhabit areas where desert shrubs grow on low sand hills, but they can also survive in barren sand dunes and windswept playas.

Extra caution is advised if you encounter a Mojave rattlesnake; their venom is the deadliest of all the North American rattlesnakes. DENNIS SHERIDAN/PLACE PHOTOGRAPHY

Animals of Upland Slopes and Mountains

The wildlife habitats of the Northern Mojave uplands are quite different from those of the lowland basins. One of the chief differences is that the upland vegetation offers animals more to eat. Mammals and birds especially benefit from the grasses and periodic crops of juniper berries and pinyon seeds available in pinyon-juniper woodlands. The other big advantage for upland wildlife is the presence of more vertical layers of vegetation. Pinyon, limber, and bristlecone pines as well as junipers and Joshua trees add an overstory component to the landscape that increases the ways in which animals can nest, hunt, and escape from predators.

Although rarely seen, the desert bighorn is the animal many people associate with the ranges of the Northern Mojave. Bighorn travel across the entire upland desert landscape but spend most of their time in rugged, high-elevation areas. Bighorn can survive on the sparsest vegetation as long as they have access to fresh water every few days. Their adaptation to mountain terrain is exemplified by their ability to use steep, rocky routes for escape. When startled, bighorn retreat to cliff faces or steep bluffs where their amazing agility places them beyond the reach of most predators. Depending on the season and forage availability, bighorn

Woodlands of pinyon and juniper trees cover the rocky slopes above Papoose Flat in the Inyo Range. Trees in these upland habitats offer wildlife shelter for nesting and roosting as well as seeds and berries for food. MARC SOLOMON

move from the lower edge of dry desert mountains to the summits of the Northern Mojave's highest ranges. Male bighorns also travel between ranges by crossing lowland hills and basins. By mixing with different herds that are located in separate upland areas, the male sheep play an important role in maintaining genetic diversity. Their movement also underscores the value of wildlife corridors that allow passage between remote mountain areas.

Before the mid-nineteenth century,

bighorn were commonly seen in nearly all of the region's mountains. In the late-nineteenth and early twentieth centuries, hunting and diseases spread by domestic sheep decimated their numbers, reducing populations to tiny remnants in the most rugged and remote terrain. By the early twentieth century bighorn faced another challenge—wild burros. Burros supplied the primary "horsepower" for desert transportation from the 1850s until well into the twentieth century. Pack strings of burros connected

mining camps with supply centers. Inevitably, some of these tough little animals escaped; additional burros were abandoned and set free as motor vehicles gradually replaced them. Feral burros were able to survive in the desert and reproduce. By the 1960s thousands of these non-native animals were roaming the Northern Mojave. Eventually it became apparent that the burros were out-competing the native bighorn for forage and water. In response the National Park Service and Bureau of Land Management (BLM) undertook controversial programs of burro reduction to protect habitat for the remaining bighorn sheep. Today, with burro control programs continuing in the desert, Northern Mojave bighorn populations have begun to rebound.

The natural predator of the bighorn and the desert's top-rung carnivore is the mountain lion, or puma. These big cats limit themselves mostly to mountain areas where sheep and deer live. The rest of the desert country they give over to their smaller cousins the bobcats; these versatile carnivores range over the great majority of the Northern Mojave, preying primarily on small mammals and birds.

Ring-tailed cats are another carnivorous species that occupies the upland slopes and mountains. They are not true felines, but instead are members of the raccoon family. These slender, agile animals have long black- and white-striped tails. They are nocturnal predators, famous for their mouse-catching abilities. Their nickname "miner's cat" comes from the fact that old-time miners often tamed the animals and kept them around their camps to control rodents.

Many species of birds prosper in the Mojave uplands. Scott's orioles, northern flickers, and ladder-backed woodpeckers are among at least 25 species that may utilize Joshua trees for nesting. Pinyon jays add color and raucous sound to Joshua tree and pinyon-juniper woodlands. These dusty-blue jays often travel in large, noisy flocks. As their name implies, they prize the mature seeds of the pinyon; they consume many and collect and cache others for later use. In a good year a flock of pinyon jays may cache over four million seeds. Many of these are never retrieved, ensuring a source of seed for pinyon regeneration.

Top: Bighorn sheep inhabit mountain ranges in the Northern Mojave and utilize steep rocky terrain as escape routes from predators.
JOHN LABONTE
Bottom: Not to be confused with crows, ravens are larger and like these two in the Panamint Range, often travel in pairs.
RANDI HIRSCHMANN

History of the Northern Mojave Before 1900

T here was no possible way to cross this high steep range of mountains anywhere to the north and the Jayhawkers had abandoned their wagons and burned them, and we could no longer follow on the trail they made. It seemed that there was no other alternative but for us to keep along the edge of the mountain to the south and search for another pass. Some who had read Fremont's travels said that the range immediately west of us must be the one he described, on the west of which was a beautiful country, of rich soil and having plenty of cattle, and horses and containing some settlers, but on the east all was barren, dry, rocky, sandy desert as far as could be seen. . . .

We had to look over the matter very carefully and consider all the conditions and circumstances of the case. We could see the mountains were lower to the south, but they held no snow and seemed only barren rocks piled up in lofty peaks, and as we looked it seemed the most God-forsaken country in the world.

We had been in the region long enough to know the higher mountains contained most water, and that the valleys had bad water or none at all, so that while the lower altitudes to the south gave some promise of easier crossing it gave us no promise of water, without which we must certainly perish. In a certain sense we were lost. . . .

—William Manly Lewis,
Death Valley in '49, 1894

Opposite: Earlier human cultures of the Northern Mojave left a legacy of beautiful rock art that is admired by visitors and studied by scholars. FRED HIRSCHMANN

Native Americans of the Northern Mojave

From the time humans first settled in the lands east of the Sierra Nevada, their lives and numbers were inescapably determined by the challenging natural environment in which they lived. Archaeological evidence from a number of locations confirms that humans have been in the Northern Mojave for at least 11,000 years. Chronometric dating of petroglyphs made in the Coso Range suggests that people were here even earlier, perhaps as long as 16,500 years ago. As recently as 10,000 years ago, semi-nomadic people made camps near the shore of receding Lake Manly and hunted in nearby savannas and marshlands. But as the last glacial period ended and the regional climate became steadily warmer and drier, this landscape was gradually transformed into a desert. Since that time the record for the Northern Mojave and Great Basin tells the story of small numbers of people responding to an arid environment. Particularly significant is the paucity of evidence that would confirm human occupation from about 7,500 to 4,500 years ago, when prolonged drought made conditions especially challenging for human survival.

Beginning about 4,500 years ago, the region's climate again became more moderate and its human population increased. A number of hunter-gatherer cultures evolved in

Archeological research, including radiocarbon dating of petroglyphs in the Coso Range, suggests that humans arrived in the Northern Mojave at least 11,000 years ago. BILL EVARTS

the region during the next several thousand years, and by the time Euro-Americans arrived in the early nineteenth century, the indigenous people had perfected a way of life that allowed them to occupy some of the most severe and forbidding landscapes in North America. For the Native Americans who lived in the Northern Mojave, the great challenge of life was finding food. That they did so successfully for millennia stands as clear testimony to their intimate knowledge of a difficult homeland.

When Euro-Americans first entered the Northern Mojave, the Native Americans who lived in the region belonged to one of four cultural groups: the Kawaiisu, Southern Paiute, Owens Valley Paiute, and Western Shoshone. The Kawaiisu were centered in the southeastern Sierra Nevada foothills and ranged into Indian Wells and Panamint valleys. They were closely related to the Southern Paiutes, who primarily lived in the southeastern corner of the region near present-day Tecopa and southward. Along the fringe of the desert, the Owens Valley Paiute established villages near Owens Lake and northward and traveled into the Inyo Mountains for hunting and foraging. The Western Shoshone lived in the arid lands at the heart of the Northern Mojave, populating basins and mountains from Saline and Panamint valleys into Death Valley and the Amargosa Desert. There were also separate bands within the groups, such as the Saline Valley and Panamint Valley bands of Shoshone. Intermarriage among the different cultural groups was not unusual, and some of the larger villages, such as Tumbisha in Death Valley, included Shoshone, Southern Paiute, and Kawaiisu people.

The harshness of the desert and its seasonal scarcity of food kept human populations small. They established villages—rarely larger than 50 to 60 people—near permanent water sources and ranged widely across the region, utilizing nearly every resource the land offered. During the course of the year, families moved between desert floor and mountain camps, harvesting seasonal plants and seeking a hospitable climate. Two staple foods provided a base: mesquite bean pods from the lowlands and pinyon pine seeds, or pine "nuts," from the mountains. The primarily vegetarian diet was supplemented by game including jackrabbits, bighorn sheep, and pronghorn. Western Shoshone populations fluctuated with conditions, but their total number in the Northern Mojave probably never exceeded 500 to 1,000 individuals. Although most of their villages are gone, a Shoshone enclave still exists near Death Valley's Furnace Creek.

A bedrock mortar and pictographs provide evidence of past human use of this small cave in the Greenwater Range. FRED HIRSCHMANN

Euro-Americans Enter the Mojave

It was not until the early nineteenth century that the desert-dwelling Paiutes and Shoshones started to feel the effects from the centuries-long European invasion of North America. Spaniards colonized coastal California beginning in 1769; their missionary efforts triggered some rebellions that sent some natives fleeing to the interior, but the impact of these events quickly faded east of the Sierra Nevada. The Northern Mojave's indigenous people would not have contact with outsiders until later, when fur trappers, traders, and pioneers began to make sporadic forays into the region.

Top: These pictographs are from the Death Valley area, one of the last places in California to be explored by Euro-Americans.
MARC SOLOMON
Bottom: The Amargosa River Canyon was along the route of the Spanish Trail, which led from Santa Fe to Los Angeles. DAVID LANNER

The transcontinental journey of Lewis and Clark, completed in 1806, set the stage for the interior West's first industry—fur trapping. By the late 1820s, however, trappers were exhausting the stock of beaver in the Rocky Mountains. This drove the impulse for exploration farther west into the more arid expanses of the Great Basin. Among the explorers was an American citizen, Jedediah Smith, who in 1826 made his way to California from the Great Salt Lake, traversing what would later become the states of Utah and Arizona. He entered Mexico's Alta California through the Mojave Desert. When he eventually left the Mexican province he crossed the Sierra Nevada just south of Lake Tahoe, passed through the Great Basin Desert and returned to the Great Salt Lake. Feeling his way through unknown country, Smith had wisely avoided the rugged lands east of the Sierra Nevada's highest peaks.

In the winter of 1829-1830 another party crossed the Mojave Desert, but these men were traders, not fur trappers. The small group, led by Spaniard Antonio Armijo, struck out from northern New Mexico with the goal of blazing a trail to Alta California. To connect these two northernmost frontier provinces of the Republic of Mexico, Armijo needed to find a reliable route across more than a thousand miles of little-known country. By early December 1829,

Armijo reached the eastern edge of the Mojave Desert (in what is now the southwestern corner of Utah) by linking trails developed in the eighteenth century. Jedediah Smith had passed through this same area four years earlier, but Armijo wanted a more direct route to the west than Smith's, which had crossed the Colorado River farther south, near present-day Needles. Sending out scouts and waiting patiently, Armijo eventually found his route. Traveling west from the springs where the city of Las Vegas now stands, Armijo's new trail took him west to the Amargosa River near modern Shoshone. Armijo then followed the Amargosa south until it turned sharply to the northwest and began its final descent into the sink of Death Valley. At this point Armijo left the Amargosa, but not before he skirted the southern end of Death Valley and thus became the first Euro-American to view North America's lowest desert basin.

In the years that followed, Armijo's route became known as the "Spanish Trail." It was initially used by New Mexican traders who packed woven goods to California and returned with mules and horses. By the early 1840s emigrants bound for California had begun to travel the route. With the opening of the Spanish Trail, one corner of the Northern Mojave had been connected to the larger world.

In 1833 Joseph R. Walker, a trapper seeking new country, crossed the northern Great Basin and climbed over the central Sierra Nevada to discover Yosemite Valley. The following spring, seeking an easier way to return to the Rocky Mountains, Walker led his group to the southern end of the San Joaquin Valley. Indian guides showed him the way east up the Kern River drainage toward a mile-high Sierran pass that now bears his name. After descending from the pass, Walker took his men north through

This is the view east from historic Walker Pass towards Indian Wells Valley.
MARK PAHUTA

Indian Wells Valley and Owens Valley. Walker was the first white man to traverse this territory, and this portion of his trek opened up yet another edge of the Northern Mojave. A decade later, in 1843, Walker was back in the region, guiding the second emigrant wagon train to enter California. This small beleaguered party of 50 emigrants worked its way south to Owens Lake where they abandoned their wagons before crossing the Sierra Nevada at Walker Pass.

By the late 1840s the logical north/south travel route that is today followed by Highway 395 had been defined, but the land to the east, the empty heart of the Northern Mojave, remained unknown to Euro-Americans. All this changed rapidly after 1848 with the advent of the California gold rush and the mass overland emigration of 1849.

Trapped in Death Valley

During the spring and summer of 1849, tens of thousands of Americans, all hoping to find their fortunes, committed themselves to the arduous journey to California. Some traveled by sea, others by land. Of those going overland most followed the proven California Trail, which led across northern Nevada and then over the Sierra Nevada to Sacramento. Others branched out to explore lesser-used routes, and some of these made terrible mistakes of

judgment. By the fall of 1849, lost argonauts were wandering all over the far West.

In early October that year, a group of 400 to 500 people with 110 wagons left Salt Lake City. Guided by Jefferson Hunt, their intention was to follow the Spanish Trail to California; by crossing the Mojave rather than the Sierra Nevada, they were assured that early snowstorms could not hinder their arrival at the goldfields. As the Hunt train moved slowly southwest across the Great Basin, it was overtaken by 20-year-old Captain Orson Smith and his small party of packers. Smith urged Hunt and other members of the wagon train to abandon the Spanish Trail; he insisted that they would more quickly reach the goldfields by taking a little-known desert trail known as Walker's Cut-off.

Convinced that Smith's shortcut would expedite their journey, 100 wagons voted to break away from the Hunt train. At a spot near the southwestern corner of Utah, they left the Spanish Trail and headed west. After encountering a deep canyon only 25 miles into the shortcut, Smith and most of his followers realized their folly. The disillusioned emigrants returned to the Spanish Trail and successfully completed their journey to the gold country. A portion of the group, however, consisting of about 27 wagons and 100 people, made their way around the canyon and

Some of the pioneers who blundered into Death Valley while seeking a short cut to California's gold fields in December 1849 followed this route down Furnace Creek Wash. JEFF GNASS

continued due west. By late December, exhausted, hungry, and splintered into little groups, all these argonauts had wandered into Death Valley.

The first to arrive were a band of 11 men, traveling on foot, who had once been among Smith's party. This unfortunate group, led by a '49er named Pinney, soon ran low on food. Pinney and one other man split off and made their way west to Owens Lake, where they were nursed back to health by the Paiutes before crossing the Sierra Nevada. The skeletons of nine men, presumed to be from Pinney's original party, were reportedly found north of the Death Valley Sand Dunes in about 1862.

The next party to blunder into Death Valley consisted of 40 to 50 Illinois men known as the "Jayhawkers." Some of this group crossed into Death Valley by traversing the rugged Funeral Mountains, but most of them skirted around the south edge of the range. About Christmastime they descended into Death Valley, passing through the Western Shoshone settlement of Tumbisha at the mouth of Furnace Creek. The villagers watched the strange procession of foreigners from a safe distance.

Another splinter group known as the "Bugsmashers" soon caught up with the Jayhawkers. After realizing that the two-mile-high wall of the Panamints blocked any direct west-ward advance, both parties turned north up the valley. Somewhere on the valley floor near Salt Creek, they killed their emaciated oxen and burned their wagons to dry the meat. With little more than oxen jerky to sustain them, the desert travelers doggedly continued north and west. They split up into still smaller units, crossing the Panamints at places now named Jayhawker Pass, Towne Pass, and Emigrant Canyon—only to face Panamint Valley. (Amidst this travail, several of the men found rich samples of silver-lead ore in the Panamint Range, which they packed out with them. One particularly nice piece was later made into a gunsight, and in subsequent years many prospecting parties tried unsuccessfully to locate the "Lost Gunsight Lode" of Death Valley.) Remarkably, with the exception of two of the Jayhawkers who died while crossing the Slate Range near Searles Valley, all of these argonauts eventually found their way to the base of the Sierra Nevada.

The last and perhaps most famous contingent to descend into Death Valley that December was the Bennett-Arcan group. Their party consisted of 7 wagons and about 30 men, women, and children. After entering the valley, they decided to turn south rather than follow the Jayhawkers. They eventually came to rest at the edge of the salt pan near the foot of Telescope Peak. Exhausted and lost, blocked from further westward progress by the huge mountains, the group concluded that further advance would be futile. The site of their bleak encampment is probably today's Bennett's Well.

Two of the group's young bachelors, William Lewis Manly and John Rogers, volunteered to venture on alone, find help, and return. Traveling on foot, they made their way over the Panamint and Slate ranges to Searles Valley; they then swung west to cross Indian Wells Valley before turning south. They continued across the western edge of the Mojave and eventually reached help at a large rancho near present-day Saugus. While Manly and Rogers were gone, several of the group, led by Harry Wade, decided to push on. They headed southwest through Wingate Wash—a route later used by borax-hauling teamsters—and rejoined the Spanish Trail near Barstow. Of the 27 wagons that entered Death Valley that fateful December, Harry Wade's and one other wagon were the only ones to make it out.

Twenty-six days after leaving their companions, Manly and Rogers triumphantly returned to rescue the remaining members of the Bennett-Arcan group. In the interim only one of these stranded '49ers had perished. Like the others before them, these hardy survivors walked out of the huge desert sink that had so nearly trapped them. As they trudged over

This bluff in the northern Panamints overlooks Emigrant Canyon, which takes its name from the lost '49ers who walked up the canyon in their escape from Death Valley. JEFF GNASS

the southern Panamints, someone in the party reportedly looked back and uttered "Goodbye death valley," bestowing an unforgettable name on North America's deepest basin.

It is hard for modern travelers to comprehend how utterly alien this desert must have seemed to the lost emigrants. In a world where people knew only the places in which they were born, how could Midwesterners and Easterners have ever anticipated Death Valley? The land they knew was largely flat, green, well-watered, and predictable. Death Valley taught them a lesson about how extreme the Western environment could be, and the tales of their hardships and escapes hold our fascination to this day.

The Search for Silver

During the decade that followed the accidental discovery of Death Valley, knowledge of the Northern Mojave region increased, particularly as a result of the 1855 California Boundary Survey. But until the late 1850s, most attention remained focused on the Mother Lode west of the Sierra Nevada crest. The formal place name of Death Valley would not even appear until 1861.

As California gold mining became a more capital-intensive industry, frustrated individual miners began to broaden their search. In 1859 prospectors made the first strikes on Mount Davidson near present-day Reno, and within a few years these

Top: *Beginning about 1874, Freeman Station in Indian Wells Valley was a key stop for stage and freight companies serving the Northern Mojave's mining camps.* EASTERN CALIFORNIA MUSEUM
Bottom: *Working alone or in teams, prospectors like this man made major gold and silver discoveries that turned the region into a mining mecca.* SEARLES VALLEY HISTORICAL SOCIETY

mines grew into the famous Comstock Load, with its boom camp of Virginia City. As the enormous wealth of the Comstock became apparent during the 1860s, the mining community received two clear messages. The first was that the Great Basin held mineral wealth; the second, equally important, was that the wealth would come from silver as well as gold. Emboldened by these lessons, prospectors moved out to find other "Comstocks" in the arid lands east of the Sierra Nevada.

Eventually the search for silver in the Northern Mojave paid off. About 1865, after the final subjugation of the Owens Valley Paiute by U.S. Army troops, a prospector named Pablo Flores recorded a silver claim near the summit of the southern Inyo Mountains east of Owens Lake. Over the next several years this claim grew into the silver-mining camp of Cerro Gordo. Despite its remote, difficult location, Cerro Gordo had grown into a sizeable mining camp by the early 1870s. Before the mines closed for the first time in 1879, more than $10 million of silver had been extracted. During peak production in the mid-1870s, heavy bars of silver-lead bullion accumulated at Cerro Gordo's smelter at the edge of Owens Lake much faster than they could be removed. Among the lasting legacies of Cerro Gordo's heyday was the establishment of a major freight route—largely traced today by Highways 395 and 14—that linked this corner of the Northern Mojave with the fast-growing town of Los Angeles and its nearby port at San Pedro.

The rich discoveries at Cerro

Gordo and the continuing excitement of the Comstock Load inspired much additional prospecting across the Northern Mojave. The next bonanza emerged suddenly in 1873 with the announcement of a major silver discovery in the Panamint Range a few miles south of Telescope Peak. Even more remote than Cerro Gordo, the new camp of Panamint City nevertheless drew hundreds of eager miners and entrepreneurs to the very rim of Death Valley. By 1875 more than a thousand people occupied the camp, which became famous for its lawlessness. At one point the mine superintendent ordered that all silver bullion produced at his mill be cast into balls weighing 750 pounds each so they could not be stolen. Inspired by the riches of the Panamints, prospectors looked closely at the surrounding region, and by 1875 another mountain camp, known as Lookout, blossomed in the Argus Range above the west side of Panamint Valley. Farther north, in a high basin between the Argus and Coso ranges, the mining camp of Darwin also prospered for a time in the 1870s. While the heady excitement generated by big gold or silver discoveries drew most of the attention, much of the region's mining was decidedly small-scale and often involved no more than a handful of men working a pocket of ore. They were known as pocket miners.

Precious metal prospecting was not confined to the high country. In 1875 brothers William and Robert Brown, who had enjoyed some success at Darwin, uncovered a rich vein of silver-lead ore near Resting Spring, an important water hole along the Spanish Trail. The Browns soon had the backing of George Hearst and other prominent investors, and their mining district attracted several hundred souls to the new townsite of Brownsville, later renamed Tecopa. But the operation was plagued by problems: lack of water to cool the smelter, the high cost of milling the ore, tense relations with the Ash Meadow Paiute-Shoshone band, and the biggest obstacle of all—the high cost of transporting ore to an outside smelter. One of the mine's subsequent owners even built and patented a self-propelled steam wagon in a futile attempt to profitably ship the Tecopa ore to the distant railhead at Daggett. By 1880 the excitement over Tecopa had subsided.

The Northern Mojave was not fated to become a new Comstock. Panamint City was as short-lived as it was wild, and by 1880, with its rich ore deposits exhausted, the camp had emptied. Lookout dwindled rapidly after its mines closed in 1879, and Darwin dissipated about the same time, although it would come back to life a quarter century later. Tecopa languished until 1906 when a new railroad helped revive its mines.

Many Native Americans were uprooted by the influx of miners, merchants, and homesteaders to the Northern Mojave; some, like this family at Furnace Creek, remained near their ancestral homes. J.C. BACK / NATIONAL PARK SERVICE, DEATH VALLEY NATIONAL PARK
Bottom: By 1874 the silver-mining frenzy in the Panamint Range was centered in Panamint City, population 2,000. The camp's crowning glory was this stamp mill at the head of Surprise Canyon. U.S. BORAX COLLECTION

Mining the Ancient Lakebeds

With the decline of Cerro Gordo, and the demise of camps like Panamint City, Lookout, Tecopa, and Darwin, the Northern Mojave silver excitement soon abated. Just when the region's silver-mining fever started to wane, a new lakebed mineral began to attract increasing interest: borax. In the early 1870s it became apparent that borax, which was now in growing demand for industrial purposes, occurred naturally in many of the dry lakebeds of the western Great Basin. Initial discoveries in western Nevada were followed by finds in eastern California.

Borax was probably first discovered in the Northern Mojave in 1862 by John Searles, who found rich deposits on the lakebed that now carries his name. By 1876 John and Dennis Searles had formed the San Bernardino Borax Mining Company and were shipping their product via 20-mule-team wagons to the railhead at Mojave. Later owners built a rail line to Searles Lake, and the site is still a mining center today.

Borax was found on the mineralized playas of Death and Saline valleys in 1873, but modest initial efforts at these remote and inhospitable sites eventually faltered and failed. The "rediscovery" of borax west of Furnace Creek, however, triggered the first truly successful effort to tap the vast bonanza on the salt flats of Death Valley. It began with Aaron and Rosie Winters, who eked out a living on their small ranch in Ash Meadows east of Death Valley. After passing prospectors left samples of Death Valley borax with the Winters, they quietly contacted William Tell Coleman and Francis Marion Smith, the nation's two leading producers of borax. Smith and Coleman's agents traveled to Death Valley and confirmed the existence of the rich deposits. By November 21, 1881 Coleman and Smith had organized the 4,000-acre Death Valley Borax and Salt Mining District. Winters sold out for the handsome sum of $20,000. He soon discovered another borax deposit near Resting Spring east of Tecopa and once again was bought out by the borax magnates.

William Coleman built the Harmony Borax Works near the mouth of Furnace Creek in 1882. The operation, which relied heavily on Chinese laborers, was a relatively simple affair that involved scraping up the silty "ore" from the playa and

A pair of huge wagons and a water tank pulled by 18 mules and 2 draft horses was used for transporting borax from processing plants at Death Valley and Tecopa to the railroad at Mojave in the 1880s. Searles Lake borax was also transported this way. WILLARD COLLECTION / PALM SPRINGS DESERT MUSEUM

Left: The original borax wagons displayed in Death Valley are an impressive sight, with their 7-foot-high rear wheels and 6-foot-deep beds that carried 10 tons of borax. FRED HIRSCHMANN
Above: Chinese workers, like these men gathering borax on the Death Valley lakebed in the 1880s, were a vital part of the early-day work force in the Northern Mojave. U.S. BORAX COLLECTION

then dissolving and boiling it in the presence of other chemicals to produce crystals of additional purity. Coleman's company maintained an industrial plant at the hottest and possibly the most remote work site in the United States. It was too hot, in fact, to crystallize the borax during the summer months, and from June to October Coleman shifted the operation to his Amargosa Borax Works, located near Tecopa. Utilizing the huge 20-mule-team wagons that later became synonymous with the public image of Death Valley, Coleman shipped out more than a million dollars worth of borax—more than any Death Valley gold and silver mines had ever yielded. By 1888 borax from mines in Death Valley, Amargosa, and Calico had flooded the market. Prices collapsed, and Coleman closed

Harmony Borax Works and declared bankruptcy. Francis Smith purchased Coleman's holdings in 1890, but borax mining did not return to Death Valley until the next century.

Still Almost Untouched

Despite several decades of mining activity, the vast Northern Mojave remained largely untouched as the nineteenth century drew to a close. The water-rich Owens Valley, bordering the western edge of the region, had changed the most. The Paiutes had been driven out, although many returned from the reservations to work as laborers on the ranches that now occupied their homeland. River-

bottom lands sprouted new farms, cattle ranches, and towns, and the narrow-gauge Carson & Colorado Railroad connected the valley's communities and ran north to meet the main transcontinental line at Carson City, Nevada. To the east and south, however, the enormous emptiness of Indian Wells, Saline, Panamint, and Death valleys remained intact despite prospecting and the temporary boom camps it provoked. As the century wound down, the Northern Mojave's indigenous people must have wondered if they might ultimately regain exclusive use of their domain. It appeared that the white men really didn't want it.

History of the Northern Mojave After 1900

I didn't get in early enough at Tonopah and Goldfield, and so I wandered south and followed the Keane Wonder excitement in the Funeral Range. . . . When I found I couldn't get anything good at the Keane Wonder, I remembered the blowout and decided to go back to it. E. L. Cross was at the Keane Wonder; he was there afoot.

"Shorty, I'd like to go with you," said Cross.

"Your chance is good," I said. "Come along."

. . . when we came to Daylight Springs I told Cross I had passed up a country some time before and as it looked good to me, we would go back to it. . . .

. . . Next morning we started west. Cross started down to the little hill to the south, which Beatty later located as the Mammoth, and I went over to the blowout. I found lots of quartz all aver the hill and started to break it with my pick. Cross hadn't moved over 400 feet from me when I ran against a boulder, and I called out, "Come back; we've got it."

The quartz was just full of free gold, and it was the original genuine green bullfrog rock. Talk about rich rock! Why, gee whiz, it was great. We took the stuff back to the spring and panned it, and we certainly went straight up. The very first boulder was as rich in gold as anything I had ever seen.

—Shorty Harris,
The Rhyolite Herald, 1909

Opposite: A symbol of the Northern Mojave's boom and bust mining history is Rhyolite's ornate Cook Bank building, which was completed in 1908 and closed that same year. LARRY ULRICH

New Towns and Railroads

If any Native Americans in the Northern Mojave held quiet hopes of regaining exclusive use of their home-land during the 1890s, events at the turn of the century must have brought them enormous disappoint-ment. Large bodies of gold and silver ore were discovered in two districts that fringe the region, and another wave of prospectors poured into the desert. More important, the new min-ing districts fueled the construction of railroads, highways, and permanent settlements that brought the outside world even closer to the once-remote territory of the area's Shoshone, Paiute, and Kawaiisu inhabitants.

The first big turn-of-the-century strike took place in the Rand Mountains, south of present-day Ridgecrest, where three prospectors found gold in 1895. Their Yellow Aster Mine soon became the hub of Randsburg, a company town whose population rapidly swelled to 14,000. By 1897 a 28-mile-long spur linked the Rand Mining District's depot of Johannesburg with the mainline of the Atchison, Topeka & Santa Fe Railroad at Kramer Junction. The mining of gold, silver, and then tung-sten continued in the Randsburg area until the 1950s, eventually yielding $25 to $50 million. Finally, beginning in the late 1980s, the Yellow Aster site was reworked with a large, open-pit mining operation.

Central western Nevada was the scene of the other significant mineral discovery to reverberate through the Northern Mojave at the start of the twentieth century. This mining boom began with a seemingly inauspicious event in May 1900. A prospector

Celebrants hold a flag-raising ceremony at Randsburg's Yellow Aster Mining and Milling Company in 1896, where gold was found the previous year by F. M. Mooers (fourth from left in white suit). EASTERN CALIFORNIA MUSEUM

named Jim Butler picked up a rock to throw at a misbehaving pack burro. The rock caught his eye, and instead of throwing it he took it home to be assayed. It turned out to contain silver—lots of silver.

Within months the site of Butler's discovery grew into a mining camp called Tonopah. By early 1902 Tonopah's silver mines had already demonstrated real potential, and more than 1,000 people were living in the new desert city. By the time the first railroad to Tonopah opened in July 1904, the district's miners were working 300 to 500 feet below the surface in large bodies of rich ore. Late in 1902 gold had been discovered 25 miles south of Tonopah. By September 1905 Tonopah's new neighbor, Goldfield, also had rich mines and a railroad connecting it to the outside world. Western Nevada's second great mining boom had begun.

Inevitably, the mineral fever kindled by the enormous wealth at Tonopah and Goldfield spread south into the adjoining Death Valley region. In August 1904 prospectors Ed Cross and Shorty Harris staked out the Original Bullfrog claim northeast of Death Valley. By 1905 a new mining camp named Rhyolite was filling with hopeful prospectors and merchants near Cross and Harris's strike in the Bullfrog Hills. Within three years Rhyolite had swelled to 5,000 residents and its main street

boasted three-story buildings. Three railroads connected the town to the outside world, with daily trains running north to Goldfield and Tonopah and south to Las Vegas and Ludlow.

The arrival of the railroads changed everything. Where half a century earlier '49ers had wandered about hopelessly lost, desert travelers now rolled along in chaircars and sleepers. The arrival of automobiles in the camps also made a difference. The new machines, despite their sometimes unreliable habits, were enormously faster and more versatile in desert country than horse-drawn wagons. Together, in just a few short years, trains and automobiles shattered the age-old silence and distance that had so long dominated the Northern Mojave.

Top: Rhyolite sprang to life after a 1904 gold strike in the adjacent Bullfrog Hills, and it soon swelled to over 5,000 people. When this photograph was taken in 1909, the town was already on the wane, soon to empty out.
WILLIAM ALEXANDER / NATIONAL PARK SERVICE, DEATH VALLEY NATIONAL PARK
Bottom: Rhyolite's Bottle House, built in 1906 with 50,000 empties—and still standing today—is shown in this 1907 photo with then-owners Jack and Eve Bennett.
EASTERN CALIFORNIA MUSEUM

Stagecoaches, like this one with its passengers at Skidoo on July 4, 1907, connected the Northern Mojave's towns with the outside world. EASTERN CALIFORNIA MUSEUM

Supported by new cities like Rhyolite that offered genuine urban comforts, and inspired by the wealth of Tonopah and Goldfield, prospective miners fanned out into the Northern Mojave seeking signs of mineral "color." They found much to interest them.

West of Rhyolite, in the Funeral Mountains overlooking Death Valley, prospectors returned to the Chloride Cliff area. Early mining attempts here during the 1870s had been defeated by isolation, but the Bullfrog boom brought new opportunities to the Funerals. In 1906 development work began on the Keane Wonder Mine, including the construction of a bucket tramway and a 20-stamp mill, and by September 1907, 1.5 million pounds of freight had been teamed to the site from Rhyolite. During the next five years, the mine produced nearly $1 million in gold before the ore body was exhausted and the mine closed.

West of Death Valley, at the northern end of the Panamint Range, several short-lived mining camps developed. By far the most significant of these was Skidoo. Development began on the Skidoo mines in 1906, and surveyors laid out a townsite at the same time. To supply the mine and town with water and to power the new stamp mill, the Skidoo Mines Company constructed a 21-mile-long pipeline from a spring in the high Panamints near Telescope Peak. The pipeline opened in 1907, and for the next decade Skidoo enjoyed the oddity of a water-powered mill in the midst of some of the nation's driest terrain. By 1917, when the mill closed and the pipeline was scrapped, the mine had produced $1.3 million in gold.

Boom to Bust

Compared to the riches of Tonopah, or even Rhyolite, the wealth produced by Skidoo was relatively modest. Yet even Skidoo was judged a success in a region where precious metal mines rarely turned a profit. New mining districts that opened with great fanfare would often collapse within a year or two, leaving little more than broken dreams and worthless stock. Among the many mining failures in the Northern Mojave, few can compare to Greenwater, which blossomed out of empty desert just east of the Black Mountains.

With rich copper ore plainly visible on the surface and mining hysteria near its peak, men and money flowed unchecked into the new camp of Greenwater. Within 18 months stock with a par value of $140 million had been issued to cover the district's new mining properties, and Montana copper interests had begun buying out claims. In November 1906 the district was growing by 100 people a day as potential miners and shopkeepers stampeded to the site. Near the peak of the Greenwater boom, a set of 16 untested properties sold for $275,000. By early 1907 more than 2,000 people lived in the dusty camp which for a while even had its own magazine, *The Death Valley Chuck-Walla*. But Greenwater declined nearly as quickly as it had grown. None of the area's mining companies were able to find the large bodies of subsurface ore needed to convert the district's copper prospect into profitable mines. Fire struck the camp in June, destroying the office of the *Chuck-Walla* and other buildings. Barely a year later the post office closed; no one was left to receive the mail.

The Tonopah boom mentality had reached its ultimate expression at Greenwater. Genuine wealth at Tonopah, Goldfield, and Randsburg had fueled the intense economic activity, but at Greenwater speculation and hope, not actual mineral wealth, drove the short-lived boom. The camp grew out of the desert and faded back into it with incredible rapidity. Only four years passed between the first rush to the site and the final abandonment of the last deep prospecting effort at the bottom of a vertical shaft 1,439 feet deep. In 1917, just 12 years after the boom began, a visitor noted that only one building remained to mark the site.

Other Northern Mojave camps were even more ephemeral than Greenwater. The winter of 1906-1907 witnessed the short flowering of the Echo-Lee Mining District in the Funeral Mountains northeast of Furnace Creek. The district straddled the crest of the rugged range and included several townsites. In Echo Canyon, on the Death Valley side of the mountains, promoters laid out the town of Schwab in December 1906. Before the end of January, 77 lots were reported as sold, and local optimists announced that the population was approaching 400. February saw the initiation of scheduled stage service from Schwab to Rhyolite, and by March telephone wires were being extended into the townsite from Nevada. April brought a United States Post Office and a miners' union. By the end of year, however, the town was gone—the post office closed and the miners' union disbanded. In its short life Schwab never had an enclosed wooden building, only tents.

In 1906 the Inyo Mine showed enough potential to attract high-profile investors like Charles Schwab, but closed without shipping any ore. It had a brief revival in the 1930s. MICHAEL SEWELL

Surprisingly, Rhyolite, with its three-story concrete buildings, did not prove much more durable than Schwab or Greenwater. Despite the enormous investment poured into the Bullfrog Mining District's mines, mills, towns, and railroads, Rhyolite also declined rapidly. The last big mine closed in 1911, the last train left town in 1914, and in 1916 the Nevada-California Power Company dismantled its electrical line to the dying city.

With little wealth flowing from beneath the desert's surface, Rhyolite had no reason to exist.

By 1910 the Tonopah mining boom also had largely spent itself, a victim of diminishing mining revenue and the general financial depression that began in 1907. Before the excitement ended, however, thousands of prospectors had probed the Northern Mojave's mountains and canyons. Only a few found wealth; most found only emptiness. Of far greater significance than what they found was what they left behind—an infrastructure offering transportation and supply centers, and a body of knowledge detailing the desert's many paths.

Not all the communities vanished when the mines were played out. Towns such as Tonopah, Goldfield, Beatty (near Rhyolite), and Shoshone persevered and became permanent, if modest, centers of commerce to the east of Death Valley. To the west, towns such as Lone Pine, Independence, and Bishop fought off their own problems and survived. But between the western edge of Nevada and Owens Valley, the great empty zone of the Northern Mojave endured. Scattered across it were the abandoned efforts of twentieth-century human activity: mines, mills, abandoned towns, campsites, telephone lines, broken automobiles, and garbage dumps. This is what was left in trade for the land's gold and silver.

Top: The Funeral Mountains contain remnants of the "sky railroad" that served the Keane Wonder Mine, one of Death Valley's few successful mining ventures. JEFF GNASS
Bottom: Little remains of Ashford Mill, which is named after two brothers who owned it and spent nearly 30 years working their nearby gold mine in the Black Mountains. ERIC WUNROW

Other Dreams of Treasure

Taking advantage of the infrastructure left behind by earlier silver and gold seekers, a new generation of miners attempted to redefine the Northern Mojave's worth. A host of minerals attracted their attention, and by the 1930s the Northern Mojave mining scene had expanded to include gypsum, sulfur, lead, salt, talc, and clay.

The Tecopa mines, located near the Spanish Trail, were among the earliest beneficiaries of the region's new transportation infrastructure. After an initial burst of development in the mid-1870s, the Tecopa district languished because there was no way to economically ship its ore to a smelter. The mines' revival began in 1906 when tracks for the new Tonopah & Tidewater Railroad reached Amargosa Canyon, just 12 miles away. Its renaissance accelerated

Two passengers board the Tonopah and Tidewater Railroad. NATIONAL PARK SERVICE, DEATH VALLEY NATIONAL PARK

under the ownership of Nelson Graves, a lead-paint manufacturer who wanted a reliable supply of lead for his plant in Philadelphia. Graves built a rail spur from the mines to the Tonopah & Tidewater in 1910, and his mines produced a relatively steady supply of ore until declining lead prices forced him to cease operations in 1928. Overshadowed by more famous bonanzas, the Tecopa district quietly yielded nearly $4 million, ranking it among the biggest metal producers in Northern Mojave history. Although gold seekers discovered the site, 75% of its mineral wealth was eventually derived from lead.

Not far from Tecopa, near China Ranch, the Gypsy Queen Mine produced 1,000 tons of gypsum a month beginning in 1915. A steep one-mile track connected the Tonopah & Tidewater with the mine. The Gypsy Queen's bad luck began when a loaded train derailed during the descent from the mine, killing the locomotive's fireman. The operation closed in 1918 when the works caved in, killing two miners.

In Saline Valley northwest of Death Valley, the dry lakebed was known to contain a mineral that had yet to be extracted from the region: table salt. The extreme isolation of the site had precluded commercial interest in these deposits until 1911, when the Saline Valley Salt Company mounted an ambitious effort to mine

and market the salt. The primary problem facing such an endeavor was the wall of the Inyo Mountains, which separated Saline Valley and its salt from the railroad in neighboring Owens Valley. To overcome this obstacle, the company constructed one of the great engineering works of the

Top: Salt on the Saline Valley playa was scraped into piles and then consolidated for shipment over the Inyo Range (in background). EASTERN CALIFORNIA MUSEUM
Bottom: A worker rides in one of the buckets of the aerial tramway that carried salt from Saline Valley across the Inyos to Owens Valley. EASTERN CALIFORNIA MUSEUM

Top: *Bulk potash, mined from the bed of Searles Lake, is shoveled into carts at a Trona processing plant in 1919.*
Bottom: *A thermometer is lowered from a wagon derrick into a well to take brine temperatures from Searles Lake in 1914.*

time—an aerial tramway running 13.5 miles over the Inyo Mountains. From the company's salt works, the tramway climbed 7,600 vertical feet up the east side of the Inyos—one of the steepest escarpments in the West—to the mountains' crest and then plunged downward more than 5,100 feet to the shores of Owens Lake. In July 1913 the electric-powered tramway began carrying salt across the mountains in 286 rust-resistant buckets. Despite the sophisticated engineering that had gone into the tramway, the salt mining did not prove to be sufficiently profitable, and by 1920 the tram was idle. A new owner, the Sierra Salt Company, refurbished the tram and used it from about 1928 until 1933 when financial problems and plunging commodity prices closed the operation for good.

At Searles Lake southwest of Death Valley, evaporated mineral deposits of another type generated a more successful enterprise. Beginning in 1873 the playa of Searles Lake was mined for borax. By 1910 improved methods of extraction led to a process that could also yield potash, soda ash, and cake salt from brine pumped from beneath the lakebed's surface. A railroad was laid from Searles Lake and its new town of Trona southeast to the main line at Searles Station. With the Trona Railway operational in 1914, the Northern Mojave gained a permanent town. The mineral deposits at Searles Lake proved to be economically workable and have remained so to this day. The amazing productivity of Searles Lake was never replicated at nearby China Lake. This playa in Indian Wells Valley is named after the Chinese laborers who mined borax here during the 1920s.

In the Crystal Hills southwest of Searles Lake, the discovery of Epsom salt deposits in 1919 stimulated a short-lived mining operation that became famous for its novel mode of transportation. The Epsom deposits were found by Thomas H. Wright, a florist and amateur prospector from Los Angeles who had a penchant for grand schemes. Rather than ship his product out via the old Harmony Borax road that passed through nearby Wingate Wash, Wright set his sites on the more distant Trona Railway siding at Searles Lake. Beginning in 1922 Wright spent two years building a 28-mile-long monorail. Supported by a 3-foot-high wooden trestle, the single steel rail ran through Wingate Wash, across the southern end of Panamint Valley, over the Slate Range, and around the south end of Searles Lake to the railroad siding at Magnesium, about six miles from Trona. Although plagued with mechanical problems, the monorail attracted national attention and was featured in magazines such as *Scientific American* and *Popular Mechanics*.

In 1927, after extracting and shipping about 1,000 tons of crude salt, Wright shut down his unprofitable company and eventually returned to work as a florist.

Although the Northern Mojave was isolated, population growth in adjacent southern California reverberated all the way into the remote corners of the desert. Housing booms in Los Angeles and other coastal communities during the 1910s and 1920s fueled the demand for the white talc used in paint, wall tile, and sewer pipe. High-quality talc was mined in the Darwin Hills, but most of the talc mining was centered in a broad belt that ran from the southern Panamints across Death Valley and into the lower Amargosa Desert. Many of these mines took advantage of their close proximity to sidings along the Tonopah & Tidewater Railroad. Among them was the area's first major talc mine, the Pacific Tile and Terra Cotta Company. Discovered in 1908, this mine east of China Ranch eventually yielded several million dollars worth of talc. The China Ranch deposits, along with talc operations in the Ibex Hills, Silurian Hills, Panamint's Warm Springs Canyon, and elsewhere were some of the region's authentic bonanzas. After borax, talc has been one of the Northern Mojave's greatest sources of mineral wealth.

While the growth of Los Angeles was a boon to some segments of the Northern Mojave's mining industry, it was the city's unslackening thirst for water at the start of the twentieth century that ultimately had the greater impact on the region. Los Angeles's audacious acquisition of Owens Valley land and water rights, and the completion in 1913 of its 233-mile-long aqueduct to deliver this water from north of Independence to San Fernando, stirred great resentment and quashed any dreams of establishing an agricultural mecca in Inyo County or eastern Kern County. The Inyokern Land and Water Company had sought its own aqueduct to deliver enough Owens River water to irrigate 55,000 acres in the Indian Wells and Fremont valleys, but Los Angeles was first to grab the prized resource. The seven-year construction of the aqueduct, along with the railroad that was built to supply the project and the highways that later paralleled much of the aqueduct's route, helped open the way to tourism along the western edge of the Northern Mojave. Travelers availed themselves of this new infrastructure to discover the area. Hollywood filmmakers began their long love affair with Red Rock Canyon as a scenic backdrop and adventurous motorists headed farther afield to destinations such as Coso Hot Springs or to Panamint Valley where they could connect with a new toll road into Death Valley.

Top: A section of steel pipe for the first Los Angeles Aqueduct is pulled by a team of 52 mules at the Jawbone Station construction camp near Red Rock Canyon.
EASTERN CALIFORNIA MUSEUM
Bottom: As highways improved and automobile ownership increased, more sightseers ventured into the Northern Mojave. These tourists are on the road between Death Valley and Rhyolite in 1926.
BANCROFT LIBRARY / UNIVERSITY OF CALIFORNIA, BERKELEY 1978.027:46

Top: *John Ryan, shown at a tunnel entrance in the Greenwater Range in 1914, and his boss Francis "Borax King" Smith, developed highly productive borax mines near Death Valley in the early twentieth century.* EASTERN CALIFORNIA MUSEUM

Bottom: *The Death Valley Railroad ran from Death Valley Junction to the mining camp of Ryan.* EASTERN CALIFORNIA MUSEUM

Borax Mining Returns to Death Valley

Of all the early twentieth-century mining endeavors, it was borax mining in the Furnace Creek area that most changed the history of the Northern Mojave, for its reemergence between 1910 and 1920 ultimately led to the recognition of Death Valley as a tourist attraction.

In 1890, two years after William Coleman closed his Harmony Borax Works at Furnace Creek, Marion Francis "Borax King" Smith acquired his Death Valley holdings. With a steady borax supply from its mines at Calico in the central Mojave during the 1890s, Smith's Pacific Coast Borax Company emerged as the nation's biggest producer of borax and claimed a near monopoly on the product. But by 1900 the Calico deposits were facing depletion, and Smith turned to long-dormant claims near Furnace Creek and the Amargosa Valley to supply his borax empire. In 1904 he reopened the Lila C. Mine just west of Death Valley Junction, where promising deposits of colemanite, a borate-rich ore, were first discovered in 1882.

In 1905 Smith began work on the 167-mile-long Tonopah & Tidewater Railroad, which would connect then-booming Rhyolite to the Santa Fe's mainline near Ludlow, with a branch to the Lila C. and its company town, Ryan. Although Smith lost the race to build the first railroad to Rhyolite— two other railroads arrived ahead of his—the Tonopah & Tidewater provided a vital transportation link for the Lila C. With the railroad completed in 1907, borax ore flowed steadily from the Lila C. for 6 years, producing a whopping $8 million. Despite the success of the Lila C., losses in Smith's other ventures wreaked havoc on his personal fortune. His assets were liquidated in 1913, and Smith never again reclaimed the title of "Borax King."

When borate production at the Lila C. began to dwindle, a reorganized Pacific Coast Borax Company shifted its focus to the Biddy McCarty Mine on the west slope of the Greenwater Range. The company constructed the narrow-gauge Death Valley Railroad to provide needed transportation to the new mining district. The new rail line stretched about 20 miles from its junction with the Tonopah & Tidewater (at Death Valley Junction) to a mining camp, also named Ryan, or New Ryan. The Death Valley Railroad opened in 1916, and for a decade colemanite was shipped from the Biddy McCarty and its neighboring mines—the Widow, Played Out, Lizzy V. Oakey, and Grand View. By the mid-1920s, however, Pacific Coast Borax began shifting its mining operations to remarkably pure borax deposits near Boron, west of Barstow. In 1927, with the closure of the mines near Ryan, both the Tonopah & Tidewater and the Death Valley Railroad appeared to have outlasted their purposes.

From Borax to Tourism

Ever resourceful, Pacific Coast Borax developed new plans for its railroads and Death Valley real estate. As the company phased out its mines in the region, it began marketing Death Valley as a winter tourism destination. To facilitate this shift, it constructed the Amargosa Hotel at Death Valley Junction and the Furnace Creek Inn at the mouth of Furnace Creek Wash. The company also remodeled Ryan into a resort hotel complex.

As Pacific Coast Borax promoted the new resorts, it stressed their convenient access via the Tonopah & Tidewater and Death Valley railroads. For a few short years in the late 1920s, winter Pullman sleeper service brought hotel patrons to Death Valley Junction from Los Angeles over the Tonopah & Tidewater, and then the Death Valley Railroad took them on to Ryan, overlooking Death Valley. In 1928 both rail lines purchased new rail motor cars especially for this service, but it was all for naught. The new hotels caught on as tourist destinations, but the popularity of rail travel was on the decline. The Death Valley Railroad was abandoned in 1930, and Pullman service on the Tonopah & Tidewater was

discontinued. That same year the Pacific Coast Borax Company shifted hotel operations from Ryan to its Furnace Creek Ranch property on the floor of Death Valley. With both the luxurious Furnace Creek Inn and the more rustic Furnace Creek Ranch properties to promote, the company had firmly entered the resort business. Death Valley was on its way to a totally unexpected future as a tourist destination.

While Pacific Coast Borax was promoting rail travel to its new hotels at Ryan and Death Valley Junction, Inyo County was taking steps to encourage auto excursions into Death Valley via Owens Valley. In October 1925 the county granted Bob Eichbaum a permit to build the 38-mile Death Valley Toll Road, which would run from Darwin Wash in Panamint Valley over Towne Pass and

Top: In 1926 Bob Eichbaum completed the Death Valley Toll Road from Panamint Valley to his Stovepipe Wells Hotel, which consisted of 20 open-air bungalows. EASTERN CALIFORNIA MUSEUM
Bottom: Pacific Coast Borax converted some of its mining infrastructure into tourism assets, such as these sightseeing cars on narrow-gauge tracks near Ryan. EASTERN CALIFORNIA MUSEUM

By the 1920s tourists were coming to the Northern Mojave for recreational camping, like this couple in Death Valley. BANCROFT LIBRARY/UNIVERSITY OF CALIFORNIA, BERKELEY 1978.027:11

down to the Death Valley Sand Dunes. Eichbaum had been an electrical engineer in Rhyolite before moving on to open sightseeing businesses in Southern California; he had long dreamed of returning to tap Death Valley's great potential for tourism. Eichbaum's toll road opened in May 1926, and at its terminus he built 20 open-air bungalows, a filling station, store, and restaurant. Named Stovepipe Wells Hotel, Eichbaum's establishment opened in November and was the only resort in Death Valley until Pacific Coast Borax completed the Furnace Creek Inn the following year.

In January 1927 Pacific Coast Borax organized a special tour of its new resorts. The company invited officials of the Union Pacific Railroad, along with Stephen T. Mather, Director of the National Park Service, to evaluate the tourism potential of the area. Mather was familiar with the region: he was once an employee of Pacific Coast Borax and actually invented the brand name of "20 Mule Team Borax." Mather privately encouraged the borax company to proceed with its resort plans, but he did not think the area could be successfully added to the national park system. Since California already had a number of national parks, and because Mather's previous association with Pacific

Coast Borax was well-known, he was reluctant to lobby for a new park.

Mather suffered a major stroke in late 1928, and in January 1929 he relinquished directorship of the National Park Service to his assistant, Horace M. Albright. A native of nearby Owens Valley, Albright knew the Northern Mojave both by reputation and by personal experience. He had been with Mather during his 1927 inspection of Death Valley and agreed that the region deserved protection. Unlike Mather, however, Albright was convinced that Death Valley could be added to the National Park system. Barely one year later, responding to Albright's lobbying, President Herbert Hoover temporarily set aside two million acres of the Death Valley region for evaluation as possible parklands. Albright then sent Roger Toll, superintendent of Yellowstone National Park, to make a careful study of the area. Following Toll's recommendations, Albright prepared for Hoover a presidential proclamation establishing Death Valley National Monument. Both Pacific Coast Borax and the Union Pacific Railroad strongly supported the move. On February 11, 1933, during the last month of his administration, President Hoover signed the proclamation. Several months later Congress added a provision declaring that the new National Monument would remain open to mining activity, including new claims.

A "Wasteland" Worth Loving

The creation of Death Valley National Monument in 1933 represented a fundamental shift in human perceptions of the Northern Mojave. Since the 1830s, when Euro-Americans first arrived in the region, it was perceived as a hostile place—a landscape that rewarded a fortuitous few with wealth, while most other visitors were punished with hardship and poverty. Only a few misfits loved the land; most individuals came and went quickly, glad to leave with whatever they had garnered.

There had been a few exceptions. In 1903 Houghton Mifflin published *The Land of Little Rain* by Mary Austin. An intense young woman with a determination to express herself through written words, Austin moved to the Owens Valley in 1888, where she wrote her book, now regarded as a classic of desert literature. Austin's land of little rain stretched eastward from the Sierra Nevada "over a very great assemblage of broken ranges beyond Death Valley, and on illimitably into the Mojave Desert." She wrote sympathetically of the landscape and its human and animal residents. Her interests included not only forgotten shepherds and prospectors, but also the region's Native Americans and Hispanics. *The Land of Little Rain* came out just as the Tonopah boom began to break across the Northern Mojave, and the book

contradicted nearly every value held by the eager miners. A few years later Austin moved out of the region. *The Land of Little Rain* is still in print and is perhaps appreciated more by each new generation of readers.

If Mary Austin defined the allure of the Northern Mojave for subsequent generations of desert lovers, Albert Johnson established another model. A self-effacing insurance millionaire from Chicago, Johnson initiated construction of his Death Valley Ranch in 1922. Located in Grapevine Canyon, near the northern end of Death Valley, Johnson's palatial estate grew over time into a Moorish castle associated in the public mind not with its owner, but rather with Johnson's close friend, Death Valley Scotty. A mining speculator left over from the Tonopah boom days, Scotty fascinated Johnson with his stories and occasional outrageous behavior. Johnson, in turn, used Scotty as a front during the building of the castle, letting the world believe that it belonged to Scotty and was being paid for by a secret gold mine. The two carried on the charade for several decades.

One pocket of the Northern Mojave that defied the term "wasteland" was Indian Wells Valley. During the mid- to late-nineteenth century, the basin's abundant forage made it an important stop on huge, annual spring sheep drives from western

Top: Death Valley Scotty, at the entrance to Scotty's Castle, gladly perpetuated the myth that his gold mine paid for construction of the fabulous estate where he lived in the Grapevine Mountains.
EASTERN CALIFORNIA MUSEUM
Bottom: Burro Schmidt, seen at his one-room cabin in 1953, spent 32 years hand-digging a tunnel in the El Paso Mountains that led to nowhere. MATURANGO MUSEUM

Kern County to Mono County. By the 1870s a steady stream of stagecoaches and freight wagons were crossing the valley while traveling between Los Angeles and mining camps such as Cerro Gordo and Panamint City. Although its stage stations and watering holes were important stops on the

"Bullion Road," it was not until the Lone Pine Branch of the Southern Pacific reached the area in the early twentieth century that the valley had its first permanent town. This community became known in 1913 as Inyokern, and like several other pioneer settlements in Indian Wells Valley, it prospered as a commercial center during construction of the first Los Angeles Aqueduct. Farmers near Inyokern established dairies and tapped into the valley's groundwater to irrigate alfalfa fields and orchards. During the Great Depression additional settlers were attracted to the area by the Desert Entry Act, which offered 160-acre homesteads to those willing to clear and plant the land.

New Directions

Beginning in 1933 the National Park Service assumed the leadership role in converting the public's perception of Death Valley—changing it from hostile wasteland to a protected natural treasure. The Park Service campaign greatly benefited from the region's previous decades of mining-driven development. During the early part of the twentieth century, railroads and highways had reduced the extreme isolation of the Northern Mojave. Pacific Coast Borax, in particular, played a major role: initially by using Death Valley's image to sell borax and later by building and marketing the Furnace Creek resort complex in the 1920s.

Using labor from the newly established Civilian Conservation Corps, the federal government initiated the development of Death Valley as a park. The winter headquarters, with an administration building and residences, was built a few miles north of Furnace Creek on land that remained a private holding of Pacific Coast Borax. The Park Service erected automobile campgrounds in the hills adjacent to the borax company's resorts and along the valley floor they developed a series of auto-touring roads. Eichbaum's toll road became a state highway in 1933, and President Franklin D. Roosevelt enlarged the national monument by 306,000 acres in 1937. Thus, by the end of the

Top: In addition to its luxury hotel at Furnace Creek, Pacific Coast Borax built modest tourist lodgings like these cabins, also called "sizzlers." NATIONAL PARK SERVICE, DEATH VALLEY NATIONAL PARK *Bottom: In February 1931 more than 3,000 people gathered at Red Rock Canyon to celebrate the opening of a new stretch of paved highway through the area.* EASTERN CALIFORNIA MUSEUM

Hundreds of CCC enrollees worked on the new national monument's infrastructure.
N.P.S., DEATH VALLEY NATIONAL PARK

1930s, Death Valley had received the basic accoutrements of a national park and had been embraced by the public as a recreational destination.

As the Park Service worked to reorganize Death Valley into a landscape preserved for tourism, it found itself confronted with a human population the federal government had chosen not to recognize. Despite the enormous changes that occurred in the region during the early decades of the twentieth century, the Death Valley, or Timbisha, band of Shoshone had endured. Still tied to the land in a way totally foreign to miners, tourists, or park managers, the Timbisha Shoshone wanted nothing more than to continue practicing their native lifestyle and religion. Sadly, the new laws governing their homeland made no such allowances.

Congress had ensured that miners could continue to exploit the Death Valley landscape, but no exception had been made to preserve the rights of the region's indigenous population. Lacking any clear instructions regarding the status of these people, the Park Service built them a village of adobe houses at Furnace Creek but prohibited the continuation of their subsistence lifestyle. Since none of the valley had been set aside for them as a reservation, the Timbisha had no option but to accept the situation.

At the same time that Death Valley's Native Americans were being confined to a small enclave near Furnace Creek, miners were returning to the region in unprecedented numbers. The Great Depression of the 1930s displaced a generation of industrial workers, and quite a few of them retreated into desert mining regions like the Northern Mojave—not to work for big mining companies, but rather to operate small, marginal mines. By the late 1930s the Northern Mojave had more active mines than at any other time in its history, and many were located within the new national monument. Most Depression-era mines were small, supporting a few pocket miners and their families. Despite the scattering of miners and small concentrations of winter tourists, the great majority of the Northern Mojave remained empty and unvisited.

Top: This basket weaver and her student (in about 1920) were among the small Shoshone community that remained in Death Valley. EASTERN CALIFORNIA MUSEUM
Bottom: By the end of the 1930s, when this photo was taken, nearly 500,000 people had visited Death Valley National Monument, established February 11, 1933. NATIONAL PARK SERVICE, DEATH VALLEY NATIONAL PARK

This northwestern edge of Indian Wells Valley lies outside the Naval Air Weapons Station at China Lake, but most of the valley and the Argus and Coso ranges are within it. JOHN EVARTS

Competing Visions

Soon after the beginning of World War II, the emptiness of the region attracted a new player—the military. In 1943 the United States Navy took control of a huge tract of land in the Indian Wells Valley and adjoining Coso Range and designated it as the Inyo-Kern Naval Ordnance Test Station (today known as the Naval Air Weapons Station at China Lake). Here, in the privacy of the empty desert, the Navy began testing weapons. South of Death Valley the Army established Camp Irwin, taking control of another gigantic stretch of the Mojave. After the war the military bases and their associated civilian communities, such as Ridgecrest, continued to be a permanent part of the Northern Mojave's changing landscape.

During the post-war years, good roads, inexpensive motor vehicles, and a rapidly growing urban population in Southern California began the final dismemberment of the Northern Mojave's famous isolation. Never before had the desert been so easy to visit or so popular. A few decades earlier, visiting the Northern Mojave had required something akin to a formal expedition; now, suddenly, the region could be enjoyed on a weekend outing from Los Angeles or San Diego. At Furnace Creek the Park Service expanded its campgrounds with giant overflow parking areas for holiday weekends. Some visitors, seeking the privacy that was less and less available in places like Furnace Creek, began to visit more remote areas like Saline Valley and the dunes in Eureka Valley.

As tourism increased, two divergent visions of the Northern Mojave gradually came into focus. To some, especially those who lived in or near the region, it remained what it had always been—a place to scratch out a living by mining, ranching, or in some way harvesting whatever it had to offer. For many others, however, the Northern Mojave's greatest treasure was not its extractable resources but rather its enormous, quiet empty spaces and intact natural environments. Inevitably, these two views came increasingly into conflict.

Not surprisingly, when Death Valley's third borax boom began in 1971, the renewed mining activity was regarded with both enthusiasm and dismay. Colemanite ore deposits near the head of Furnace Creek Wash were developed at the Boraxo, Billie, and Inyo mines. The Boraxo Mine was especially controversial, because its waste dumps and open pit were located within the national monument. Prodded by public concern over Death Valley's Boraxo and other mines on western parklands, Congress passed the Mining Act of 1976, which gave the National Park Service greater control over mining claims within park holdings. More than 4,000 claims existed in Death Valley National Monument in 1975, but with the aid of the new legislation, the total was whittled down to less than 150 by 1994.

A National Park for Future Generations

By the late 1970s two opposing political coalitions had emerged to debate the issue of land-use in the California deserts. One side supported continued use of the desert in the traditional sense, with emphasis on preserving opportunities for mining, desert grazing, and unrestricted vehicular recreation; the other side increasingly saw the desert as requiring active protection from those very activities. Because the United States government controlled most of the area, the resulting political wars were largely federal in nature; the competing coalitions sought to influence the federal agencies that managed the land, as well as Congress itself. The real question, of course, was what role the Northern Mojave would play in the twenty-first century and beyond.

The military lands and Death

Valley National Monument already operated under relatively clear mandates from Congress. The growing debate about land-use management in the Northern Mojave therefore focused primarily on the vast public acreage outside their boundaries, most of which belonged to the Bureau of Land Management. Congress attempted to bridge the gap between the increasingly hostile desert coalitions when it established the California Desert Conservation Area in 1976. The implementation plan for the area tried to accommodate a wide range of interests, but it ultimately failed to still the debate. Pressure mounted for a new congressional mandate.

Finally, at the suggestion of the Sierra Club, California Senator Alan Cranston introduced a bill in 1986 to

Top: Mining is still an important industry in the Northern Mojave. These are tailings at talc mines in the Kingston Range. DAVID LANNER
Bottom: Tourists, such as these photographers at Zabriskie Point, play an increasingly important role in the Northern Mojave's economy. FRANK BALTHIS

Many areas with sensitive archeological sites, such as the Greenwater Range where these ancient house rings are located, were included in the new Death Valley National Park. JOHN DITTLI

radically change desert land management priorities. Cranston's California Desert Protection Act took aim at the California deserts as a whole, but it targeted the Northern Mojave for some of its most far-reaching provisions. His legislation proposed that Death Valley National Monument be enlarged by more than one million acres and elevated to national park status. Among the areas to be added to the new park were Saline Valley, Eureka Valley, and most of the Greenwater Valley. Cranston's plan also designated large tracts as federal wilderness, including much of the Panamints, Inyos, and parts of many other ranges in the region. It enlarged Red Rock Canyon State Park and created the 1.6 million-acre Mojave National Preserve to the south.

Cranston's bill initially went nowhere until after he retired in 1992, when two new California senators, Barbara Boxer and Diane Feinstein, were elected. They both strongly supported passage of the Desert Protection Act and worked to end the stalemate that had stalled the legislation. During 1994 the House of Representatives and the Senate passed similar versions of the legislation, but final resolution lingered into the ultimate hours of the session. In its last days, the bill took on an additional significance when it became the center of an intensely partisan national debate. As it came down to the wire, the real issue was no longer the future of the California deserts, but the relative power of the embattled Democratic President and a fiercely hostile group of opposing Republican legislators. In the waning hours of the 103rd Congress, Feinstein, who was carrying the bill in the Senate, finally mustered a slender majority to cut off a filibuster and the bill sailed onto the floor, where it passed easily. President Clinton signed it into law on October 31, 1994.

One of the most significant changes to occur to the bill during the final months of debate over its future was the addition of a section calling for the establishment of a reservation for the Timbisha Shoshone. Confined to a 60-acre tract at Furnace Creek since the establishment of the national monument in 1933, the Timbisha began lobbying to regain access to their native lands in the 1970s. In 1983, in their first major political success, the tribe gained formal federal recognition. From this platform they initiated an effort to regain title to part of their original lands. With the passage of the California Desert Protection Act, they came within striking distance of achieving their goal. The bill not only authorized the creation of Death Valley National Park but also ordered that a study be undertaken to find reservation lands for the Timbisha within their native region. This resulted in the Timbisha Land Act, enacted in November 2000, which created a 300-acre homeland for the Timbisha at Furnace Creek. The act also recognized a special use area, known as the Timbisha Shoshone Natural and Cultural Preservation Area, for traditional Timbisha religious activities.

With the passage of the California Desert Protection Act, Congress provided a clear direction for the future management of the Northern Mojave. In effect, they had declared that the highest and best use for this spectacular desert country is to preserve it largely intact for the enjoyment of present and future generations. The enactment of this landmark legislation, however, has not entirely stilled the debate over land-use in the region. The Timbisha Shoshone tried unsuccessfully to halt a gold mine on BLM land in Panamint Valley because it could damage sacred cultural sites in their ancestral homeland. Conservationists are opposing the U.S. Army plan to take over and close off 326,000 acres of public land for expansion of the Fort Irwin National Training Center, just outside Death Valley National Park's southeastern boundary. Ranchers fought a court order to restrict grazing on BLM land that resulted from lawsuits to protect desert tortoise habitat. The residents of Shoshone have joined with many

others to fight plans to transport the nation's nuclear waste through their town enroute to storage at nearby Yucca Mountain in Nevada.

Barely a century ago the Northern Mojave was one of the least-known corners of America. Today the region is home to the largest national park in the contiguous United States and attracts more than a million tourists each year. Where emigrants found only hostility, modern-day visitors perceive both beauty and fragility. Where people once chafed against desolation, they now relish the healing quiet of empty space. Perhaps we are finally beginning to appreciate what Mary Austin had to say about this land of little rain.

Top: The Eureka Dunes and much of Eureka Valley became part of Death Valley National Park in 1994. DENNIS FLAHERTY
Bottom: The 5,200 square-mile Death Valley National Park contains this riparian corridor in Darwin Canyon. STEPHEN INGRAM

Indian Wells Valley Region

This district, located . . . approximately twenty-five miles north of Mojave, is one of the best known scenic spots in Southern California. It contains unrivaled examples of acute arid-climate topography. Its coloring, its vegetation and its pinnacled natural architecture are most unique. It attracts visitors every day of the year. . . . It is, however, not merely interesting to casual tourists, but is fully as instructive for scientific purposes. Within it is a wonderful example of a fault. . . . On the north slope of the fault block lie sediments about a mile in thickness tipped up to angles as steep as thirty degrees and then transected so as to show the folded structure more clearly than a text-book figure. A variety of rocks make up these strata, including conglomerate, sandstones, pumice beds, volcanic ash and lavas. It is one of the most instructive places for students desiring to glean a concept of the construction and structure of the earth's crust that can be found in the country. . . . The locality yields an extraordinary record of mountain making, volcanism, sedimentation and erosion. I think the district well merits being set aside as a State Park; it should be better known. Certain simple facilities might be provided for visitors, and perhaps certain limitations placed upon conduct in the area.

—John P. Buwalda,
Letter to the State Parks Commission, 1928

Opposite: Red Rock Canyon is a major gateway to the Northern Mojave, and its distinctive landforms have long intrigued desert travelers, artists, and filmakers. JIM STIMSON

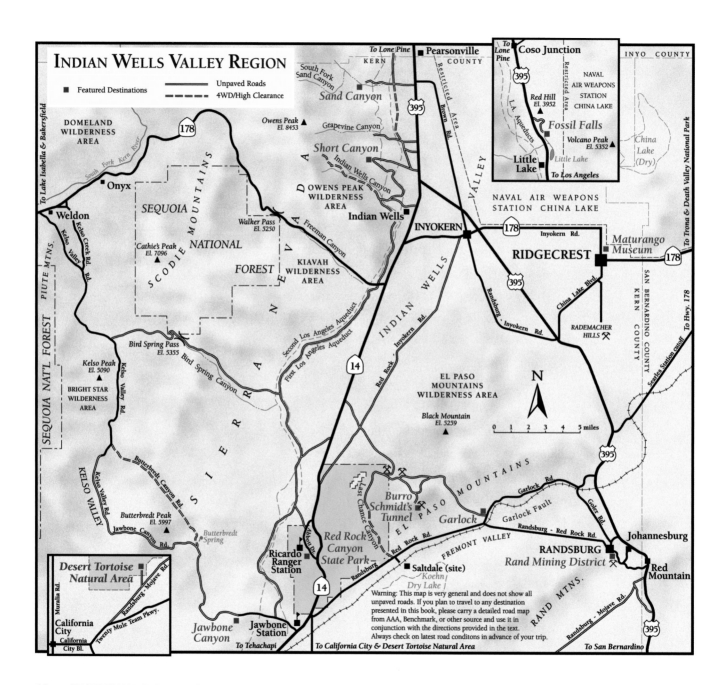

INDIAN WELLS VALLEY REGION

■ Featured Destinations

═══════ Unpaved Roads

▬ ▬ ▬ 4WD/High Clearance

To Lake Isabella & Bakersfield

South Fork Kern River

DOMELAND WILDERNESS AREA

178

Onyx

SEQUOIA NATIONAL FOREST

Weldon

Kelso Creek Rd.

PIUTE MTNS.

SEQUOIA NATL FOREST

Cathie's Peak El. 7096 ▲

Kelso Peak El. 5090 ▲

BRIGHT STAR WILDERNESS AREA

KELSO VALLEY

Kelso Valley Rd.

Butterbredt Canyon Rd.

Butterbredt Peak El. 5997 ▲

Jawbone Canyon Rd.

Butterbredt Spring

Jawbone Canyon

Jawbone Station

To Tehachapi

SCODIE MOUNTAINS

Walker Pass El. 5250

KIAVAH WILDERNESS AREA

Freeman Canyon

SIERRA NEVADA

Bird Spring Pass El. 5355

Bird Spring Canyon

Second Los Angeles Aqueduct

First Los Angeles Aqueduct

Owens Peak El. 8453 ▲

Grapevine Canyon

Short Canyon

Indian Wells Canyon

OWENS PEAK WILDERNESS AREA

Indian Wells

South Fork Sand Canyon

Sand Canyon

395

KERN COUNTY

Pearsonville

To Lone Pine

Brown Rd.

Restricted Area

INYOKERN

178

INDIAN WELLS VALLEY

14

Red Rock - Inyokern Rd.

EL PASO MOUNTAINS WILDERNESS AREA

Black Mountain El. 5259 ▲

Randsburg - Inyokern Rd.

RIDGECREST

Inyokern Rd.

395

China Lake Blvd.

RADEMACHER HILLS ⛏

KERN COUNTY

SAN BERNARDINO COUNTY

NAVAL AIR WEAPONS STATION CHINA LAKE

Maturango Museum

178

To Trona & Death Valley National Park

To Hwy. 178

Searles Station cutoff

N

0 1 2 3 4 5 miles

Last Chance Canyon

Abbott Dr.

Ricardo Ranger Station

Red Rock Canyon State Park

14

Burro Schmidt's Tunnel ⛏

Garlock

Red Rock Rd.

EL PASO MOUNTAINS

FREMONT VALLEY

Randsburg - Red Rock Rd.

Saltdale (site)

Koehn Dry Lake

Garlock Rd.

Garlock Fault

Goler Rd.

Randsburg - Red Rock Rd.

RANDSBURG

Rand Mining District ⛏

RAND MTNS.

Johannesburg

Red Mountain

Randsburg - Mojave Rd.

395

To San Bernardino

Warning: This map is very general and does not show all unpaved roads. If you plan to travel to any destination presented in this book, please carry a detailed road map from AAA, Benchmark, or other source and use it in conjunction with the directions provided in the text. Always check on latest road conditons in advance of your trip.

To California City & Desert Tortoise Natural Area

Desert Tortoise Natural Area

Muralia Rd.

Randsburg - Mojave Rd.

Twenty Mule Team Pkwy.

California City

California City Bl.

(Inset, top right)

To Lone Pine

395

Coso Junction

INYO COUNTY

NAVAL AIR WEAPONS STATION CHINA LAKE

Red Hill El. 3952 ▲

L.A. Aqueducts

Restricted Area

Fossil Falls

Volcano Peak El. 5352 ▲

China Lake (Dry)

Little Lake

Little Lake

To Los Angeles

Desert Tortoise Natural Area

With a little luck and good timing, visitors to the Desert Tortoise Natural Area (DTNA) may be rewarded by an encounter with California's official state reptile—the desert tortoise. A warm day in early March to May offers the greatest chance of viewing desert tortoises, as spring is their most active season. This is when these high-domed, terrestrial turtles have emerged from their burrows after winter hibernation to eat wildflowers and grasses. Once a common sight in the Mojave, desert tortoises are now listed as threatened by both California and federal wildlife agencies. (For more information on tortoise biology, see pages 43-44.)

Arranging a spring visit to the DTNA in a year with good rainfall adds an opportunity to appreciate colorful desert wildflowers. Lupines, gilias, phacelias, coreopsis, and alkali goldfields are some of the many annual flowers that provide a feast for human eyes and food for tortoises. Prolific here in some years is an unusual looking annual plant known as "desert candle," which gets its name from its conspicuous, yellow or light-green inflated stems. The preserve lists over 160 different plants within its boundaries and pamphlets for the self-guided 0.4-mile-long Plant Loop Trail help identify many common Mojave perennials, such as creosote bush, spiny hop-sage, and burrobush.

Warm spring weather brings out other reptiles in addition to the desert tortoise. If you arrive at midday the tortoises may have retreated to their burrows to escape the heat, but you are likely to spot western whiptail, horned, side-blotched, or leopard lizards as they dart across the trail or scurry under a desert shrub. You can follow the 0.5-mile-long Animal Loop Trail to learn more about the habitat of the DTNA's animal residents. The informative trail brochures caution visitors to "be aware of rattlesnakes;" both the sidewinder and the Mojave rattlesnake live in the preserve.

The Desert Tortoise Preserve Committee joined with the BLM to establish the DTNA on the western edge of the Rand Mountains in 1976. The following year, the BLM completed a mesh fence around most of the preserve to keep motorized vehicles and livestock out. The committee played a large part in the design and content of the permanent outdoor information display in the kiosk situated at the entrance to the preserve, which was dedicated in 1980.

The DTNA spreads across gently undulating terrain that is dissected by more than 100 narrow washes, or "stringers." One of the reasons desert tortoises thrive here is that the vegetation they depend on is often more abundant in washes. The DTNA was established at this site to protect this ideal tortoise habitat and the high

An ideal time to visit the Desert Tortoise Natural Area is early spring, when tortoises are more active and visible. DAN SUZIO

population densities of tortoises that it harbors. This is the only Tortoise Preserve in California, and it now encompasses nearly 40 square miles. The committee continues to raise funds to purchase private inholdings within the DTNA and to work for the protection of the desert tortoise throughout its range.

Directions: *From Highway 14 take the California City exit and proceed to California City. Drive all the way through town to its east end and turn left off California City Boulevard onto Randsburg-Mojave Road. Continue 1.2 miles to a junction with a sign for the DTNA where you turn left and leave the pavement. (If you go right at this junction, you are on Twenty Mule Team*

In good wildflower years, the Desert Tortoise Natural Area has colorful displays of desert candle (shown here). DENNIS FLAHERTY

Parkway, which proceeds east along the historic borax freight-wagon route from Death Valley to Mojave.) Continue about 4 miles up the sometimes-washboard Randsburg-Mojave Road to a left turn into the DTNA; follow signs to the parking area. You can also reach the preserve from Highway 58 in the south by taking California City Boulevard north to Randsburg-Mojave Road. The preserve is open year-round, but an on-site naturalist is only present during the spring. For more information, contact the Desert Tortoise Protection Committee at (909) 683-3872.

Jawbone Canyon to Kelso Valley Tour

"The bears played a game of ball, running over the mountains and causing deep canyons to form . . ."
—From a Kawaiisu story

The Kawaiisu's homeland embraces the rugged canyon country where the southern Sierra Nevada meets the western edge of the Mojave Desert. A scenic auto tour from colorful Jawbone Canyon to Kelso Valley and Kelso Creek and east over Walker Pass provides a good introduction to this area. The Kawaiisu frequently traveled the corridor from Kelso Valley through Jawbone Canyon. One of the reasons they came down from this upland valley was to gather salt from the surface of Koehn Dry Lake, located several miles northeast of the mouth of Jawbone Canyon. Their trail later became a wagon road into the mountains. Much of this route is still unpaved today, and it remains a quiet backcountry road.

Begin this tour at the BLM's Jawbone Station, located at the entrance to Jawbone Canyon on Highway 14. The station offers information, pamphlets, maps, and books. The road first passes through the popular Jawbone Canyon Off-Highway Vehicle Recreation Area. About 1 mile after turning off Highway 14, you pass the second Los Angeles Aqueduct pipeline, built in 1970. At 2.8 miles you encounter the

first Los Angeles Aqueduct pipeline, built in 1913, and its famous Jawbone Siphon, which plummets down an exceedingly steep slope. Despite these human impacts, the canyon remains strikingly beautiful, with green, white, and reddish-brown sedimentary rock decorating its floor and walls. At 5 miles from the highway look for Blue Point, located on the north side of the road near the mouth of a side canyon. Geologists classify its blue-green rock as welded tuff-breccia, which spewed from a

The road to remote Kelso Valley follows the wash of Jawbone Canyon before climbing into the mountains. MARC SOLOMON

volcanic eruption 8 to 12 million years ago.

The road soon leaves the Jawbone Canyon wash, turning right (north) and climbing up Hoffman Canyon. Along the way there are pullouts that offer dramatic views, especially to the southeast. Near the top of the ridge you enter a zone of granitic rock where numerous white quartz dikes are visible in the roadcuts. After reaching a saddle, the road heads down into another drainage where it is joined by a road coming up on the right. About 0.6 mile past this junction, a cattleguard and sign on the right mark the turnoff to Butterbredt Spring Wildlife Sanctuary.

A steep, 0.9-mile descent on Butterbredt Spring Road leads to a shaded seep and dense grove of cottonwoods teeming with bird life. More than 230 different avian species visit the oasis in Butterbredt Canyon. During spring and fall, this isolated wetland acts like a magnet, drawing in large numbers of birds as they pass through on long migrations. A granite outcrop above the springs and parking area provides a nice view up Butterbredt Valley and of Butterbredt Peak to the northwest. These landmarks were named after Frederick Butterbredt, a German miner who married a Kawaiisu woman. He found her hiding with her baby in a willow grove after her husband was killed by soldiers in a massacre near Lake Isabella in 1863. Butterbredt called his new wife Betty, and together they raised a large family at their homestead in the canyon.

Return to Jawbone Canyon Road to continue the tour and reset your trip odometer. About 3 miles beyond the Butterbredt Springs Road, you reach a crest before descending into scenic, mountain-rimmed Kelso Valley. Joshua trees pour down the slopes on the east side of the valley, while gray pines cover its west side, extending toward the 7,702-foot-high summit of Sorrell Peak. A narrow band of pastureland separates the two distinct woodlands, and ranch buildings dot this bucolic landscape. At 6.2 miles Jawbone Canyon Road comes to a junction where you swing right (north) onto a road that merges into Kelso Valley Road and heads toward Weldon. (Straight ahead goes west across the valley and then up into the Piute Mountains.) Your route continues north and soon enters an extensive Joshua tree woodland.

The road climbs to a 4,850-foot-high summit that divides Kelso Valley from the actual drainage of Kelso Creek. The Pacific Crest National Scenic Trail crosses the road at this point. From here you follow Kelso Creek toward its confluence with the South Fork of the Kern River near Highway 178. A good entry point to explore Kelso Creek, which is bordered by a mixture of public and

A small but verdant grove of cottonwoods marks the presence of water at isolated Butterbredt Springs. JOHN EVARTS

private land, is located along the left shoulder of the road, about 3 miles down from the summit. A BLM sign, "Foot Travel Welcome," marks a side road (closed to vehicles) that provides hiking access. Naturalists have spotted a number of intriguing birds along this section of the creek, including the yellow-billed cuckoo and the American redstart.

The drainage broadens as you continue north on Kelso Valley Road. Just after the road passes a cluster of houses, look for a large wooden sign on the right side at the junction with Bird Spring Pass Road. The sign commemorates the 1845 route of John C. Frémont. That year, his expedition party found the established route over Walker Pass blocked by snow; the group swung south and became the first Euro-Americans to travel over 5,300-foot-high Bird Spring Pass. (If you have a high-clearance vehicle, you can also return to Highway 14 by traveling east on unpaved Bird Spring Pass Road. Near the summit of the pass, turn south on a good road to make the 3-mile side trip to Wyley's Knob, which offers some of the finest views in the region.)

From its junction with Bird Spring Pass Road, Kelso Valley Road continues 6.2 miles to a "Y" where you bear right onto Kelso Creek Road; continue 4.5 miles to reach Highway 178. Turn right (east) at Highway 178 to continue towards Walker Pass and back down to the Mojave. The historic Onyx Store, built in 1881, is located 2 miles up on the right side of the highway. Highway 178 soon leaves the South Fork of the Kern River and follows Canebrake Creek for several miles before climbing to mile-high Walker Pass. A historical marker near the summit commemorates Joseph R. Walker, who, with the help of Tubatuabel Indian guides, opened this route in 1834. From Walker Pass you descend through Freeman Canyon and its magnificent Joshua tree woodland before rejoining Highway 14, just 8 miles from the summit.

Directions: *Allow at least a half-day to make a leisurely trip of the Jawbone*

Canyon-Kelso Valley tour. Jawbone Canyon Road heads west from Highway 14, about 20 miles north of Mojave or 6 miles south of the entrance to Red Rock Canyon State Park. The first 4 miles of the route are paved. The next 19.5 miles are over good, graded dirt, with occasional washboard. Pavement begins again just over the summit between Kelso Valley and the Kelso Creek drainage and continues the rest of the way. Following rain, a 4-wheel-drive vehicle is recommended for the side trip to Butterbredt Springs (it's also a pleasant walk). Jawbone Station is open daily from 9 a.m. to 5 p.m., except in summer (June through September) when it is open five days per week. For information, call (760) 373-1146.

Red Rock Canyon State Park

At high noon on a cloudless day, the Mojave Desert may appear monotonous. Motorists roll past dusty lakebeds and shrub-dotted basins that seem to stretch to the horizon. Along Highway 14, in the midst of one such section, the sudden appearance of the vibrant cliffs at Red Rock Canyon comes as a surprise. Here the road enters a deep, curving gorge cut into low foothills, revealing a layer cake of sedimentary and volcanic deposits. The bluffs resemble fluted columns of a gigantic pipe organ. Shades of white, pink, rose, and rusty-red undulate across their surface. Many of these colorful palisades have eroded

into spires, chutes, and castellated forms, and they have been given fanciful names such as Closed Cathedral, Acropolis, Temple of the Sun, and Alabaster Knoll.

Red Rock Canyon is the largest state park in the Mojave Desert. It owes much of its beauty to the nearly 7,000-foot-thick Dove Springs Formation (formerly known as the Ricardo Formation), which comprises deposits of sand, clay, silt, and gravel, interspersed with layers of volcanic ash and debris, basalt, and a distinctive bed of pink tuff-breccia. Most of the Dove Springs' sediments accumulated on the bottom of a land-locked basin about 7 to 12 million years ago. Subsequently exposed by uplift, many

Above: The colorful sediments in Red Rock's cliffs first accumulated in a land-locked basin 7 to 12 million years ago. STEPHEN INGRAM
Opposite: Volcanic rock and sandstone cap Red Rock's bluffs, protecting the softer deposits below from rapid erosion. LARRY ULRICH

of the softer deposits would have been eroded away long ago were it not for a protective cap of harder volcanic rock and sandstone.

When the Dove Springs Formation was laid down, the region's climate was mild and relatively wet (about 30 inches per year), and much of the vegetation was savanna or grassland inhabited by a variety of animals. Within the Dove Springs Formation, paleontologists have discovered one of California's largest, and perhaps most diverse, assemblage of mammal fossils. They have excavated eight kinds of prehistoric horses, seven species of camels, three types of rhinoceroses, four varieties of pronghorn, three types of mastodons (known as gomphotheres), as well as deer, saber-toothed cats, rabbits, and geese. Petrified plant remains have also been unearthed, and together with its animal fossils, the Dove Springs Formation has furnished a fascinating five-million-year record of Miocene life forms. Paleontologist David Whistler, who has led the excavations, described it as a "textbook lying in the landscape."

The El Paso fault, part of the extensive Garlock fault zone, uplifted the Dove Springs deposits and also thrust up the El Paso Mountains, which reach their western terminus at Red Rock. The El Pasos contained enough mineral deposits to trigger a small mining rush during the late

Red Rock Canyon State Park has over 160 plant species, including many wildflowers. LARRY ULRICH

1800s, but most of these ore bodies were small and hard to develop. Still, Red Rock Canyon saw its share of mining-related excitement. During the 1870s and 1880s, the springs here were a well-known watering hole on the freight route that linked the Cerro Gordo mines in the Inyo Mountains with the sea port at San Pedro, and later, with the railroad at Mojave. Driving mule-drawn wagons, the teamsters hauled silver-lead ingots south from Cerro Gordo's smelters to the port. After delivering their cargo, they purchased fresh provisions in Los Angeles and retraced their route north to the mining camps.

Following Cerro Gordo's heyday, Red Rock Canyon continued to be a rest stop on the north-south transportation route between Owens Valley settlements and the fast-growing town of Los Angeles. In 1896 prospector Rudolf Hagen had the foresight to get out of mining and gradually acquire land and water rights in the canyon. Hagen purchased the old stage stop in 1900 and named the settlement Ricardo, after his son Richard. Hagen was a Renaissance man of the desert. He not only ran the stage station, but also established a post office, general store, campground, farm, and pie-in-the-sky oil drilling operation. As if to spite Hagen's resourceful industry, a flashflood washed away the stage stop in 1909. Ricardo served as a way station for desert travelers up until 1958 when the highway was relocated and its gas station and store were abandoned.

The 4,000-acre Red Rock Canyon State Recreation Area was established in 1973, and park headquarters were located at the old site of Ricardo. Red Rock was reclassified as a state park in 1980, and by 1989 it had grown to 8,000 acres. With passage of the Desert Protection Act in 1994, it expanded to approximately 28,000 acres, making it the sixth largest state park in California. In September 1997 damaging flashfloods revisited the canyon, filling buildings with silt, destroying park roads, and washing out sections of Highway 14.

The most evident attraction at Red Rock Canyon is its colorful geology, but the park is also famous for ephemeral displays of spring wild-flowers. The Hagen Canyon area is especially noteworthy for its floristic diversity. During exceptional wild-flower years several dozen species may be in bloom here at the same time. Look for sand verbena, desert primrose, Bigelow's coreopsis, desert dandelion, chia sage, popcorn flower, and various species of peppergrass. Later in the season you might spot the small, yellow flowers of the endemic Red Rock tarweed around moist seeps. Listed by the State of California as a rare species, this member of the sunflower family has probably grown here for more than 10,000 years.

A visitor center, campground, and nature trail system are found in the heart of the park at Ricardo. The visitor center provides information about the ever-changing conditions of local backcountry roads, along with interesting exhibits on the area's natural and cultural history. The campground offers 50 sites nestled among Joshua trees and along the base of 160-foot-high cliffs. At the east end of the campground, a short guided nature trail provides a good introduction to the area. It leads up to a saddle where two other trails begin: one climbs to Whistler Ridge and a viewpoint of the El Pasos and the vast Mojave; the other drops into Hagen Preserve, one of two scenic park areas accessible only to hikers.

Red Rock has long been a favorite location for film crews. Its dramatic canyon walls have served as backdrops for more than 140 movies and television commercials. The setting lends itself to stage robberies, thundering chase scenes, romantic cowboy-cowgirl interludes, and other standard Western fare. Some first-time visitors may sense that they have already seen this place.

Directions: *Red Rock Canyon State Park straddles Highway 14 about 25 miles north of the town of Mojave, or about 21 miles south of the junction of Highways 14 and 178 West. The old stage route, now called Abbott Drive, is a spur off the west side of the highway that provides access to the park visitor center, campground, and picnic area. For information, call the State Park's Mojave Sector office at (661) 942-0662.*

El Paso Mountains and Burro Schmidt's Tunnel

The El Paso Mountains rise abruptly from the Garlock fault zone to encompass a landscape of subtle beauty and geologic complexity. Volcanic mesas, weathered granite ridges, and pastel sedimentary deposits are folded into this 50-square-mile territory, which is packed with cultural and natural treasures. Most of the range is administered by the BLM as a "limited use" area, but additional sections are protected

The El Pasos contain many mining sites, including the Holly Ash Mine where pumice was extracted from volcanic deposits. JOHN EVARTS

Top: *Burro Schmidt's tunnel and his ore-cart track abruptly end on the steep southern face of the El Pasos.* JOHN EVARTS

Bottom: *It takes visitors 15 minutes to walk through (one-way) the tunnel that Schmidt completed after 32 years of hand digging and blasting.* JOHN EVARTS

within the El Paso Mountains Wilderness Area and Red Rock Canyon State Park. For those with a high-clearance vehicle, a curiosity about small-scale mining, and a sense of adventure, the El Pasos make a rewarding destination.

The high point of the El Pasos is 5,259-foot-high Black Mountain, a lava-covered peak located at the eastern edge of the wilderness area. Archeologists theorize that Black Mountain was once a Native American ceremonial center, perhaps due to its proximity to major trading routes and quarries. Ancient village sites, house rings, and petroglyphs near its flat-topped summit are now within an archeological district listed on the National Register of Historic Places and protected by law. The El Pasos are also home to Bonanza Gulch, Grubstake Hill, Last Chance Canyon, Petrified Forest, and Copper

Basin Mine—places whose names reflect the area's more recent history as a haven for prospectors, rock hounds, and desert dreamers. Although miners swarmed into the range's canyons to work at placer gold diggings in the early 1890s, the El Pasos' real riches were found in its deposits of volcanic ash, which were mined in several locations beginning in 1923 for use in well-known household products such as "Old Dutch Cleanser."

Unlike most other ranges in the Northern Mojave, the El Pasos never had a mining boomtown with its attendant fame and notoriety. Instead, it was the solitary labors of one person, William Henry Schmidt, that ultimately brought the El Pasos to the attention of the outside world. Schmidt arrived in Kern County as a young man in 1894 after a doctor had advised him that moving to a warm, arid climate might spare him from the tuberculosis that killed six of his siblings in his native Rhode Island. He eventually established several mining claims in the El Pasos, including one high on the side of Copper Mountain. Equipped with little more than a pick, shovel, hand drill, four-pound hammer, and wheelbarrow, Schmidt began digging and blasting a tunnel through the mountain's solid granite in 1906, a project that would take him 32 years to complete.

Schmidt believed that a tunnel

offered the most direct route for transporting his ore out of the then-remote El Pasos to processing facilities in the south. By the 1920s, however, a good haul road entered the range by way of Last Chance Canyon, and his tunnel was no longer necessary. Yet Schmidt persisted with his daunting endeavor, installing rails and an ore cart to help carry shattered rock out of the ever-deeper hole. Throughout these years he lived an extremely frugal existence at his one-room cabin near the tunnel's north entrance. Since his only companions were his burros, Jack and Jenny, he became known as "Burro." He worked each summer as a ranch hand near Weldon to support himself.

In 1938, after having excavated an estimated 5,800 tons of rock, Burro Schmidt finally punched through to daylight on the south side of the mountain. The completed tunnel was more than 2,000 feet long, averaged 7 feet high by 5 feet wide, and included several side tunnels. Schmidt, who was then 67, sold the claim and moved to a nearby site in Last Chance Canyon where he lived until his death at age 83. (His photo is on page 77.)

Today, a resident caretaker greets visitors to the tunnel and can show you the inside of Schmidt's one-room shack on Copper Mountain. Its interior is filled with memorabilia and the walls and ceiling are covered with magazine, newspaper, and box covers that date to the 1930s. The tunnel begins a short distance west of the cabin. You will need a flashlight (available for rent on the site) and about 15 minutes to walk one-way through the 0.4-mile-long tunnel. It emerges on a steep slope with sweeping views of the Fremont Valley basin about 2,500 feet below. The last stretch of the tunnel is smaller and lower because Schmidt was increasingly stooped and frail near the end of the project. As you imagine Schmidt, chipping away at solid rock beside the faint glow of a kerosene lantern, you can only marvel at his determination and wonder why this tunnel to nowhere became his obsession.

One of Schmidt's neighbors was Walt Bickel, who worked eight adjoining claims—one in the name of each of his children—in Last Chance Canyon from 1934 until 1980. A short side trip off the main route to Schmidt's tunnel takes you to Bickel's camp, which is well worth a visit. The first thing you notice when approaching the site are the amazing heaps of

Bickel Camp is now a historic site that contains the original cabin, workshop, and equipment collection that were part of a small gold-mining operation dating to 1934. JOHN EVARTS

rusting machinery, spare parts, motors, tools, and countless other mining-related implements. These castoffs surround Bickel's small cabin and the shop where he made much of his own equipment. The entire place is largely preserved just as he left it. A caretaker lives next door, keeping a careful watch over this world-class collection of junk. The nearby Bickel gold diggings are still being worked by hand with the time-tested techniques of dry-washing and panning, giving this desert hideaway the feel of a living history museum.

Directions: *From the junction of Highways 14 and 178, drive south 7.3 miles on Highway 14 and turn left onto unpaved Hart Road, which intersects the highway between two huge billboards. From the Ricardo entrance at Red Rock Canyon State Park, it is 9.6 miles north to this turnoff. Hart Road heads straight for the El Pasos in a southeasterly direction. It crosses the dirt Redrock-Inyokern Road and then gradually climbs past Joshua trees near the southern edge of the wilderness area, with Black Mountain looming on the left. At 4.5 miles from Highway 14, a side road on the right leads a short distance to the Holly Ash Mine, located just inside the boundary of the state park. Between the 1940s and mid-1960s, the layer of tuff-breccia here was mined for pumice and volcanic ash that went into products such as abrasives, paint, and toothpaste. About*

Only a handful of structures remain at the site of Garlock, a mining supply center that sprang to life in the 1890s and then quickly faded when nearby Randsburg boomed. MARC SOLOMON

0.25 mile beyond the turnoff to the mine, the road reaches a crest, and you can look across the basin to spot a few buildings at Burro Schmidt's tunnel, perched on the left flank of Copper Mountain. At 6.25 miles from the highway you reach Last Chance Canyon wash and turn left to go up the drainage. (Those with 4-wheel drive might want to make a side trip by taking the right fork, which goes down the wash and passes colorful sedimentary cliffs, following the 1850 route of Manly and Rogers, discussed on page 59.) At 7 miles you reach a junction where the left fork leads about 0.25 mile to Bickel Camp. At 8.5 miles you turn right off the main road to make the climb up to Burro Schmidt's. From Highway 14 to Burro Schmidt's totals 9.2 miles.

Garlock Fault and the Site of Garlock

The powerful Garlock fault zone slashes diagonally across the Mojave Desert for more than 150 miles, extending from Frazier Mountain near the town of Gorman to southern Death Valley. The Garlock is the largest transverse (east-west) fault system in California. Vertical uplift along this fault zone has formed the abrupt south face of the El Paso Mountains, which now stand 2,500 feet above the adjacent floor of Fremont Valley. Horizontal displacement along the fault zone has been even greater: the valley and mountains have moved up to 40 miles in opposite directions during the last 13 million years. The

El Paso Mountains' stream channels provide vivid evidence of this horizontal offset; in many places they jog abruptly at right angles to their natural downhill course.

Amid all this geologic turmoil lies the site of Garlock. Not much is left of this historic community that once supplied the area's early mining camps. A weathered log cabin on the west side of Garlock Road and a roofless stone building (now stucco-covered) on the east are some of the last remnants; both are on private land. The stone structure was once a saloon, bawdyhouse, and stage stop. Across the street from the saloon was the Doty Hotel, the "Taj Mahal" of its day. From its second story it was said that "one could look farther and see less than at any point in the surrounding country." Scattered piles of adobe, rock, and wood in the nearby brush denote such former landmarks as Jennie's Bar, the Wells Fargo office, a blacksmith shop, the post office, Granny Slocum's boarding house, and several mill sites, including an old Mexican-style arrastra, or drag mill. Cars on Garlock Road speed past, giving the place a lonesome feel, as if life passed it by—which is what actually happened in 1898.

Springs at the foot of the El Paso Mountains were a rest stop for the 20-mule-team wagons hauling borax from Searles Valley to the railroad at Mojave. In the 1890s a small settlement named Cow Springs grew up alongside this freight road. When its first post office was built in 1896, the town was renamed after Eugene Garlock, who built a mill here that served nearby mines. Initially, Garlock was a supply center for the placer gold workings in nearby Goler Gulch. These mines were soon overshadowed by the Rand Mining District in the mountains just to the southeast, which began to boom with the discovery of gold in 1895. Water was pumped from Garlock to the new town of Randsburg, which in turn began shipping its ore to Garlock to be milled. The arrangement was short-lived. Randsburg's Yellow Aster Mine turned out to be so rich it warranted its own mill and railroad. By 1898 the settlement of Johannesburg, only a mile over the hill from Randsburg, became the new railroad depot and supply center. The Yellow Aster developed its own water supplies, further diminishing the role of Garlock. Because building materials were in such demand in the desert, most of Garlock's structures were eventually moved to Randsburg. Saddened citizens watched as the town packed up and left, leaving only memories of the huge horseshoe games on Main Street, presentations of the Literary Society, and the laughing shrieks of children as they rode burros, bikes, and dog-pulled wagons through the dusty streets.

The Randsburg-Red Rock and Garlock roads run along the southern base of the El Pasos, providing a good look at the Garlock fault zone. The spectacular escarpments near Garlock gave this fault system its name. Drive a few miles east from the historic site of Garlock to view fault scarps on your left. A well-defined graben—or sunken block between two parallel branches of a fault system—is located between 4.3 and 5.5 miles east of Garlock. This 100-foot-deep trough runs along the north side of the road (about 0.25 mile to the north) yet remains just out of sight.

About 5 miles west of Garlock, a short spur road branches south to the site of the company town of Saltdale on the edge of Koehn Dry Lake. Salt was harvested here from 1911 until the 1970s by evaporating the waters that accumulated on this playa.

This broad wash rimmed by low bluffs is a graben along the massive Garlock fault at the foot of the El Pasos. STEPHEN INGRAM

Directions: To reach Garlock from the west, exit Highway 14 at the Randsburg-Red Rock Road 4 miles south of Red Rock Canyon State Park, or just over 20 miles north of Mojave. Continue 12.2 miles east on the Randsburg-Red Rock Road to a fork where you head left onto Garlock Road. Continue east just under a mile to reach the townsite. From the east drive 9.6 miles south on Highway 395 from the China Lake Boulevard exit, or drive 4 miles north of Johannesburg to reach the turnoff for Garlock Road. Drive 7.4 miles west on Garlock Road to reach the townsite. The east end of the graben begins 2 miles west of Highway 395.

Rand Mining District

The rounded volcanic knob of mile-high Red Mountain watches over a cluster of mining towns known as the Rand Mining District. Named after the famous Witwatersrand gold-mining district ("The Rand") in South Africa, this region of the Mojave became one of the biggest gold and silver producers of its day. The towns of Randsburg, Johannesburg, Red Mountain, and Atolia all flourished for a time, nestled around the rich ore of Red Mountain and the Rand Mountains to the west.

When approaching Red Mountain from the south via Highway 395, the first mining ruins to come into view are abandoned buildings and scattered head frames of Atolia. This settlement boomed during World War I as a supplier of much-needed tungsten. It was primarily a short-lived tent city, so not much remains. The community of Red Mountain, about three miles north of Atolia, was known for its silver mines, especially the Kelly. Between 1919 and 1923 it produced $7 million in silver. One carload of ore alone brought $54,000 during the mine's first year of operation. This heady success helped to make Red Mountain a well-known party town, famous for its painted ladies, saloons, and dance halls.

The fading railroad supply center of Johannesburg, locally called "Joburg," is located another two miles north on the highway. Established in 1897, it was the railhead for a spur line that ran 28 miles south to join the Atchison, Topeka & Santa Fe mainline at Kramer Junction. Although Joburg was always thought of as nearby Randsburg's "little sister," it once boasted a grand hotel that even had a skating rink. While writer Edna Brush Perkins was a guest in 1921, she wrote: "The big hotel at Joburg, which was attractively built around a court and which could accommodate twenty or thirty guests, was empty save for us. We looked at and admired innumerable specimens of ore. They were everywhere, in the hotel-office, in the general store, in the windows of the houses. Everyone

Buildings from Randsburg's early-twentieth-century heyday line its main street. JOHN EVARTS

had some shining bit of the earth which he treasured."

This fascination with ore also defines the neighboring town of Randsburg, just two miles over the hill. At its heart is the Randsburg Desert Museum, a shrine devoted to the area's fabulous ore. Beautiful rock-work terraces and steps lead up to the entrance. Inside, the tiny rooms smell of rocks. On a kitchen table in the center of the front room is a "meal" of rocks whose shapes and colors resemble food. Behind a heavy curtain, dusty shelves are crammed with specimens that glow with eerie fluorescent colors. Display cases in the back room hold gem and mineral samples. Above them hangs a framed patchwork of obsidian arrowheads resembling a diamond-patterned quilt. The museum grounds contain gold-mining equipment, including an impressive five-stamp mill and a locomotive that once pulled ore cars from the deep "glory hole" of the famous Yellow Aster Mine.

Prospectors Austin Burcham, John Singleton, and F. M. Mooers founded the Yellow Aster in 1895. Disappointed with their meager success at the nearby Summit Dry Diggings, the trio had slipped off to look for something better and discovered rich ore at the northeast end of the Rand Mountains. With a grubstake from Burcham's wife (Dr. Rose LaMonte Burcham, a successful San Bernardino

physician/midwife), they established the Yellow Aster Mining & Milling Company. In 1899 the mine fired up its thundering 130-stamp mill, which literally shook the ground. Randsburg was the Yellow Aster's company town, and during its heyday at the turn of the century, the population swelled to 14,000. Over the course of 47 years, the Yellow Aster produced about $25 million in gold before shutting down in 1942.

Sporadic, small-scale mining of the old claims kept Randsburg alive for many years. During the 1990s, however, the site of the Yellow Aster experienced a major renewal of mining activity. Like other hardrock gold-mining districts in the California desert, the area was reworked with the open-pit, heap-leach process. The old diggings yielded gold that previously was not cost-effective to mine. Using huge earth-moving equipment, the Glamis-Rand Mining Company dug out the entire glory hole of the Yellow Aster in its quest for the precious metal.

The simple beauty of the Rand Mining District may be one of the reasons it persists, fighting off the ghosts of neglect and decay. Its weathered buildings, scattered shacks, and old mine sites have million-dollar views across the Fremont Valley to the El Paso Mountains and southern Sierra Nevada. Because Red Mountain rises a few thousand feet above the

This table, set with a "meal" made from rocks, is one of the more whimsical exhibits at the informative Randsburg Desert Museum. FRANK BALTHIS

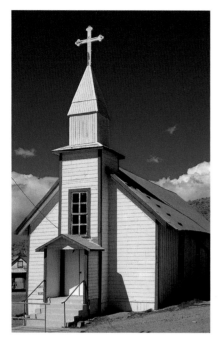

Randsburg's picturesque Church of Santa Barbara was built in 1904. JOHN EVARTS

surrounding basins, it often wrings enough extra moisture from winter storms to nurture a carpet of spring wildflowers.

The community of Randsburg retains much of the historic ambiance that justifies its claim to being a "living ghost town." False-front buildings dating back to the start of the twentieth century line the town's main street, Butte Avenue. One of the older structures is the Randsburg General Store, which has been in continuous operation since 1896. It still serves up old-fashioned malts at a marble-countered soda fountain that was shipped around the Horn from Boston and delivered from Pasadena by an eight-horse freight wagon in 1904. As it climbs out of town, Butte Avenue passes the picturesque Church of Santa Barbara (ca. 1904) and offers views over Randsburg and the Yellow Aster operation. During winter holidays, when tiny homes and historic churches are ornamented with strings of lights, this old mining town on a hill puts out a welcome glow that seems to reflect the residents' enduring love for this piece of earth.

Directions: The Rand Mining District straddles Highway 395 about 14 miles south of the China Lake Boulevard exit to Ridgecrest, or about 26 miles north of Kramer Junction (Four Corners). The town of Randsburg is located on a 4-mile-long loop west of the highway. The loop's southern entrance is near Red Mountain, while the north entrance is about 1 mile west of Johannesburg. Motorists in Randsburg can also take a back way into Johannesburg by turning left on Johannesburg Road, less than 1 mile out of town. Randsburg can also be reached from the west on the Randsburg-Red Rock Road, which comes up Fremont Valley. The Randsburg Desert Museum is open from 10 a.m. to 5 p.m. on weekends and holidays, except for Thanksgiving, Christmas, and New Year's Day.

Maturango Museum and Ridgecrest

Only one museum is fully dedicated to interpreting the Northern Mojave: Maturango Museum. This nonprofit institution has been educating people about the natural and cultural history of the region since 1961. The focus of its work is the preservation of the prehistoric, historic, and natural heritage of the Northern Mojave. Located in Ridgecrest, the museum is an essential resource for anyone who loves this arid, rugged country.

The museum features a well-stocked bookstore and gift shop, the Sylvia Winslow Gallery with changing art shows, a hands-on discovery area for children, and an exhibit room with displays on local history, plants, and animals. The permanent exhibits here include: "Ecology Islands," which presents Northern Mojave habitats; a geology section with local rocks, Coso Range volcanism diagrams, and a

Maturango Museum features Northern Mojave natural and cultural history. JOHN EVARTS

geothermal video; a paleontology area with ancient mammoth and bison bones and the skull of a sabertoothed cat from China Lake; and an aboriginal inhabitants display with local artifacts. Other exhibits feature Searles Lake, upper Mojave history, and the Naval Air Weapons Station. The museum building is surrounded by a garden of native plants, labeled for identification.

The Maturango Museum offers many tours and outreach programs, including field trips to view wildflowers or local mining and geologic sites. During fall and spring, trips are offered to Petroglyph Canyon Historical Monument on the nearby Naval Air Weapons Station at China Lake. (See pages 102-103 for more about Petroglyph Canyon.) Children and adults will enjoy the labyrinth on the museum grounds. It was laid out with tufa blocks recycled from a dismantled residence. Some of the early houses in Ridgecrest were constructed with tufa collected from Salt Wells Valley, just east of Indian Wells Valley. One of these historic tufa-block structures is located a short distance from the museum at the southwest corner of Norma Street and Ridgecrest Boulevard.

Another interesting facility in the Ridgecrest area is the BLM's Wild Horse and Burro Corrals just east of town. Many domestic horses and burros, abandoned during the early

mining era, successfully adapted to life in the wild. Today, feral populations of these animals threaten native wildlife by competing with them for limited water and grazing resources. To keep their numbers at acceptable levels, BLM wranglers gather wild horses and burros from public lands. The animals are gentled and offered for adoption to good homes, and many become horse show and rodeo stars, successful breeding stock, pack animals, or great pets.

To round out your Ridgecrest itinerary with some nearby hiking, head to the BLM's Rademacher Hills on the south edge of town. This former mining area was closed to off-highway vehicles in the early 1990s and is now dedicated to passive recreation along a 12-mile network of trails. A good introduction to the hills is a 1.1-mile loop section of the Rademacher Hills Trail. This hike begins at Sunland Trailhead and heads east about 0.25 mile to the Ron Henry Interpretive Site, where many of the desert plants are identified with signs. Take a left fork here to climb about 300 feet in 0.25 mile to reach the summit of Sky Point and its sweeping views of the Indian Wells Valley. From the bench at Sky Point you can retrace your steps or descend to the north (toward Ridgecrest) and turn left at the first intersection to return to the trailhead, completing a counter-clockwise circuit.

Some wild burros are brought to BLM corrals at Ridgecrest for adoption. SCOTT T. SMITH

Directions: *The Maturango Museum is located at 100 E. Las Flores Avenue, on the corner of Las Flores and China Lake Boulevard/Highway 178, and it is open every day from 10 a.m. to 5 p.m. For information on changing exhibits and programs, call (760) 375-6900. To reach the Wild Horse and Burro Corrals, drive 4.5 miles east on Ridgecrest Boulevard from its intersection with China Lake Boulevard/Highway 178 and turn right onto the Randsburg Wash Road; the facilities are less than 0.2 mile farther. They are open Monday through Friday, 7 a.m. to 4 p.m. Visitors are welcome and tours can be arranged by calling the Ridgecrest BLM office at (760) 384-5400. For adoption appointments and general information, call (760) 446-6064 or (800) 951-8720. To access the Rademacher Hills Trail, drive about 1 mile south on China Lake Boulevard from its intersection with Ridgecrest Boulevard and turn left onto College Heights Boulevard. Continue about 3.5 miles, turn left (east) onto unpaved Belle Vista Road, and follow it 0.5 mile to the Sunland Trailhead.*

Petroglyph Canyon National Historic Landmark

Petroglyphs appear on nearly every rock surface of Big Petroglyph, Little Petroglyph, Sheep, and other more inaccessible canyons that wind through the volcanic mesas of the Coso Range north of Indian Wells Valley. The walls of these canyons comprise a stunning gallery of native rock art filled with thousands of images. At Little Petroglyph Canyon (formerly known as lower Renegade Canyon), for example, bighorn sheep "run" across 1.5 miles of stone surfaces. Human-like figures appear, their elongated bodies covered with elaborate designs; likenesses of dogs, deer, mountain lions, snakes, and medicine bags decorate the panels. The variety is overwhelming. More than 5,000 different designs have been recorded in these remote canyons, and the Coso Range is now recognized as having one of the largest concentrations of rock art on Earth.

Aboriginal artists made the petroglyphs by pecking, abrading, or grinding these images into the dark desert varnish that forms a patina over the Coso's basalt rocks. Since desert varnish continually builds up, the exposed stone in the petroglyphs has been gradually recoated, causing the images to fade. Based on various dating techniques, scientists now believe that the oldest Coso petroglyphs were created more than

Above: Canyons of the volcanic Coso Range north of Ridgecrest contain one of the world's largest concentrations of rock art. DENNIS FLAHERTY
Opposite: Bighorn sheep are frequently depicted in the art at Petroglyph Canyon National Historic Landmark. FRED HIRSCHMANN

12,000 years ago, with some art estimated to date back 16,500 years.

Although no one knows exactly why the petroglyphs were made, the prevailing theory today is that the art is associated with shamanistic activity, hunting, and possibly vision quests. The art potrays elaborately attired figures with great headdresses who may be shamans with supernatural powers. Many scenes depict hunting, such as men armed with atlatls or bows stalking sheep. Although it is impossible to be certain of the petroglyphs' original meanings, they continue to communicate the human concerns and artistry of another time.

Directions: The 99-square-mile national historic landmark is located within the Naval Air Weapons Station, where it has been protected from unrestricted public access since 1943. Visitation is only allowed as part of an escorted tour group. The Maturango Museum offers tours to Little Petroglyph Canyon on weekends in spring and fall. The 90-mile round trip departs from the Maturango Museum in Ridgecrest. Basic tours leave at 8 a.m. and return about 4:50 p.m. Specially trained tour guides accompany the group. For information, call (760) 375-6900.

Short Canyon

Short Canyon is a scenic destination treasured for its biological diversity and wildflower displays. Located where the Northern Mojave meets the southern Sierra Nevada, it harbors desert and mountain species that overlap in rich natural communities. Nearly 300 different plants are found in the canyon, which straddles the boundary of the Owens Peak Wilderness just west of Indian Wells Valley. A short drive and well-marked trail offer easy entry points for exploring this ecological transition zone.

A typical Mojave creosote scrub community covers the upper part of the broad alluvial fan that spills out of the mountains here. The road up the canyon crosses the 1970 Los Angeles Aqueduct pipe before it climbs up from sand hummocks that lie on the canyon floor. About 3 miles in, the road splits. One fork stays low, traverses a sandy wash, and then follows it to an abrupt end at the base of some granite cliffs; the other continues straight ahead up to a parking area with trail access to the Owens Peak Wilderness.

At the terminus of the lower canyon you can clamber up to a small waterfall that plummets from a deep cut in the rocks. Below the falls, the stream disappears into the sand; above them, the creek usually flows year-round. In a wet year the road to the falls is lined with a spectacular display of wildflowers. Even after a low-rainfall winter, spring visitors may see a splash of color from hardy annuals, such as desert

The rare Charlotte's phacelia is found in Short Canyon. STEPHEN INGRAM

Granitic peaks of the southern Sierra Nevada loom above Short Canyon, which is known for its spring wildflowers and a plant diversity that exceeds 300 species. JIM STIMSON

dandelion, Bigelow's coreopsis, and desert primrose.

The creek above the falls is easily accessed via a hiking trail that begins from the parking area at the end of the upper canyon road. From the parking area, the path immediately ascends steeply for about 300 feet to a saddle that offers wonderful views of the upper stream basin and the granite spires that rim the drainage. (Even if you don't plan to hike, the view from here is worth the short climb up.) The trail then descends to the stream, where willow, ash, and cottonwood flourish in the riparian zone. The music of running water and the songs of canyon wrens fill the air. The dry, dusty odor of the desert is overpowered by the sweet scents of green leafy growth.

Hike farther up the creek and you'll encounter a rich combination of plants, including cholla and beavertail cactus, rabbitbrush, bitterbrush, and sagebrush. Amid lush tangles of native grapevines, Parry nolina—uncommon in much of the Northern Mojave—sends up glorious stalks of cream-colored blossoms in spring. Clumps of Joshua trees are dispersed among stands of canyon oak, Utah juniper, and gray pine. All this vegetation eventually chokes the path and makes it difficult to follow the stream. Heading back down the trail, the many textures and colors of the canyon's rocks and plants stand out against the expansive plain of Indian Wells Valley.

Directions: Exit the highway at Brady's Gas Station, located about 0.5 mile north of the junction of Highways 395 and 14. Follow the highway frontage road north about 0.5 mile and turn left (west) onto a graded dirt road where you will see the first of several BLM signs directing you to Short Canyon. After 0.4 mile turn left (south) onto a power-line road, which you follow for about 0.5 mile before reaching an intersection where you'll turn right and resume heading west into the canyon. After crossing the white aqueduct pipe, stay on the main fork of the road, which soon enters a sandy section that is almost always passable for 2-wheel-drive vehicles. About 3 miles from the frontage road you come to a junction with a partially paved road. Straight ahead is a fence with a cattle guard and another BLM sign for Short Canyon. Go this way about 0.3 mile to reach the trailhead for the creek and Owens Peak Wilderness entrance. To reach the base of the waterfall, turn left onto the short section of paved road and follow it across the wash. Immediately after crossing the wash, turn right onto a dirt road. Stay right at the forks on this road and follow it about 0.5 mile to where it dead-ends. From here, a short scramble leads to the falls.

Sand Canyon

Sand Canyon contains one of the Northern Mojave's longest stretches of riparian habitat. A perennial stream that flows out of the southern Sierra

Nevada and into the desert sustains this strip of water-loving vegetation. It supports a tremendous variety of plants and animals, including stands of cottonwoods and willows that provide refuge for more than 100 species of resident and migratory birds. Sand Canyon is so important to migratory songbirds that the BLM has designated 2,300 acres here as an Area of Critical Environmental Concern. Plants from the Mojave and Great Basin deserts and the Sierra Nevada contribute to the canyon's diverse flora, which ranges from creosote bush scrub at the lower elevations to coniferous woodlands on the flanks of Lamont and Sawtooth peaks. Sand Canyon is also rich in human history, which adds to the allure of this large drainage.

The lower section of the canyon is easily accessible on a good dirt road that passes serene, creekside groves. In the early 1900s, however, this place buzzed with activity during construction of the first Los Angeles Aqueduct. The 230-mile-long aqueduct was engineered to rely on the force of gravity to carry water from its intake at the Owens River, at an elevation of around 4,000 feet, to the San Fernando Valley, about 700 feet above sea level. Since the pipeline required sufficient gravitational force to push water southward over a crest near Red Rock Canyon, its route in this area did not drop into Indian

Wells Valley but instead remained at a higher elevation, where it had to traverse canyons along the base of the mountains. In building the stretch through Sand Canyon, aqueduct workers initially dug shafts into the north and south slopes of the canyon. The concrete and steel-reinforced shafts, called pressure tunnels, were designed to funnel water into, then out of, a 550-foot-long German-manufactured steel pipe that crossed the canyon floor. The original design was flawed because the water leaving the canyon via the pressure tunnel on the south slope was at a higher level than the water entering it on the north. The pressure resulting from this hydrologic logjam caused the steel pipe to buckle and then rupture, sending a flood of water down Sand Canyon and delaying the much-anticipated delivery of water to Los Angeles. The failed pipe was replaced by a multi-sectioned siphon that still plummets down the canyon's north slope about 50 feet above where the original pipe broke out of the cement cradles that held it.

Patrolmen for the Los Angeles Aqueduct and their families lived in isolated Sand Canyon up until the 1940s. Their job was to patrol, on foot and horseback, an approximately 20-mile-long section of the pipeline to inspect it and protect it from vandalism or sabotage. Concrete slabs, a toppled chimney, and partial rock

walls are all that remain of the homes and outbuildings of these families. If you look carefully on the south side of the road about 100 yards up from the aqueduct, you can find the small, rock-walled swimming pool they filled in summer with ice-cold water drawn from the pipeline.

You can explore the upper canyon by following an easy trail—an abandoned jeep road—that begins at the parking area on the boundary of the Owens Peak Wilderness. Near the start of the trail you will see Joshua trees and an occasional gray pine.

The first Los Angeles Aqueduct crosses Sand Canyon at a spot where aqueduct patrolmen and their families once lived. JOHN EVARTS

Cottonwoods, gray pines, and Joshua trees thrive in upper Sand Canyon. JOHN EVARTS

This unusual botanical pairing is possible because gray pine reaches its easternmost distribution here as it extends far down Sand Canyon. The path is never far from the sound of running water, and it ascends gently for the first 1.5 miles before it splits. The trail up the north fork (straight ahead) climbs gradually for another mile before reaching a pleasant gray pine woodland and the ruins of the Whortley Ranch. A Native American village was also located at this site, as evidenced by numerous mortar holes in granite boulders, scattered flakes of obsidian, and a few pictographs. The trail up the south fork (left, across the creek) is steeper and reaches scenic Rodecker Flats in about 0.75 mile. Experienced hikers can continue farther up both forks of Sand Canyon for superb vistas.

Directions: From the intersection of Highways 395 and 14 proceed about 5 miles north on Highway 395 to Brown Road. Turn left, crossing the highway and a frontage road, and head west on a paved road. Not long after leaving the highway—just before intersecting a power-line road—you cross the faint track of the historic, nineteenth-century freight and passenger road that connected Cerro Gordo's mines and Los Angeles. At 0.8 mile from the highway, near the entrance to a sand and gravel quarry, you swing left onto a dirt road that continues into the canyon. At 1.3 miles several roads intersect; remain on the road that goes up the canyon. At 2 miles there is a BLM sign for the Sand Canyon Management Area. At 2.4 miles you can see the old aqueduct cement cradles, which are broken off on their upstream side. The entrances to the tunnels that connected the original pipe to the pressure tunnels in the canyon's north and south slopes align with the cradles, but are now blocked off. Just beyond this point the road goes under the black 1913 aqueduct pipe. Campers or other high-profile vehicles can pass beneath the pipe via a lower fork that crosses a seep that smells of sulfur; most other cars and trucks can take the upper fork. At 2.9 miles you pass an aqueduct service road that forks to the left; follow the main road, which crosses the creek, and continue a short way to the trailhead at the boundary of Owens Peak Wilderness. Beyond the parking area, the canyon

broadens and the trail swings northwest, hugging the western base of stark Boulder Peak (on your right) until the route forks. Remember that archeological resources in Sand Canyon, and elsewhere, are protected by law, and unauthorized collecting of artifacts or disturbance of sites is illegal.

Fossil Falls

The Fossil Falls area provides a vivid introduction to volcanism and climate change in the Northern Mojave. Within the last 400,000 years, at least three different eruptions in the Coso Range and adjacent Rose Valley have produced lava flows that are visible near Fossil Falls. Some of this basalt spilled into the path of ice-age Owens River, which flowed southeast from the Sierra Nevada during periods of high glacial run-off. At Fossil Falls the river cut a path through the lava beds, and its sediment-laden water scoured out deep potholes and polished the basalt as it swirled over the

Carpets of goldfields erupt near the Red Hill cinder cone. MARK PAHUTA

rocks. When the climate gradually became drier about 10,000 years ago, the river ceased flowing through this channel, exposing a "fossilized waterfall."

Volcanic landforms abound near Fossil Falls. The trail to the "falls" winds through a field of craggy lava. Rising to the immediate north is 630-foot-high Red Hill, a rusty-red cinder cone composed of porous volcanic rock called *scoria*. The most recent lava flow in the area is less than 20,000 years old and originated from the vent on Red Hill. Older cinder cones and lava flows are also visible in the Coso Range to the southeast. An impressive palisade of columnar basalt flanks the east side of Highway 395 just a few miles south of Fossil Falls.

The area surrounding Fossil Falls contains numerous reminders of human habitation from centuries past when the climate was less arid and water and game were more abundant. You may see obsidian chips, petroglyphs, grinding holes, and wide circles of stones—the foundations of temporary shelters built by the Shoshones. These and all other Native American artifacts are protected by law and should be left in place, undisturbed.

A good time to visit Fossil Falls is during spring, when delicate annual wildflowers bloom amidst the black, tumbled lava. A short trail takes you

The ice-age Owens River cut a deep, narrow swath through these lava beds before it eventually dried up about 10,000 years ago, leaving behind this "fossilized waterfall." BILL EVARTS

to the overlook at the edge of the Fossil Falls gorge. (Keep children back from the edge.) The falls' intricate maze of water-sculpted lava can be further explored—but this should only by attempted by those who are agile and sure-footed. The BLM administers Fossil Falls and has designated it an Area of Critical Environmental Concern.

Directions: *Fossil Falls is located just east of Highway 395 in Rose Valley. To reach Fossil Falls from the south, drive 3 miles north of Little Lake on Highway 395 to the exit for Cinder Road. From the north, drive 5 miles south of the Coso Junction Rest Area to reach the exit. Follow Cinder Road 0.5 mile east to a right curve and another 0.5 mile south to the parking area and trailhead.*

Searles and Panamint Valleys Region

At the extreme northern end of the bowl we found an attenuated wraith of a road leading up into a heavily wooded canyon. . . . It brought us to a small, level spot where, made of rocks like the mountains and indistinguishable until we were right on them, stood seven immense charcoal-kilns like a row of giant beehives. . . .

. . . Everywhere men have left their footprints on the Mojave, sojourners always, never inhabitants. The seven kilns were the most impressive testimony of brief possession that we saw, more impressive even than the twenty-eight-mile-long trench that brought the water to Skidoo. . . . They will still be eloquent in that remote fastness long after Keane Wonder and Rhyolite are gone.

Behind the kilns a dim path climbed the mountain-side to a little, secret spring . . . so deftly hidden that we wondered what prospector first had the joy of finding it. From the elevation of the spring we could look along the length of Wild Rose Canyon, where the sagebrush smoothed to a blue and green and purple sea, and through its narrow opening to the white serenity of Mount Whitney. Thus framed the white peak seemed to float in the blue sky. Very swiftly Mojave brushes men off, but always with a fine gesture. From the midst of her most obliterating desolations she never fails to point at some far-off shining.

—Edna Brush Perkins,
The White Heart of the Mojave, 1922

Opposite: Wild buckwheat and creosote cover
this alluvial fan that slopes toward the long,
deep basin of Panamint Valley. JIM STIMSON

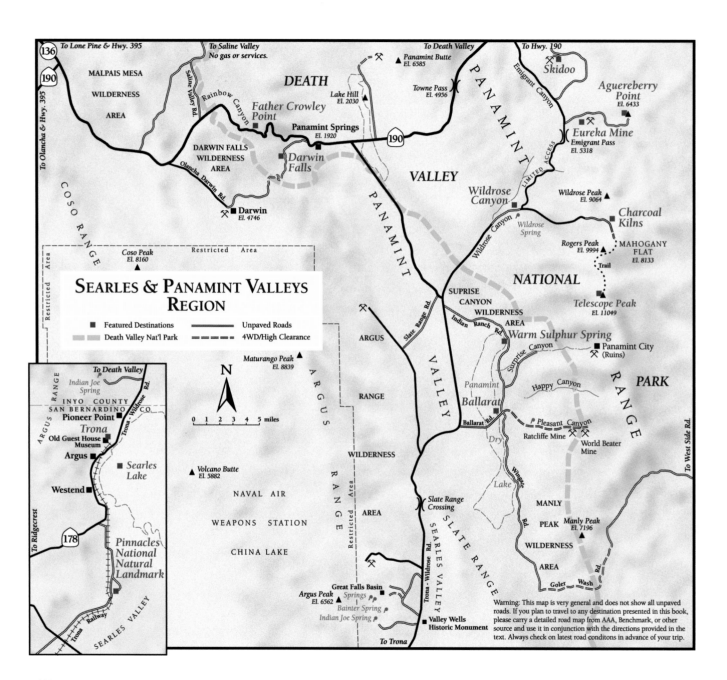

To Lone Pine & Hwy. 395 — **136**
190
To Olancha & Hwy. 395

To Saline Valley
No gas or services.

To Death Valley

To Hwy. 190

MALPAIS MESA
WILDERNESS
AREA

Panamint Butte
El. 6585

Skidoo

PANAMINT

Aguereberry
Point
El. 6433

DEATH

Emigrant Canyon

Saline Valley Rd.

Rainbow Canyon

Father Crowley
Point

Lake Hill
El. 2030

Towne Pass
El. 4956

Panamint Springs
El. 1920

190

Eureka Mine
Emigrant Pass
El. 5318

DARWIN FALLS
WILDERNESS
AREA

Olancha Darwin Rd.

Darwin
Falls

VALLEY

Wildrose
Canyon

Wildrose Peak
El. 9064

Charcoal
Kilns

Wildrose Canyon

Wildrose
Spring

Darwin
El. 4746

C O S O   R A N G E

Restricted   Area

Coso Peak
El. 8160

Rogers Peak
El. 9994

MAHOGANY
FLAT
El. 8133

Trail

SEARLES & PANAMINT VALLEYS REGION

National

Telescope Peak
El. 11049

SUPRISE
CANYON
WILDERNESS
AREA

Slate Range Rd.

Warm Sulphur Spring

Indian   Ranch   Rd.

Panamint City
(Ruins)

ARGUS

RANGE

PARK

■ Featured Destinations
    Death Valley Nat'l Park

Unpaved Roads
4WD/High Clearance

Maturango Peak
El. 8839

N

0 1 2 3 4 5 miles

Suprise Canyon

Happy   Canyon

To West Side Rd.

To Death Valley

Indian Joe
Spring

Panamint
Ballarat

INYO COUNTY
SAN BERNARDINO CO.

Pioneer Point

Trona

Old Guest House
Museum

Argus

Westend

Searles
Lake

ARGUS   RANGE

Trona - Wildrose Rd.

Volcano Butte
El. 5882

N A V A L   A I R

W E A P O N S   S T A T I O N

C H I N A   L A K E

WILDERNESS

AREA

Restricted   Area

Ballarat
Ballarat Rd.

Dry

Pleasant   Canyon

Ratcliffe Mine

World Beater
Mine

Lake

MANLY

PEAK

Manly Peak
El. 7196

178

Pinnacles
National
Natural
Landmark

SLATE   RANGE

Slate Range
Crossing

Wingate Rd.

WILDERNESS

AREA

Manly
Rd.

Goler   Wash   Rd.

To Ridgecrest

Trona   Railway

SEARLES VALLEY

Searles Valley Rd.

Trona - Wildrose Rd.

Argus Peak
El. 6562

Great Falls Basin
Springs

Bainter Spring

Indian Joe Spring

Valley Wells
Historic Monument

To Trona

Warning: This map is very general and does not show all unpaved
roads. If you plan to travel to any destination presented in this book,
please carry a detailed road map from AAA, Benchmark, or other
source and use it in conjunction with the directions provided in the
text. Always check on latest road conditons in advance of your trip.

Trona Pinnacles National Natural Landmark

As dawn approaches, the Trona Pinnacles emerge like a dream landscape from the parched bed of Searles Lake. The silhouettes of over 500 strangely shaped towers cluster together against a vast plain rimmed with distant hills. Old-timers called it Cathedral City, an apt name for such a mysterious-looking place.

Although it may be hard to imagine, the Trona Pinnacles once protruded from the bottom of a deep lake. During ice ages that occurred between 10,000 and 100,000 years ago, runoff from the Sierra Nevada periodically coursed into Searles Lake via Owens Lake and China Lake to the north and west. During peak times of glacial runoff, ancient Searles Lake reached a depth of 640 feet and may have overflowed into neighboring Panamint Valley. High above the playa of Searles Valley, wave-cut terraces from these past lake levels are etched into the slopes.

The pinnacles consist of an unusual "rock" called tufa. It resembles limestone and forms entirely underwater. Like other desert lakes, Searles was high in carbonates and salts. Mixing with the salty lake were the waters from springs, rich in dissolved calcium, which flowed out of fissures along fault lines on the lake bottom. When the calcium-rich waters came in contact with the carbonates

The tallest of the Trona Pinnacles rises nearly 140 feet above the lakebed. STEPHEN INGRAM

in the lake water, calcium carbonate, or tufa, precipitated out. Blue-green algae growing in the lake bonded with the calcium carbonate, giving the growing tufa a living framework. A tower, permeated with hollow passages for the rising water, formed above each spring. Some of the towers are nearly 140 feet high. The unusual qualities of this landscape were officially recognized in 1968 when the site was declared a National Natural Landmark.

There is no set way to explore the Trona Pinnacles. Miles of dirt tracks and trails wind throughout the 14-square miles of Cathedral City, so plan to stay a few hours if you wish to see it all. Mountain bikes are a great way to tour the area, provided you keep to established trails. You can access an informal nature trail by following the main road over the

natural embankment just north of the Trona Pinnacles, turning left at the bottom, then staying to the right at the forks until reaching a sign, visitor register, and handicapped-accessible restroom. Proceeding south from this sign, look to the left for a large rock with a brass plaque, and next to it, a post displaying a hiking trail symbol. These landmarks are just below a small, fenced tailings pile. Along the trail, little nooks at the base of tufa towers make good spots to sit and observe this wonderfully strange landscape.

As you drive to Trona Pinnacles from Ridgecrest, the highway drops into Poison Canyon when you approach Searles Valley. An ancient river that flowed into Searles Lake carved this canyon. At one of the sharp bends near the mouth of the canyon, rocks painted (in modern times) with fish heads come into view, about 2 miles before the turnoff to Trona Pinnacles; mud hills just across from the "Fish Rocks" contain fossils of freshwater snails and clams dating to 20,000 years ago. To see wave-cut terraces from ancient Searles Lake, look up at the hills on the left (west) side of the highway, beginning about 1 mile north of the turnoff to the Trona Pinnacles as you approach the Westend chemical plant and Trona.

Directions: From the south, it is 16.5 miles on Highway 178 from the intersection of China Lake Boulevard/Highway 178 and Ridgecrest Boulevard to the turnoff (on the right) onto unpaved Pinnacles Road. (Highway 178 ends at Pinnacles Road and becomes Trona-Wildrose Road.) From the north, drive about 6.8 miles south from the roadside rest in Trona on Trona-Wildrose Road and turn left onto Pinnacles Road. A historic landmark commemorating the John and Dennis Searles wagon route of 1873-1895 is located at the turnoff. You come to a fork about 0.5 mile after leaving the highway; stay to the right here. At 1.3 miles you cross the tracks of the Trona Railway and turn south. (Where Pinnacles Road crosses the tracks is near the site of Magnesium, which was the terminus for a 1927 monorail, described on page 72.) The total distance from the highway to the edge of the Natural Landmark is about 5 miles. Pinnacles Road is usually accessible to passenger vehicles but may be completely closed after rain due to mud. The Trona Pinnacles are managed by the BLM; for more information call (760) 384-5400.

Searles Lake and Trona

From a distance Searles Lake looks like any other Mojave Desert salt pan. But this playa is different: its deep lakebed sediments contain 98 of the approximately 112 elements. The chemicals came from the briny waters of ice-age Searles Lake. Dissolved minerals carried in with the waters, as well as minerals released from nearby geothermal areas, accumulated in the lake and the lake-bottom mud. Since the basin that held Searles Lake rarely overflowed, the chemical brew in the water steadily became more concentrated. About 10,000 years ago, as the climate warmed and grew more arid, Searles Lake gradually evaporated, exposing the lakebed's mineral riches. (See page 111 for more about Searles Lake.)

Due to its amazing mineral content, Searles Lake has been a mining center for more than 125 years. The site is named after John Searles, who discovered crystals on the lakebed in 1862 that he later determined to be

The tracks of the Trona Railway, built in 1914, follow the shore of Searles Lake, which has been a center of lakebed mining since the 1870s. FRANK BALTHIS

borax. Searles returned in 1872 to drive his first claim stake into the lakebed. The following year, he formed San Bernardino Borax Mining Company with his brother Dennis and other partners, and they were soon shipping out one million pounds of borax per year. The Searleses' mining process was simple; borax was scraped from lakebed crust and leached with hot water, allowing the mud to settle and clean borax to recrystalize as it cooled. The brothers noticed that worked-over areas were replenished with new borax in just three to four years as evaporating groundwater drew more borax crystals to the surface. John and Dennis Searles initially shipped their product to the port at San Pedro, some 250 miles away. They kept a stable of 250 mules, which would pull immense wagons that were the forerunner to the famous 20-mule-team wagons from Death Valley's Harmony Borax Works. After the Southern Pacific was extended to Mojave in 1876, the Searleses developed two wagon roads that allowed their teamsters to deliver borax to the railroad year-round.

Pacific Coast Borax Company bought out the Searleses' operation in 1897, but closed it down the following year because of financial problems. The property changed hands again in 1908 when the California Trona Company purchased the business. Its successor, the American Trona Corporation, founded the town of Trona and completed the 31-mile Trona Railway to Searles Station in 1914, which connected with the Southern Pacific Railroad. (The town, company, and railroad all took their name from trona, the dominant salt in the lakebed, which consists of sodium carbonate and bicarbonate.) In addition to borax, American Trona also produced potash. This turned out to be a lucrative venture because much of the nation's supply of potash then came from Germany; when the Allied blockade cut off this source during World War I, domestic potash prices skyrocketed and the town of Trona boomed.

Over the years, mining operations at Searles Lake and the Trona Railway have changed hands several times. In 1918 "Borax" Smith established a large chemical plant that became known as the Westend Facility. The massive Argus plant just south of Trona, built by Kerr-McGee Chemical Corporation, came on line in 1978. IMC Chemical currently owns the three plants at Trona, Argus, and Westend, which receive brine that is pumped to them from below the dry lake. They extract minerals before discharging the brine back into the lakebed. Soda ash, sodium sulfate, potash, and boron are some of the products derived from the processing. Soda ash is used in glass manufacturing, petroleum refining, water treat-

This caboose and the nearby History House and Old Guest House Museum pay tribute to Trona's mining heritage. JOHN EVARTS

ment, and pulp and paper production. Boron is used in detergents, glass production, home insulation, ceramics, solder flux, and leather tanning, while potash is used in fertilizers, paper manufacturing, sewage treatment, and industrial chemicals.

Trona is primarily a company town, and the silver smokestacks of the Trona Facility form a gleaming backdrop to the community. The distinctive red and silver Trona Railway engines can sometimes be seen at the plant; they haul cars south with Trona's mineral products and return with coal to fuel a cogeneration power plant. The thrum of the engines and hum of the plant permeate the center of town. The smell of bacteria in the ponds and sulfur released by the facilities sometimes greets the traveler long before Trona comes into view. Offensive at first, the

You can walk this section of the historic Nadeau Trail where it crosses the Slate Range. JOHN EVARTS

odor becomes less noticeable over time. As old-timer Dr. O. N. Cole wrote in his book *Trona,* "You've been in Trona too long when . . . you think the Westend Plant is beginning to smell like lilacs."

The Searles Valley Historical Society has acquired two historic properties in Trona. The Old Guest House Museum is located in one of the oldest buildings in Searles Valley. Built in 1917, the guest house consists of 12 rooms, with 8 rooms of displays on local history. The History House, constructed in 1920, is one of Trona's first residential structures. A 1958 Trona Railway caboose and small railroad museum are also on the grounds. A good bike path runs along the west shore of Searles Lake, connecting a chain of little communities and providing great views of the lakebed and valley. About 5.5 miles north of the center of Trona, on the east side of Trona-Wildrose Road, is Valley Wells Historic Monument. Look for the stone landmark near the turnoff to the company recreation complex. The monument commemorates the 1849 route of several parties of emigrants who struggled through Death Valley and passed by this site on their way to the Sierra Nevada goldfields.

To view the historic Nadeau Trail, continue 9 miles beyond Valley Wells Monument to a small pullout on the right side of the summit of the Slate Range Crossing. (Use extra caution when approaching this narrow, unmarked stop, which has space for about one vehicle.) Built by Chinese laborers in 1874 and used by freight hauler Remi Nadeau, this wagon road carried up to 300 tons of freight a month to and from the mines of the Panamint and Argus ranges. As you face Panamint Valley from the pullout, you can trace the Nadeau Trail as it climbs the Slate Range to the east of the present-day highway. In the distance there is a very straight stretch of the trail—a section known as the "Shotgun Road"—where it runs up the far west side of Panamint Valley; the road visible to its right (east) is the more recent Nadeau Road, which serviced a mine in Panamint Valley. The Nadeau Trail intersects the highway near the pullout, and you can walk down it to get a closer look at the impressive stone buttressing that was required to hold the road against these steep slopes.

Directions: *Trona is 32.5 miles from Highway 395, via Highway 178 and Trona-Wildrose Road. To reach the Old Guest House Museum in Trona, turn off the highway onto Center Street (opposite the roadside rest area and the Searles Lake Borax Discovery Site Historic Landmark). Go two blocks to Main Street, turn right, and the museum will be on the corner on the right. To visit the History House, return to Main Street and continue two blocks, then make a left on Panamint Street. The History House is on the right at 83001 Panamint Street. The Old Guest House Museum is open Monday through Saturday from 9 to noon, and the History House is open by appointment only. For information call (760) 372-5222 or (760) 372-4800.*

Ballarat and Warm Sulphur Springs

During the early years of the twentieth century, the Northern Mojave towns of Rhyolite and Ballarat anchored many drifting prospectors. Ballarat, established in 1897, was never as classy as upscale Rhyolite, but the tough little settlement at the western base of the Panamints survived longer than most mining camps of the era. Named after a famous Australian gold district, the town was a supply center for Panamint mines such as the "World Beater," "Radcliff," and "Oh Be Joyful." During its heyday, around 1900, Ballarat had about 400 residents and boasted a two-story hotel, school, Wells Fargo station, red-light district, stores, restaurants, livery stables, blacksmith shop, morgue, and jail. There were also a number of saloons and no churches—the usual recipe for a rowdy mining camp—but surprisingly, Ballarat had little in the way of excitement. Instead of gunfights, the big news one Fourth of July was a burro race undertaken by a handful of young ladies for a stake in a claim known as the "Hot Cake."

As activity at the local mines waned, so too did Ballarat. By 1907 the town was fading fast. A few diehards kept the post office open until 1917. All that remains today of this former prosperity are a few decaying adobe buildings. A small cemetery just northwest of the town center is the final resting spot for several well-known desert characters, including Seldom Seen Slim. His epitaph reflects a sentiment that could have applied to many of Ballarat's early prospectors: "Me, lonely? Hell, No! I'm half coyote, and half burro."

From Ballarat, Indian Ranch Road heads north along the base of alluvial fans that pour out of the Panamint Range's steep canyons. In about 2 miles, a side road (which can turn to 4-wheel drive only) climbs 4 miles east to Chris Wicht Camp, the trailhead for Surprise Canyon Wilderness and the 1870s silver-mining town of Panamint City. Continuing north on Indian Ranch Road, you pass lush mesquite thickets that grow among low sand hummocks along the edge of Panamint Valley's lower playa. After a few more miles the road swings east, bringing you closer to the steep, erosion-etched mountains. Water rises along fault lines to sustain Warm Sulphur Springs, a salt marsh rimmed with willow and mesquite. Permanent pools reflect the moods of the sky, while birds carry on quiet conversations in the thickets. A good area to access the wetland from the road begins about 5.5 miles north of Ballarat, although there is little space for parking. Migrant ducks and shorebirds visit this spot in fall. Just north of the marsh, the Panamints rear back from the road, revealing a

Top: The small cemetery on the outskirts of Ballarat is a reminder of the community that once existed here. JOHN EVARTS
Bottom: A few crumbling structures are practically all that remain from Ballarat's heyday as a mining supply center. JOHN EVARTS

near-vertical wall, its dark face spun through with bold white dikes.

About 1.5 miles north of Warm Sulphur Springs, Indian Ranch Road intersects a dirt road that leads a short distance east to Indian Ranch. This site was the home of George Hanson, a Western Shoshone who reportedly guided Panamint-area prospectors as early as the 1860s. Hanson, who lived to be well over 100, remembered how, as a boy, he spied on the Jayhawkers group of '49ers when they camped in Death Valley. His ranch served as a watering hole and traveler's oasis for 30 years, but is now closed to the public.

Directions: *Indian Ranch Road and Ballarat Road are well-maintained, graded dirt routes passable to any vehicle. To reach Ballarat Road from the south, drive 21.7 miles north from Trona on Trona-Wildrose Road. A stone monument and sign on the east side of the*

Low cliffs mark the fault scarp along the far side of this mile-wide graben (a depression bounded by faults) that cuts across the mouth of Wildrose Canyon. STEPHEN INGRAM

Mesquite thickets rim the shallow wetlands at Warm Sulphur Springs, located about 5 miles north of Ballarat. JOHN EVARTS

road mark the intersection where it swings north after descending the Slate Range (3.8 miles past the marked Nadeau Road). After turning onto Ballarat Road, drive east 3.6 miles to reach Ballarat. To continue the north- ward loop past Warm Sulphur Springs, turn left in the center of Ballarat onto Indian Ranch Road, which reconnects with Trona-Wildrose Road in just less than 12 miles.

To drive the loop from the north, turn off Highway 190 at Panamint Valley Road (2.5 miles east of Panamint Springs Resort) and drive 13.9 miles south to Indian Ranch Road, which begins just past the intersection of Trona- Wildrose Road and Panamint Valley Road. To visit only Ballarat it is more direct to drive 9.1 miles south on Trona- Wildrose Road to the Ballarat Road turnoff.

Wildrose Canyon and the Charcoal Kilns

Wildrose Canyon cuts a long, deep cleft in the western slope of the Panamints. The elevation gain from the mouth of the canyon to its head at a high, timbered ridge overlooking Death Valley is 7,000 feet. The nar- row, middle section of the drainage contains a spring-fed oasis filled with cottonwood, willow, and the canyon's namesake, wild rose. This inviting habitat has drawn people for thou- sands of years, including Shoshone villagers, lone prospectors, bandits, and countless desert travelers.

Wildrose Canyon is accessible from Death Valley via Emigrant Canyon Road or from Panamint Valley via Trona-Wildrose Road. This tour begins from Panamint Valley, but can be done in reverse. Heading northeast from its junction with Panamint Valley Road, Trona-Wildrose Road climbs straight up a deep alluvial fan toward the mouth of Wildrose Canyon. The Wildrose graben momentarily interrupts the ascent. The graben is a down-dropped trench, about one mile wide, that has formed between two faults; look for the short cliffs, or scarps, that delineate the faults on either side of the graben.

You reach the ruins of Wildrose Station 8 miles past Panamint Valley Road. The station was a stage stop on the run between Skidoo and Ballarat from 1906 to 1908. Wildrose was later developed into a wayside motel, restaurant, gift shop, and gas station that served travelers until 1971. About 1.5 miles farther up, Emigrant Canyon Road joins Trona-Wildrose Road at Poplar Spring (keep to the right fork here). Just up the hill on the left is Wildrose Campground, and beyond that on the right is Wildrose Ranger Station (rarely open). Beyond the ranger station the canyon widens; about halfway up this wide section look for a sign on the left that marks the path of the famous water pipeline to Skidoo. The pipe began at a spring in Jail Canyon below Telescope Peak and ran 21 miles north to this turn-of-the-century mining town. (For more on Skidoo, see pages 120-122.)

The Wildrose Charcoal Kilns are about 2 miles beyond the pipeline

These 25-foot-tall kilns converted pinyon and juniper wood—plentiful in the Panamints—into charcoal that fueled smelters in the nearby Argus Range where wood was scarce. DENNIS FLAHERTY

route, and the last 2 miles are unpaved. These 10 stone kilns, set amid a pinyon-juniper woodland, resemble a row of giant beehives. Modeled after similar kilns near Owens Lake, they were built in the spring of 1877 to provide charcoal for silver smelters at the Modoc Consolidated Mining Company in the Argus Range, located across Panamint Valley to the west. Kilns were the most efficient way to produce the

3,000 bushels of charcoal required daily by the Modoc's smelters. Each kiln was about 30 feet in diameter and 25 feet tall, capable of holding 42 cords of wood. The charcoal-making process took well over a week to complete, with each of the Wildrose kilns yielding about 2,000 bushels of charcoal per firing. The kilns still smell of wood smoke, even though it has been over a hundred years since they were last used.

The Panamint daisy is a rare plant found only on the west side of the Panamint Range below 4,000 feet in elevation. MARC SOLOMON

Close inspection of the kilns reveals how well they were constructed. A collage of colorful rocks forms the foot-thick walls. Rasp marks remain on stones lining the arching doorways. Inside, the blackened walls and floor absorb what little light enters through the low door and a small opening on the east wall. The kilns' parabolic shape was designed to concentrate the heat of the fire and speed the charcoal-making process. This unusual shape also magnifies sounds and creates strange reverberations. Vocal acoustics are amplified but do not resonate, while foot stomps in the center of a kiln sound like a booming earthen drum.

Directions: Coming from the south or west, begin your tour of Wildrose Canyon at the junction of Panamint Valley and Trona-Wildrose roads, located 31 miles north of Trona via Trona-Wildrose Road, or 14 miles south of Highway 190 via Panamint Valley Road. (From this direction part of the road in lower Wildrose Canyon is unpaved.) Coming from the north or east, exit Highway 190 at Emigrant Canyon Road (about 9 miles west of Stovepipe Wells Village) and drive 21.3 miles south to its junction with Trona-Wildrose Road near the Wildrose Station. Most of Wildrose Canyon Road is paved. The pavement ends near the upper reaches of the canyon, but it is a well-graded dirt road as far as the kilns. Motorhomes and cars with trailers that exceed 25 feet combined are prohibited on Emigrant Canyon and Wildrose Canyon roads.

Telescope Peak

"It is not the height of a mountain nor its difficulty which makes it desirable, but something in the mountain's own self. The Panamints are neither very high nor very difficult, but they are dramatic and alone." So wrote Edna Brush Perkins when preparing to climb Telescope Peak in 1921. Little has changed here since Perkins made her midwinter ascent, except that today's hikers follow a trail built by the Civilian Conservation Corps during the 1930s.

The snow-covered summit of Telescope Peak often beckons to those enduring the heat of the basins below. But climbing this mountain should not be a spur-of-the-moment outing. Hikers need ample time—a full day—and sufficient stamina to complete the 14-mile round-trip to its 11,049-foot summit. Telescope Peak Trail begins just south of Mahogany Flat Campground in a low woodland of mountain mahogany and pinyon. The trail begins its ascent right away and eventually gains 2,916 feet in the 7-mile route to the top. As you climb, the forest thins on the steep slopes, opening up expansive views to the east. During late spring and early summer, wildflowers may cover the ground; in fall their sculptured seed pods add rich colors and textures to the landscape. Plants associated with the Great Basin are abundant, including rabbitbrush, sagebrush, ephedra, and fern bush.

Rounding the first curve, the trail skirts one of the Panamints' many steep eastside canyons. The route then swings west, crosses a saddle, and heads south. As you climb the main ridge toward the peak, there are fine views of the range's westside canyons, Panamint Valley, and the distant Sierra Nevada. Along this airy middle section of the journey, the vast

Hikers on the Telescope Peak trail are rewarded with sweeping views like this, which takes in bristlecone pines, upper Panamint Valley, and the distant Sierra Nevada. STUART SCOFIELD

surrounding desert landscape seems to fall away below your feet.

The trail heads for a prominent peak on the southern skyline, but Telescope Peak lies behind this first impostor. Before the final grueling ascent, the trail crosses back to the east side of the ridge. It is hard to believe anything but bighorn sheep could continue climbing, but the path switchbacks steadily upward. The twisted, wind-sculptured trees along this last stretch are Great Basin bristlecone and limber pines. The Great Basin bristlecone, longest-lived tree in the world, grows only in high-elevation desert ranges, such as the Panamints and the Inyo-White chain to the northwest. Even these hardy trees fall away as one nears the summit. From atop the peak, surrounding Mojave ranges, valleys, and playas look like a three-dimensional topographic map. From this perspective it is easy to see how Telescope Peak lies at the geographic heart of the Northern Mojave.

After the amazing, hundred-mile views from the summit, the descent might seem anticlimactic. Fortunately, the simple beauty of the Panamints' woodlands welcomes you back to lower elevations. Mountain bluebirds surf afternoon thermals that rise up from the canyons. Quail chatter quietly from the thickets along the trail. Pine needles glisten and whoosh in the breeze. The birds and trees lend an air of intimacy to the surrounding immensity as the setting sun washes deep valleys with shades of pink, orange, and finally luminous blue.

Directions: *Telescope Peak trail is steep, but half of the elevation gain comes in the first two miles. Allow at least 6 to 8 hours to reach the top. Most hikers begin the ascent at dawn in order to have plenty of time to return by dark. This is especially important in the spring and fall when days are short. Wildflowers are usually at their best in June and July, but the early-autumn colors are equally beautiful. No water is available along the trail, so carry plenty.*

From the junction of Emigrant Canyon Road and Trona-Wildrose Road in Wildrose Canyon, drive 8.6 miles southeast on Mahogany Flat Road to reach the Telescope Peak trailhead parking area at Mahogany Flat Campground. The last 1.8 miles (after the Charcoal Kilns) are rough, narrow, and steep. Four-wheel drive is recommended, but high-clearance 2-wheel-drive vehicles can usually make the climb if driven with care and patience. This portion of the road is closed from early November until mid-May. Check with the Furnace Creek Visitor Center for road conditions and closures.

Top: Water was piped 21 miles to Skidoo from a spring high on the slopes of Telescope Peak to power a Pelton wheel that generated electricity for this stamp mill. MARC SOLOMON
Bottom: This head frame is one of the few remnants from the Skidoo mines, which produced $1.3 million in gold. MARC SOLOMON

Skidoo, Eureka Mine, and Aguereberry Point

The high Panamints experienced two mining booms; the first occurred in the mid-1870s and the second in the first decade of the twentieth century. You can tour the later era's key mining camps, Skidoo and Harrisburg, and visit one of the Northern Mojave's finest viewpoints on a leisurely auto trip into the range's high country.

In 1906, when Bob Montgomery's wife, Winnie, heard he was buying 23 mining claims in the wild Panamints, she quipped, "23 Skidoo!" The name stuck, and Bob—famous for his successful management of Rhyolite's Montgomery Shoshone Mine—was just what Skidoo needed. He immediately set to work on a 21-mile pipeline to bring water to Skidoo from Birch Spring near Telescope Peak. The pipeline supplied enough hydropower to run a Pelton wheel that, in turn, generated enough electricity to run a stamp mill. By 1907 the mine and mill were up and running. Over the next decade, Skidoo produced more than $1.3 million in gold, becoming the first and only Death Valley gold mine of the period to pay dividends to its shareholders.

Although hardly a board remains of the town of Skidoo, it once boasted a population of about 700, freight and stage runs to Randsburg and Rhyolite, and a telegraph line. At first glance, the gentle valley where the town thrived appears to be an unlikely place for gold, for there are few exposed rocks to harbor ore bodies. The famous "million dollar slope" lies hidden from view along the road leading up the hill to the southwest. Where this amazing quartz vein once ran, an impressive, gaping crevasse now exists, supported by rough sections of timber. The only building that remains near Skidoo is the mine mill, which clings to the side of a steep gully west of the townsite.

The glory of Skidoo overshadowed the nearby mining camp of Harrisburg. Shorty Harris, who helped find the gold bonanza at Rhyolite, and Pete Aguereberry, a young Basque miner, discovered this site in 1905 while on their way to Ballarat to celebrate the Fourth of July. Although Harris sold his interest early on, the camp retained his name. Nothing is left of Harrisburg since it was just a short-lived tent village, but you can see mines on the east and south sides of Providence Ridge, one of which belonged to Pete Aguereberry. He remained long after Harrisburg had faded, working his Eureka Mine off and on until his death in 1945. The white-washed cabins and shade trees of his camp still stand near the opening to his mine tunnel. Ore car tracks emerging from the mine entrance curve gently, then abruptly end, dangling over a small wash. The Park Service has stabilized the tunnel, making it one of the few in the region that are safe to enter. A gate closes the entrance during winter so that two species of bats can hibernate undisturbed.

While poking around Aguereberry's camp and Eureka Mine, you may get a sense of the unusual man who spent most of his life here. Aguereberry loved the beauty of the desert. Mining to him was more a way of life than a money-making profession. In his wanderings Aguereberry came upon a spot where the view was so spectacular he had to share it with others. Using a wheel barrow, shovel, and blasting powder, he built a rough road to his special place, now known as Aguereberry Point. Today, visitors can drive east from his cabin to a parking area on a high ridge overlooking Death Valley. A short trail leads from there to the rocky point where Aguereberry admired many sunsets.

The view from Aguereberry Point is grand, especially in late afternoon on days when the sun is breaking in and out of clouds. Bands of light play across the floor of Death Valley more than 6,000 feet below and highlight range after range of colorful mountains far into Nevada. To the west the Sierra Nevada crest scrapes the skyline. Immediately below Aguereberry Point lies Trail Canyon's astonishingly deep north fork, streaked by a huge band of creamy brown Paleozoic sediments. Above Trail Canyon to the

Clouds form on the Panamints' peaks near mile-high Aguereberry Point. FRED HIRSCHMANN

south begin the extensive pinyon groves of the Panamints. The steep slopes around the viewpoint are dotted with ephedra, its green, stick-like stems springing from the rocky soil. The quiet is often so intense here that the air seems to buzz. Aguereberry Point is a fine memorial to a man who loved this place with all his heart.

Directions: *Skidoo, Eureka Mine, and Aguereberry Point are accessible on dirt roads that intersect with Emigrant Canyon Road (closed to trailers and motorhomes over 25 feet long). From the north, Emigrant Canyon Road begins at Emigrant Junction on Highway 190, about 9 miles west of Stovepipe Wells Village, or 18.6 miles east of*

Panamint Springs. Drive 9.5 miles south to Skidoo Road (left) and continue 7.2 miles to the Skidoo site. To reach the Skidoo Mill, continue straight through the townsite and into a small canyon where the road forks. The right fork leads to a "road closed" sign (1.2 miles from Skidoo) where you can park and walk 0.25 mile to reach the bottom of the mill. You can also take the left fork and park near a tailings pile by a mine tunnel; the top of the mill is a short walk from here. (The left fork continues another 0.3 mile, but the turnaround at the end is very tight and on the edge of a steep drop-off.)

To continue south to Eureka Mine and Aguereberry Point, drive 2.4 miles past Skidoo Road on Emigrant Canyon Road and turn left on Aguereberry Point Road. This dirt road is occasionally graded and usually passable to most vehicles, although high-clearance vehicles are recommended for the last several miles of the route. About 1.5 miles after turning off Emigrant Canyon Road, a short spur road turns south (right) toward the base of Providence Ridge to reach Aguereberry's old camp and Eureka Mine. Return to Aguereberry Point Road and continue about 5 miles east to reach the parking area for Aguereberry Point. To access these sites from the south, take Trona-Wildrose Road 9.7 miles past Panamint Valley Road to its junction with Emigrant Canyon Road; continue 9.4 miles north on Emigrant Canyon Road to reach the Aguereberry Road turnoff.

Darwin Falls

The Northern Mojave has few perennial streams. Even more rare, however, are waterfalls, such as the gentle cascade that graces lower Darwin Wash. In this narrow, basaltic canyon at the north end of the Argus Range, a hard layer of bedrock forces groundwater to emerge near China Garden Spring. As it flows down the streambed, the water drops over a 20-foot rock face to fill a clear, shallow pool. An easy hike brings you to this enchanting place.

Near the trailhead, where the small stream may barely form a trickle, willow shoots try their luck along the banks of the watercourse. As you head farther up the canyon, the streamflow steadily increases; willows grow taller, watercress and cattails line the water's edge, and lush green grass even appears in season. The canyon walls gradually close in and

With its gentle cascades and lush greenery, Darwin Falls is an enchanting anomaly in a landscape largely defined by intense heat and aridity. DENNIS FLAHERTY

their rock faces, tinged with gray, green, and yellow-brown, support hanging rock gardens.

The trail threads its way through a tangled riparian woodland before reaching the cascade. Gooddings willows spread their gracefully arching branches, shading the canyon from wall to wall. The sound of falling water grows louder and you suddenly emerge from thick undergrowth, arriving at the base of Darwin Falls. The creek cascades over massive, polished boulders, forming two slender falls that plunge into a pool. Mosses and maidenhair ferns grow in spray-drenched pockets alongside the falls. This inviting setting beckons you to stay a while to breathe the cool, moist air and listen to the varied voices of water and songbirds in the trees. Near twilight the red-spotted toad may add its high-pitched trill to the chorus.

Directions: The trailhead for Darwin Falls is accessible via a well-marked dirt road that turns southwest off Highway 190 about 1 mile west of Panamint Springs. Follow this dirt road 2.4 miles up Darwin Wash, keeping right at the fork to reach the parking area. From here, a 1-mile-long trail with a 200-foot elevation gain leads to the falls.

Father Crowley Point

As it winds across the north end of the Argus Range, Highway 190 passes a stone monument built in the shape

The deep gorge of Rainbow Canyon cuts through dark volcanic tablelands. JOHN DITTLI

of a California mission. This memorial is dedicated to Father John C. Crowley, "Padre of the Desert." Father Crowley served as a missionary to the rugged region between the Sierra Nevada and Death Valley. He was killed in an automobile accident along Highway 395 in 1940. The Father's dedication to, and love of, the local people and beautiful landscape have long been remembered.

Rainbow Canyon is easily viewed from near the monument. Erosion has cut this deep drainage—which begins just uphill—exposing deep, colorful layers of lava and ancient Paleozoic rock. A dirt road continues about 0.5 mile east of the monument to a stunning overlook. Panamint Valley stretches to the east and Telescope Peak crowns the Panamint

Range to the southeast. Straight across the valley is the wildly striped face of Panamint Butte, a layer cake of ancient sediments uplifted by fault action. To the south rises the dark, largely volcanic Argus Range, home of several famous historic mines, including the Modoc Consolidated Mining Company of Comstock millionaire George Hearst. While enjoying the scenery, do not be surprised to see wild burros; activity at the overlook area seems to provide these curious creatures with good entertainment.

Directions: Father Crowley Point is located on the north side of Highway 190, about 8 miles west of Panamint Springs, or 5.6 miles east of the turnoff for Saline Valley Road.

Saline and Eureka Valleys Region

They have 18 crystallizing tanks, each of a capacity of 1000 gallons. Three tanks are emptied each day, and the yield might not quite reach that amount, as the borax does not crystallize so well as in cool weather. . . . Within a few hundred yards of the works is an Indian settlement. The borax marsh has an elevation of about 500 feet above the level of the sea. The Inyo mountains rise like a wall close to the works and attain an elevation of about 11,000 feet. . . . This is one of the grandest stretches of mountain scenery in the State.

—Anonymous
Mining and Scientific Press, 1889

In this latter locality the Indians all live at one place on the west side of the valley, at the base of the Inyo mountains and near the border of the salt-bed which covers the sink of the valley. A small stream of water flows out of Hunter's cañon, in the Inyo mountains, about a mile from the Indian village, and furnishes them with water for irrigation purposes.

They have about one hundred acres of land enclosed, and some of it planted in alfalfa. . . . They also grow melons, squashes, corn, beans, barley, and wheat. The alfalfa, barley, and wheat raised they sell readily to the Borax Company. . . .

—E. W. Nelson
American Anthropologist, 1891

In wet years runoff from surrounding areas flows onto the Saline Valley playa to create a shallow, temporary lake. CARR CLIFTON

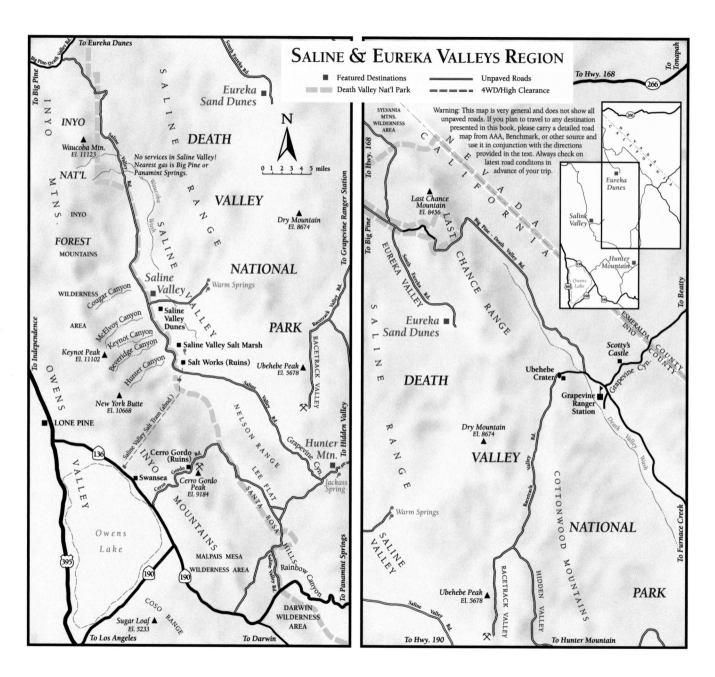

SALINE & EUREKA VALLEYS REGION

■ Featured Destinations	—— Unpaved Roads	
▨ Death Valley Nat'l Park	- - - - 4WD/High Clearance	

Warning: This map is very general and does not show all unpaved roads. If you plan to travel to any destination presented in this book, please carry a detailed road map from AAA, Benchmark, or other source and use it in conjunction with the directions provided in the text. Always check on latest road conditons in advance of your trip.

To Eureka Dunes

Big Pine-Death Valley Rd.

To Big Pine

South Eureka Rd.

Eureka Sand Dunes ■

INYO

Waucoba Mtn.
El. 11123 ▲

NAT'L

INYO

DEATH

SALINE RANGE

SALINE VALLEY

Waucoba Wash

VALLEY

N

No services in Saline Valley!
Nearest gas is Big Pine or
Panamint Springs.

0 1 2 3 4 5 miles

Dry Mountain
El. 8674 ▲

NATIONAL

To Grapevine Ranger Station

FOREST

MOUNTAINS

WILDERNESS

Cougar Canyon

Saline Valley

Warm Springs

AREA

McElvoy Canyon

Keynot Canyon

Beveridge Canyon

■ Saline Valley Dunes

PARK

Keynot Peak
El. 11102 ▲

Hunter Canyon

■ Saline Valley Salt Marsh

Ubehebe Peak
El. 5678 ▲

RACETRACK VALLEY

Racetrack Valley Rd.

■ Salt Works (Ruins)

Saline Valley Rd.

To Independence

New York Butte
El. 10668 ▲

Saline Valley Salt Tram (abnd.)

NELSON RANGE

Grapevine Cyn.

Hunter Mtn.

To Hidden Valley

OWENS

■ LONE PINE

136

■ Cerro Gordo (Ruins)

Cerro Gordo Rd.

LEE FLAT

Jackass Spring

■ Swansea

Cerro Gordo Peak
El. 9184

SANTA ROSA

VALLEY

Owens Lake

MOUNTAINS

Saline Valley Rd.

HILLS

395

MALPAIS MESA

Rainbow Canyon

190

WILDERNESS AREA

To Panamint Springs

190

COSO RANGE

DARWIN WILDERNESS AREA

Sugar Loaf
El. 5233 ▲

To Los Angeles

To Darwin

To Tonapah

266

To Hwy. 168

SYLVANIA MTNS. WILDERNESS AREA

To Hwy. 168

NEVADA

CALIFORNIA

266

Eureka Dunes

Saline Valley

Hunter Mountain

Owens Lake

395

190

198

To Big Pine

EUREKA VALLEY

South Eureka Rd.

Big Pine - Death Valley Rd.

LAST CHANCE RANGE

Last Chance Mountain
El. 8456 ▲

ESMERALDA INYO COUNTY

To Beatty

Eureka Sand Dunes ■

SALINE RANGE

DEATH

Scotty's Castle

Ubehebe Crater

Grapevine Cyn.

■ Grapevine Ranger Station

Dry Mountain
El. 8674 ▲

VALLEY

Racetrack Valley Rd.

Death Valley Wash

COTTONWOOD MOUNTAINS

NATIONAL

SALINE VALLEY

Warm Springs

RACETRACK VALLEY

HIDDEN VALLEY

Ubehebe Peak
El. 5678 ▲

Saline Valley Rd.

PARK

To Furnace Creek

To Hwy. 190

To Hunter Mountain

Hunter Mountain

Long before it became part of Death Valley National Park, Hunter Mountain was an important destination for humans because of its pinyon woodlands, freshwater springs, large game, and moderate summer temperatures. More of a plateau than a peak, Hunter Mountain is part of an upland divide that separates the Panamint and Saline valleys. Its surface is dotted with quartz monzonite, a rock similar to granite. Like many high-elevation areas of the Northern Mojave, Hunter Mountain's flora is dominated by Great Basin plants. As you ascend toward its 7,454-foot-high summit, Joshua tree woodlands give way to a mix of pinyon, ephedra, rabbitbrush, and wild rose. The Jackass Springs drainage on the plateau's west slope seems especially lush compared to the surrounding Mojave lowlands; willows line the watercourse, and in fall their bright yellow foliage cuts a brilliant path through the pines.

The pinyons of Hunter Mountain traditionally provided an important source of food for Native Americans. Western Shoshone families would camp on the mountain in late summer to gather their annual supply of pine "nuts." They also came to hunt, collect willow branches for basketry, and escape the heat of adjacent lowland basins.

The mountain is named after

William L. Hunter, who settled here in the early 1870s. His hand-hewn log cabin and some old corrals from the livestock operation can still be seen. Hunter later used his mountain ranch as a base camp for developing his copper interests in the Ubehebe Mining District 6 miles to the north. Although the ore was good, the site

The roads to Hunter Mountain and Saline Valley traverse upland areas that support extensive stands of Joshua trees, like this site on Lee Flat. FRED HIRSCHMANN

Sulfur buckwheat in bloom and Great Basin sagebrush surround an outcrop of quartz monzonite, a common rock in the Hunter Mountain area. STEPHEN INGRAM

the Northern Mojave—emerged almost unscathed from mining activity.

The road up Hunter Mountain begins near South Pass, which offers dramatic vistas into Panamint Valley to the south and down Grapevine Canyon to the north. Beyond the pass your route climbs into the moist drainage of Jackass Springs. About 3 miles from South Pass, the road crests above 7,000 feet among pinyons and junipers. From here you descend to a lovely desert landscape where Joshua trees grow in clusters, interspersed among outcrops of quartz monzonite.

Directions: *To reach Hunter Mountain, turn off (north) from Highway 190 at Saline Valley Road 13.7 miles west of Panamint Springs, or 17 miles east of the junction of Highways 190 and 136. Drive northeast on unpaved Saline Valley Road until it intersects with Hunter Mountain Road (unpaved) 15.5 miles from Highway 190. The first 7 miles of Hunter Mountain Road, which take you past Jackass Springs and to the summit, are usually accessible to high-clearance 2-wheel-drive vehicles, but the steep section of road that drops down the east side of the mountain requires 4-wheel drive; check ahead for current road conditions. Hunter Mountain Road continues east and finally reaches pavement again in about 40 miles at Ubehebe Crater. Hunter Mountain Road is usually closed from about November to May due to snow and ice.*

was too remote and copper prices too low to make the mine pay. Hunter tried to make a go of it until his death in 1902. The mine, later called the Ulida, finally had a heyday of sorts around 1906. Riding on excitement generated by speculators in the Greenwater copper boom on the east side of Death Valley, several promoters made money pushing stock in the Ubehebe Mining District revival. Little came of the excitement on the ground, however, and the Hunter Mountain region—unlike much of

Saline Valley

Desert naturalist John Van Dyke wondered in 1901, "Have immensity, space, magnitude a peculiar beauty of their own?" A glimpse into the depths of Saline Valley suggests the answer should be a resounding "yes." Cut off by rugged desert ranges, accessible by only one unpaved road, and harboring no tourist services or facilities, Saline Valley exemplifies the kind of isolation that was once common throughout the Northern Mojave. A modest number of visitors make the long, dusty drive required to reach this remote basin and experience its "peculiar beauty." Those who make the trip into Saline Valley soon discover that it offers more than solitude: old mines, salt marshes, sand dunes, and hot springs are all accessible in a tour through this lonely landscape.

Saline Valley is a flat-bottomed depression—more than 20 miles long—that lies at the eastern base of the Inyos. The range juts up 10,000 feet from the valley floor to form one of the most spectacular escarpments in the West. This magnificent mountain wall also displays textbook examples of folded sedimentary rock. The gentler, but still abrupt, slopes of the Last Chance, Saline, and Nelson ranges form the other boundaries of Saline Valley.

The only auto access to the valley is via unpaved Saline Valley Road, which begins in the south at Highway 190. After leaving the pavement, you head northeast, cross the low ridge of the Santa Rosa Hills, and in 7 miles arrive at Lee Flat, which supports one of the most extensive stands of Joshua trees in the Death Valley region. Keep to the right and continue to the head of Grapevine Canyon, 15.6 miles from the highway. Here, in a pinyon-juniper woodland, the road swings north and descends into aptly named Grapevine Canyon. Not only is the route twisty as a tendril, but native grapevines also use nearly everything in the canyon to support their luxuriant growth. Beneath the grapevine canopy, willows dominate a lush,

In Saline Valley the imposing eastern escarpment of the Inyo Mountains looms behind these ancient lakebed deposits, now covered with rocks from a volcanic eruption. JOHN DITTLI

riparian community. Water from a series of springs mingles to form a small stream flowing down much of the drainage. This relatively verdant corridor, however, soon opens into the vast, arid basin of the Saline Valley.

After leaving Grapevine Canyon, the road swings northwest and in another 15 miles you approach the Saline Valley playa (37 miles from Highway 190). Take some time at the playa to examine the wooden tramway towers that jut from the lakebed and march up the steep slopes to the west. These are remnants from an ambitious salt-mining operation that dates from the early twentieth century.

Prospectors were aware of the Saline Valley playa's unusually pure salt deposits as early as the 1870s, but the overwhelming challenge of transporting the product to distant railheads discouraged initial mining efforts. Proposals to build a railroad or a pipe to carry the salt in slurry were rejected. The Saline Valley Salt Company ultimately decided to transport the salt via aerial tram. Although mining tramlines were built throughout the Death Valley region, this one was the most remarkable. It crept 7,600 feet up the cliffs of Daisy Canyon, crossed the crest of the Inyos, then descended 5,100 feet to a railroad siding near Swansea on the shores of Owens Lake—a distance of

Glassy waters of Saline Valley's flooded playa reflect a mirror image of the Inyos, which rise over 11,000 feet to create a barrier that contributes to the area's famous isolation. RANDI HIRSCHMANN

13.5 miles. When completed, the Saline Valley Salt Tram was considered a wonder of engineering. Hydroelectric turbines in the Sierra Nevada, on the other side of Owens Valley, powered the entire operation. Although the aerial tram worked, the economics of the salt market only kept it operating from 1913 to about 1920 and again from 1928 to 1933.

The Saline Valley salt marsh, one of the largest wetlands in Death Valley National Park, comes into view a short distance north of the playa. Look for a dirt road that heads a short distance east to the marsh about 1.5 miles beyond the playa. Pools rimmed with mesquite and sedges reflect the nearby face of the Inyos. Naturalists have recorded at least

124 species of birds at the salt marsh. The Western Shoshone village of Ko-o once thrived here, and descendants of the villagers ran a successful farm and ranch a few miles to the north until the early 1950s.

About 1.6 miles past the salt marsh you pass the ruins of the Conn and Trudo Borax Works. Remnants of the operation's rock-lined tanks and evaporating ponds are visible on both sides of the road. One of the first Northern Mojave borax mines, this site produced commercial-grade borax from 1875 to 1907.

As you continue north the low-lying Saline Valley dunes cover hundreds of acres to the east of the road. Although not as tall as the Eureka or Death Valley dunes, these "sheet" dunes are a unique habitat that dune enthusiasts enjoy exploring.

The turnoff to Warm Springs, marked by a painted rock, is just north of the dunes (about 46 miles from Highway 190). Warm Springs Road, also referred to as Painted Rock Road, is accessible to high-clearance vehicles and leads 7 miles northeast to Lower Warm Springs, and a short distance farther to Palm Spring. Developed by bathers many years ago, both springs have soaking pools and informal, user-maintained campgrounds. The warm springs area has a long-standing tradition of being clothing-optional. (Skip this area if nudity offends you.) This policy and the current camping situation could change anytime, although at this writing the Park Service expects the status quo to continue.

Saline Valley Road continues 32.4 bumpy miles beyond the Warm Springs Road turnoff before reaching the pavement at its intersection with Big Pine-Death Valley Road. This last unpaved stretch takes a minimum of two hours, and occasional washouts can make high-clearance, 4-wheel-drive vehicles necessary. Once you arrive at Big Pine-Death Valley Road, continue west about 20 miles to Big Pine and the nearest services.

Caution: Due to the remote character of Saline Valley, it is important to be prepared for extremes of weather. Snow can sometimes block both the south and north passes into the valley, trapping visitors for several days; in summer the heat is brutally intense. Do not head out for Saline Valley without a full tank of gas, ample supplies of water, and an update on the latest road conditions. For safety, rangers recommend traveling with another vehicle.

Directions: *The southern end of Saline Valley Road intersects Highway 190 13.7 miles west of Panamint Springs, or 17 miles east of the junction of Highways 190 and 136. (The closest gas is at Panamint Springs.) The northern end of the road turns off Big Pine-Death Valley Road 15.3 miles east of Highway 168.*

(The nearest service station is at Big Pine.) The total length of the route is about 78 miles, and if you drive it all in one day, you may emerge with a new appreciation for pavement.

This wooden tower was part of a remarkable aerial tram that carried salt from the Saline Valley over the Inyo Mountains to a railroad siding in Owens Valley during the early 20th century. JOHN DITTLI

Eureka Dunes

Rising nearly 700 feet, the Eureka Dunes are among the tallest sand hills in the western hemisphere. The highest dunes loom before the striped face of the Last Chance Range, their smooth, sensuous lines contrasting dramatically with the sharp features of the mountains' escarpment. A hike to the uppermost sand ridges rewards you with a stunning vista of smaller transverse dunes that trail off to the south for several miles. Whether you climb to the summit or not, the Eureka Dunes are a seductive destination; it is easy to spend hours exploring on foot or simply basking on the sand, soaking in the view.

The dunes are especially dynamic on breezy days. The wind constantly resculpts their rippling surface, quickly erasing footsteps and other imprints left by visitors. Grains of sand and dried seedpods are swept along the ridges, herded forward by the rushing air. Sand pours over the dune crests, like steam from dry ice, hissing as it moves. Occasionally, on the steep upper ridges, these dunes even "sing" as cascading particles generate a deep vibrating sound.

The dunes' surface changes constantly and more grains accumulate each year, but this dune system does not move. Although Eureka Valley receives only modest amounts of precipitation, the dunes are relatively moist because of sand's ability to

The dunes in Eureka Valley rise nearly 700 feet and are among the tallest in the western hemisphere. Their beauty and solitude are rewards for those who make the long drive here. DENNIS FLAHERTY

capture and store rainwater. This moisture, coupled with the dunes' stability, creates conditions that support a surprisingly diverse flora. More than 50 plant species grow here, including the endemic Eureka Dunes evening primrose and Eureka Valley dune grass. The dune plant community is perhaps most vibrant in early May, when annual wildflowers tend to be at their peak.

As you explore the dunes, it may be hard to imagine that these sand hills once echoed with the roar of dune buggies and other off-highway vehicles. Conservationists waged a lengthy campaign to exclude motor vehicles from this fragile environment. The BLM closed the dunes to vehicle use in 1975, and in 1983 the Eureka Dunes were declared a National Natural Landmark. Today, the dunes and 200,000 acres of surrounding Eureka Valley are part of Death Valley National Park.

Conservationists succeeded in closing the Eureka Dunes to vehicles in 1975, and today the area attracts hikers, many of whom come to see the area's endemic plants. JIM STIMSON

Directions: *To reach Eureka Dunes from the north, drive 38.5 miles from the Owens Valley town of Big Pine via Highway 168 and Big Pine-Death Valley Road, turn off at South Eureka Road, and continue 11 miles to the dunes. Big Pine-Death Valley Road is paved in several sections and the rest is graded dirt, usually passable to any vehicle. South Eureka Road (also called Eureka Dunes Road) is generally well graded all the way to the picnic area; the short road south from the picnic area to an interpretive sign requires 4-wheel drive. The road leading east from the picnic area goes to several campsites and a fenced parking area near an interpretive sign. Roads beyond this point require 4-wheel drive. They make good walking paths, however, and provide great views of the dunes' south side.*

To reach the dunes from the south, drive to Grapevine Ranger Station on Scotty's Castle Road in northern Death Valley and continue 3.4 miles north to the start of the Big Pine-Death Valley Road. From here it is 32.6 miles on a bumpy, graded road (2-wheel drive) through upper Death Valley and over a pass in the Last Chance Range to the junction with South Eureka Road. Continue 11 miles farther to reach the dunes.

Northern Death Valley Region

I had ridden from Wells across country and had been on the lookout for a view of the place for two days. Finally I came in full sight of it. I was on the summit of the Grapevine Mountains, when I saw Death Valley yawning down beneath.

Now, no one has ever accused me of being superstitious, or believing in spirits, or other things of a like nature, but when I saw Death Valley for the first time a strange feeling came over me. I felt that I had found what I was looking for. I had heard a great deal about the place and had regarded the name with horror, but now when in plain view of it I felt good. . . . This place so avoided by everybody, whose very name made so many shudder, attracted me. To be plain, I felt that it was to be, some way, instrumental in bringing about a great fortune for me.

—Death Valley Scotty,
Death Valley Magazine, *February, 1908*

Low-angle light in early morning or late afternoon brings out the subtle colors, textures, and ripple patterns of the Death Valley Sand Dunes. CARR CLIFTON

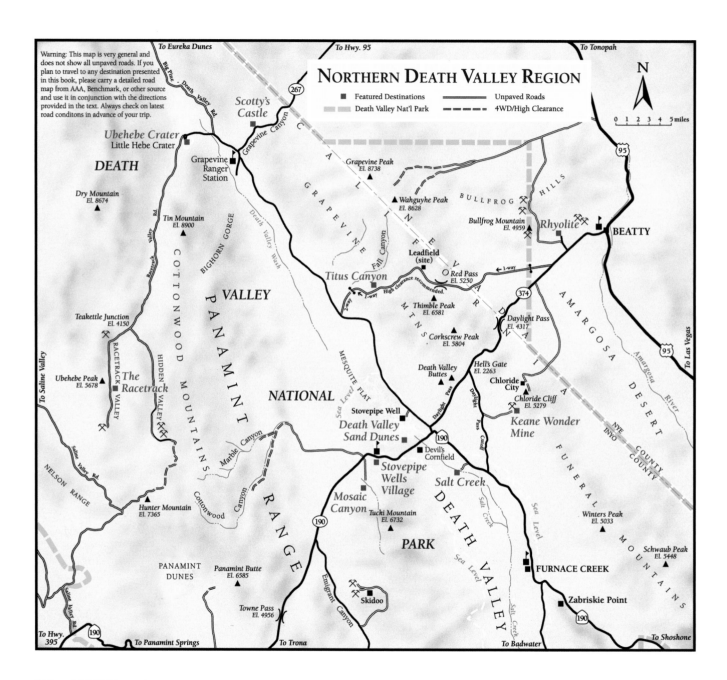

Warning: This map is very general and does not show all unpaved roads. If you plan to travel to any destination presented in this book, please carry a detailed road map from AAA, Benchmark, or other source and use it in conjunction with the directions provided in the text. Always check on latest road conditons in advance of your trip.

To Eureka Dunes   To Hwy. 95   To Tonopah

NORTHERN DEATH VALLEY REGION

■ Featured Destinations ———— Unpaved Roads
▬ ▬ Death Valley Nat'l Park - - - - 4WD/High Clearance

N

0 1 2 3 4 5 miles

Scotty's Castle

Big Pine Death Valley Rd.

267

Grapevine Canyon

CALIF

Grapevine Peak
El. 8738

Ubehebe Crater
Little Hebe Crater

DEATH

Grapevine Ranger Station

▲ Wahguyhe Peak
El. 8628

BULLFROG HILLS

95

Dry Mountain
El. 8674

Bullfrog Mountain
El. 4959

Rhyolite

BEATTY

Tin Mountain
El. 8900

GRAPEVINE

Death Valley Wash

COTTONWOOD MOUNTAINS

BIGHORN GORGE

Fall Canyon

Leadfield
(site)

ORNIA

Red Pass
El. 5250

1-way

374

Racetrack Valley Rd.

VALLEY

Titus Canyon

High clearance recommended.

2-way 1-way

Thimble Peak
El. 6581

NEVADA

AMARGOSA

Amargosa River

95
To Las Vegas

Teakettle Junction
El. 4150

Daylight Pass
El. 4317

Corkscrew Peak
El. 5804

MTNS

RACETRACK

Ubehebe Peak
El. 5678

The Racetrack

HIDDEN VALLEY

PANAMINT

NATIONAL

Mesquite Flat

Death Valley Buttes

Hell's Gate
El. 2263

Chloride City

DESERT

NYE COUNTY

INYO COUNTY

Saline Valley Rd.

NELSON RANGE

Sea Level Flat

Stovepipe Well

Daylight Pass

Chloride Cliff
El. 5279

Keane Wonder Mine

FUNERAL

Death Valley Sand Dunes

Devil's Cornfield

MOUNTAINS

Marble Canyon

RANGE

Cottonwood Canyon

Stovepipe Wells Village

Salt Creek

Salt Creek

Winters Peak
El. 5033

Hunter Mountain
El. 7365

Mosaic Canyon

Tucki Mountain
El. 6732

DEATH

Sea Level

Schwaub Peak
El. 5448

190

FURNACE CREEK

PANAMINT DUNES

Panamint Butte
El. 6585

PARK

Salt Creek

VALLEY

Skidoo

190

Zabriskie Point

190

Towne Pass
El. 4956

Emigrant Canyon

Sea Level

Saline Valley Rd.

To Hwy. 395

190

To Panamint Springs   To Trona   To Badwater   To Shoshone

Salt Creek

One of the last things you might expect to find on the floor of Death Valley is a flowing stream teeming with fish. Not only does Salt Creek defy expectations, it also preserves a living link between today's arid landscape and Death Valley's watery past.

Salt Creek begins as an underground stream beneath Death Valley Wash, rising principally from McLean Spring, located about 2 miles northwest of the Salt Creek parking area. As the subterranean water moves downstream, it encounters a layer of impermeable rock that forces it to the surface. The creek then flows above ground for 2 to 8 miles, depending on rainfall and groundwater levels. During especially wet years Salt Creek may extend all the way into Cottonball Basin, where it terminates in a shallow, briny lake.

The creek is indeed salty—about the same as ocean water. A variety of salt-tolerant plants and animals, including the tiny Salt Creek pupfish, live in and around the stream. The minnow-like ancestors of the pupfish made their home in huge Lake Manly, which covered this portion of Death Valley at the end of the last ice age. As the climate became drier, the lake gradually shrank and the dissolved salts in the water became more concentrated. This transition happened slowly enough for the pupfish to adapt to the higher salt content and

Salt grass and picklebush thrive along the banks of Salt Creek. RANDI HIRSCHMANN

higher water temperatures present in Salt Creek today. The pools along Salt Creek, and a few others located at springs elsewhere in Death Valley, represent the last living remnants of the Lake Manly habitat.

A half-mile interpretive trail on a boardwalk loops around the lower portion of the stream and provides a good introduction to its unusual ecosystem. You can also venture beyond the boardwalk on a narrow path that heads upstream. As you walk along the creek, you are surrounded by mud hills, wrinkled and creased by erosion. Their simple shapes and light colors contrast with the dark, rough mountains looming in nearly all directions. A dense carpet of picklebush (also called pickle-

weed) and salt grass grows in the creek bottom, providing cover for kangaroo rats, small birds, lizards, and insects. This tapestry of green and gold earth tones is offset by the bold colors of the sky reflected in the pools of the creek. Through this calm runs the soft song of the stream, its murmurings changing with the heat of the day and the progress of the season.

Directions: *To reach the turnoff to Salt Creek, drive 13 miles north on Highway 190 from the Furnace Creek Visitor Center, or 4 miles south from the intersection of Highway 190 and Scotty's Castle Road. Turn west at the signed turnoff for Salt Creek and continue 1.2 miles (on graded dirt) to the parking area and trailhead.*

Keane Wonder Mine

The Keane Wonder was one of the few mines in Death Valley that lived up to its optimistic name. The rich ore body here was discovered by Jack Keane in 1903, but it was not fully developed until 1907. For the next five years the mine shipped several thousand dollars of bullion a month, producing just over $1 million in gold before closing in 1916. Enough remains at the mill site and dramatic tramway—once known as the "sky railroad"—to give visitors an idea of how this successful mine functioned. You can drive to the mill and from there hike to the mine or to nearby springs.

A short trail leads from the parking area to the Keane Wonder's mill site, which is littered with rusted metal, warped boards, twisted cables, and busted pipes. These remnants look as if they had been strewn about by a whirlwind. Although the mill building is gone, an interpretive sign located at the site shows a photograph of the building during its years of operation. A short distance away are the better-preserved remnants of the tramway, its massive wooden posts and beams slowly weathering in the desert sun. The long-vanished settlement of Keane Wonder, where the miners' families lived, was located below the mill near the mouth of the canyon.

The trail to the mine is only a mile long, but in traveling its length you gain 1,500 feet in elevation. Initially, the trail heads up the ridge to the north, following the route of the old tramway. About a third of the way up, the tramway spans a steep-walled canyon. Cables sweep dramatically through space. With binoculars you can pick out several remaining buckets that hang near the tower directly across the canyon. From this vantage point it is easy to imagine how the buckets—each carrying nearly 600 lbs. of rock—slowly descended the mountain, creaking as they swayed on the cables. Although it was expensive to build, the tram was the only efficient way to move ore in such rugged terrain. Sometimes a daring miner would climb into a bucket to take the 20-minute ride down to the mill.

After passing beneath the tramway, the trail takes you up the ridge to the left and then cuts across the edge of the canyon to a saddle where the last tram tower comes into view. The mine site is located just beyond the last tower. Although not much remains of the Keane Wonder's buildings, extensive workings survive. Be extremely cautious when exploring the area since the mineshafts are cut into unstable metamorphic rock and are not safe to enter.

Water for the operation came from springs that emerge along the Keane Wonder fault zone, located about a mile north of the mill. You can access these springs by one of two routes, each of which entails a moderate 1.5-mile-long roundtrip hike. Follow the old road that starts by the rusted water tank near the mill or take a footpath that originates near the top of the parking area. Both trails parallel the original water pipeline and then converge and cross the pipeline near the springs. The main part of the spring is located uphill

The ore from Keane Wonder Mine was transported down to the mill in buckets attached to the cables on this tramway built into the steep face of the Funeral Mountains. MARC SOLOMON

from the road at the base of a small natural rock arch. The mineralized water fills a pool and then flows across the slope, its path marked by wide terraces of travertine. Despite the water's sulfurous nature, wildlife frequents this unlikely oasis. The spring is a fine place to enjoy an expansive view down into Death Valley accompanied by the sound of birds, crickets, and the trickling little stream.

Directions: *The turnoff to Keane Wonder Mine is located on the east side of Beatty Cutoff Road, 5.7 miles north of Highway 190, or 4.3 miles south of Daylight Pass Road. Although the 2.7-mile-long road to the mill is rough and rocky, it is usually passable to 2-wheel-drive vehicles.*

Death Valley Sand Dunes

Death Valley's famous dunes lie near the base of Tucki Mountain, a broad peak of the Panamint Range that juts northeast into the valley. The protruding mountain and the shape of the surrounding basin cause strong, sand-laden winds to slow down, eddy, and drop their loads. Sand has been accumulating here for about 10,000 years, gradually amassing into cream-colored dunes that now measure 100 feet high. The magnitude of this dune system, which covers 14 square miles, is especially evident from Scotty's Castle Road. In places, vegetated dunes

The popular Death Valley Sand Dunes are not the Northern Mojave's tallest, but they cover many square miles, including areas that see few visitors. CHUCK PLACE

extend across the Death Valley floor as far as you can see.

The dune's smooth, sandy slopes beckon you to stop and explore, especially during the dramatic light of early morning or late afternoon. To hike to the tallest sand peaks, you first cross vegetated dunes that teem with animal life. Since most dune residents are nocturnal, the best indication of their activities comes from the numerous tracks that crisscross the sand. The tracks are most visible in early morning before they are erased by the wind. Animal burrows, tunneled into the sand beneath mesquite trees, are another sign of dune

wildlife. Animals dig their burrows here because the mesquite roots help stabilize the shifting sand. The mesquite's flowers, leaves, pods, and beans provide sustenance to a variety of insects, birds, reptiles, and mammals. The tree's green pods (in spring) and ripe beans (in fall) were also dietary staples for the Timbisha Shoshone.

Mesquite can grow in deep, loose sand because it sends roots down 50 to 60 feet in search of groundwater. Once anchored into the soil beneath the dunes, the tree can survive despite the constant movement of sand at the surface. Sand collects at

Above: Small, clay-covered basins form at the bottom of some depressions and swales within the dune field. FRED HIRSCHMANN
Opposite: The southern edge of the dunes below Tucki Mountain are near Stovepipe Wells Village. JEFF GNASS

its base because the tree acts as a windbreak. Although sand gradually piles up, the top of the tree keeps growing. Some mesquites measure more than 100 feet from root tips to branch tops, yet only a few feet of vegetation may show above the sand.

Although surface water would seem unlikely in this environment, shallow Stovepipe Well at the eastern side of the dunes once provided a critical, if brackish, supply of drinking water for prospectors, teamsters, and others who crossed this part of Death Valley. The site got its name from a section of iron stovepipe that marked its location among the shifting sands. In 1907, when a 56-mile-long road was graded between Rhyolite and Skidoo, a small roadhouse—consisting of little more than several dugout buildings and some tents—was built near the well to serve the steady stream of people who traveled between the two mining towns. Although remote, this small rest stop claimed the distinction of having the first telephone service in Death Valley. The well and roadhouse have long since disappeared, but it is still possible to imagine a freight wagon struggling through the sand at the edge of the dunes, its driver urging his team on toward the little water hole.

Directions: *The most direct access to the tallest dunes is from broad turnouts along the north side of Highway 190 about 2 miles east of Stovepipe Wells Village. You can access historic Stovepipe Well and the low, vegetated east side of the dunes via a graded dirt road that intersects the west side of Scotty's Castle Road, 3 miles north of Highway 190. Once off the pavement, it's about 0.3 mile to the grave of Val Nolan, a prospector whose body was discovered here in 1931 by a film crew. Continue about 0.5 mile south on this road to reach the sign that marks the site of the original Stovepipe Well.*

Stovepipe Wells Village

Stovepipe Wells Village overlooks the Death Valley Sand Dunes from an alluvial fan at the base of Tucki Mountain. The resort was the brain-child of Bob Eichbaum, who had worked in Rhyolite around 1908 before he became a tour operator at Catalina Island. He foresaw the potential for tourism in Death Valley and eventually returned to the Northern Mojave with big plans.

Before he could build his resort, Eichbaum had to contend with what

was then a major obstacle to Death Valley tourism: a lack of decent access roads for automobiles. His original idea was to build a toll road from the south that would run up the east side of the valley and terminate at a luxury hotel near Hell's Gate in the Amargosa Range. Pacific Coast Borax, preferring their roads, objected to the idea of a new toll road. Eichbaum then successfully petitioned Inyo County for a permit to build a toll road from the west. It would begin in Darwin Wash near Panamint Springs, cross Towne Pass, and drop down to the historic Stovepipe Well on the eastern edge of the sand dunes. (For more on Stovepipe Well, see page 141.) Eichbaum's Death Valley Toll Road was completed on May 4, 1926. The charge to travel the scenic route was $2 per car plus 50¢ per occupant.

Ironically, the toll road never extended to Eichbaum's proposed hotel at Stovepipe Well. The trucks that carried in his building supplies had hard rubber tires and quickly bogged down in the dunes. Undaunted, Eichbaum simply built the resort on the western side of the dunes—about 4.5 miles short of his intended destination—and had water trucked in from Emigrant Spring. The cost of constructing the toll road had diminished his capital, and when the resort opened in November 1926, it was a modest affair consisting of 20 open-air bungalows.

Eichbaum's establishment, named Stovepipe Wells Village, became Death Valley's first full-service tourist facility. The complex eventually contained a store, gas station, swimming pool, tennis court, makeshift golf course, and a restaurant topped by a searchlight to guide travelers. Eichbaum offered Easter services and "skiing" contests on the nearby dunes. He took visitors on tours to the decaying walls of the original Stovepipe Road House, Mosaic Canyon, and Aguereberry Point.

A few things have changed since the early days at the village. The tennis court, golf course, and searchlight on the roof of the restaurant are things of the past. Modern motel rooms have replaced the bungalows, and the resort now has a saloon, gift shop, and a camping area with full hookups for recreational vehicles. A Park Service ranger station and campground are nearby. The Death Valley Toll Road was acquired by the state in 1934 and became part of Highway 190.

Directions: *Stovepipe Wells is located on Highway 190, 24.1 miles north of the Furnace Creek Visitor Center. From Highway 395 at Olancha, it is 75 miles on Highway 190 to Stovepipe Wells.*

Mosaic Canyon
Mosaic Canyon derives its name from the polished rock breccias that curve through its narrows. Breccia (pro-

nounced brecha) means "fragments" in Italian and refers to pieces of rock held together in a natural cement. Where smoothed by water, the breccias resemble mosaic art forms in their intricate beauty. The narrows in Mosaic Canyon present excellent examples of polished breccias and white marble exposed along a fault in the Noonday Dolomite Formation.

The walls in the canyon's narrows beg to be touched. Countless flash floods have carved them into soft curves and slick chutes. Look closely at one of the breccias: each rock embedded in the mosaic differs from its neighbor. Some have small white stripes winding through a dark matrix. Others are solid, creamy white, slate gray, or gold, while a few are conglomerates of even smaller rock fragments.

Natural beauty and fascinating geology, exemplified by these polished breccias, draw visitors to Mosaic Canyon. DENNIS FLAHERTY

A desert holly's silver-gray leaves contrast with a rust-colored wall in Mosaic Canyon, a gorge that has been repeatedly filled and scoured out by rock debris. JEFF GNASS

A half-mile of easy walking and boulder-hopping takes you through the canyon's first narrows and into an airy amphitheater. Colorful slopes of green and pink-orange sediments spill down on the left. A side canyon enters on the right, forming a low wall of breccia. A little trail runs along the top of this wall, allowing you to view both washes at once. Voices echo off the east side of the canyon, and even the quietest sounds reply.

The wash in the amphitheater is home to at least four different kinds of buckwheat, including pagoda buckwheat. This Northern Mojave endemic has tiny, intricate branches that crisscross tightly to form "stories," one on top of the other. When in bloom its tiny white or pink flowers hang down under each "story." The one- to two-foot-high plants are reminiscent of Japanese pagodas, and their graceful shapes against colorful boulders create beautiful miniature landscapes.

Beyond the amphitheater, Mosaic Canyon squeezes down into a second narrows. This section involves some easy boulder scrambling around a few rockfalls and dry waterfalls. The canyon then opens again for a short way before constricting into a third narrows. Up to this point, you have come just under 2 miles from the parking area. The going gets far rougher and more technical for the next 3 miles to the head of the canyon.

Each season brings a different highlight to Mosaic Canyon. Spring decorates the rocky cliffs and flat wash with wildflowers. In summer, the deep narrows provide a shady escape from the glare and heat of the valley floor. During autumn, it's cool enough to indulge in a lengthy exploration of the many side canyons along the route. In winter, the low sun angle can make the polished marble of the inner gorges shine like pewter.

Directions: To reach Mosaic Canyon, take the well-signed, graded dirt road just west of Stovepipe Wells Village. The 2.3-mile-long road climbs 1,000 feet up the alluvial fan of Tucki Mountain to the mouth of the canyon. It's an easy quarter-mile walk to the beginning of the first narrows.

Rhyolite

"Big freight teams, hundreds of horses, mules and burros, dogs, dust clouds, swarms of flies and no screen doors. Ah, those were the good old days!" Thus George Probasco described life in the blossoming mining town of Rhyolite in 1905. In just a few short years, optimistic residents turned the young community into the most modern metropolis in southern Nevada. No less than three railroad lines served the city of 5,000 to 10,000 inhabitants. Nearly every

Lightening bolts etch the sky above the crumbling shell of Rhyolite's Cook Bank building, a three-story edifice that was built of concrete and faced with local stone. PHIL KEMBER

house had running water and electricity. A telephone exchange and newspaper kept the populace in touch with the rest of the country. Oddly, all this happened before a single gold mine in the district proved to be a steady producer.

The excitement started in 1904 when prospectors Frank "Shorty" Harris and Ed Cross found gold in the Bullfrog Hills northeast of the Amargosa Range near modern-day Beatty. They located the precious metal embedded in knobby green rock and named their claim the Bullfrog. When word of their discovery got out, the last great American gold rush was underway. Claims were staked throughout the new Bullfrog Mining District. The town of Rhyolite, named after the surrounding hills' rose-colored volcanic rock, sprang up about a mile southwest of the district's most promising mine, the Montgomery Shoshone.

Thousands of people arrived with dreams of riches. Their enthusiasm convinced urban investors to front the funds to open the mines and build the town. Rhyolite was no canvas-tent-and-miner's-shack affair. Although most of this remarkable settlement has crumbled away, a walk down the main thoroughfare, Golden Street, clearly shows the place was meant to last. The ruins of the Cook Bank building still stand three stories above the sidewalk. It once featured a front with plate-glass windows, wrought iron trim, and a facing of local stone. A fragment of its original decorative brick trim remains near the top. The large concrete walls of the schoolhouse still endure, as well as the cut-stone facade of the Porter brothers' store. Up the hill stands the Mission-style Las Vegas & Tonopah railroad station, with its deep, inviting porches and decorative tile work.

Although millions were spent on fancy buildings in Rhyolite, the most famous remaining structure was made of empty bottles fetched from the back doors of saloons. Tom Kelly completed the Bottle House in February 1906. Using adobe made from local clay, he embedded some 50,000 bottles into the walls of his house. Time and wind have imparted a beautiful sheen to the bottles, whose colors range from brown and frosted green to purple and ice blue. The glass glitters when the afternoon sun hits the west-facing walls, far outshining what is left of the posh stone buildings up the street.

Many mining towns founded in the early twentieth century persist, but with Rhyolite's dreams built on shallow ore, it could not survive.

Investment money dried up when the 1906 earthquake leveled San Francisco, removing the city as a source of capital. Then followed the financial panic of 1907 that gripped the nation. Although the Montgomery Shoshone proved to be a productive mine, everyone had expected it to be a "world beater." The mine closed in 1911 after yielding more than $1.4 million in bullion. In the census of 1910, a little over 600 people still lived in Rhyolite, but by 1922 only one person remained. A local story tells of a mummified cow found at the railroad station; the unfortunate animal had missed the last train out.

Directions: Rhyolite is located at the end of a 1.5-mile paved road that turns north off Highway 374. From the Furnace Creek Visitor Center, drive 36.3 miles via Highway 190 and the Daylight Pass Cutoff Road, which becomes Highway 374 in Nevada, to reach the turnoff to Rhyolite. From Beatty, the turnoff is 4 miles west of town. There are BLM Volunteer Hosts present at Rhyolite to answer questions and furnish interpretive tours of the Kelly Bottle House.

These substantial building ruins convey the ambitions and confidence of Rhyolite residents during the town's heyday, which lasted less than a decade. MICHAEL SEWELL

Titus and Fall Canyons

In June 1905 a small man with a dark goatee scrawled the following message in a remote drainage: "Hurry On! I'm going down to investigate the spring. —Titus." The young tenderfoot, bent on prospecting in the Panamints to the west, was never heard from again. His name endures, however, at Titus Canyon, one of the most scenic destinations in northern Death Valley. Today, the route of the ill-fated Titus is roughly traced by a one-way road that crosses over the colorful Grapevine Range, winds

The deep narrows of Fall Canyon are accessible to hikers on a trail that begins at adjacent Titus Canyon. JIM STIMSON

through a deep set of narrows, and emerges into the valley beyond. Along the way, visitors can see spectacular geologic features, an old mining camp, petroglyphs, and a spring.

Titus Canyon Road begins off Daylight Pass Road near Rhyolite. It gradually climbs west into the Grapevine Mountains, crossing White Pass in a little under 10 miles. The route descends into the upper drainage of Titanothere Canyon, named for the fossilized remains of a large, rhinoceros-like mammal found here in 1934. Titanotheres roamed the region 35 to 40 million years ago when the climate was much moister. The road then climbs out of Titanothere Canyon, cresting at mile-high Red Pass where a dramatic view of upper Titus Canyon unfolds. The pass straddles a fault zone that marks a dramatic geologic juxtaposition: to the east are 15- to 20-million-year-old volcanic rocks while to the west are 500-million-year-old limestone formations.

From the summit tight, steep switchbacks wind down to what remains of the short-lived mining camp of Leadfield. Titus Canyon Road was built in 1926 to bring supplies from Beatty to promoter C. C. Julian's Western Lead Mine and the Leadfield camp. The ore at Leadfield looked good on the surface, but it petered out at depth. Julian strived to make sure his investors never knew the facts. To allay his skeptics, he

announced a free chartered train excursion from Los Angeles on March 15, 1926. "COME UP or SHUT UP," he challenged. About 340 curious people made the train and auto journey to Leadfield, where another 800 motorists from Tonopah and Goldfield joined them. Imagine over 1200 people and hundreds of cars clustered in this rugged, isolated drainage. Julian's guests devoured a free barbecue lunch, listened to a six-piece jazz band and heady speeches from Julian's mining experts, and then toured the mine. The event was a huge success and Western Lead Mine's stock jumped to a new record. Two days later, however, the state announced an investigation into Western Lead. State commissioners went on to discredit Julian and his mining experts. Stock prices plummeted and Leadfield died a quick death. The town lasted barely a year.

Beyond Leadfield the route continues 2.5 miles down canyon to Klare Spring. The water here is essential for wildlife, especially bighorn sheep. The presence of petroglyphs on rocks just upstream from the spring suggests that this was an important water source or sheep-hunting area for Native Americans. (As with all petroglyphs, please do not touch, climb on, or deface them. They are irreplaceable.)

From Klare Spring the road meanders nearly 4 miles down the wash before plunging into deeply carved narrows. The canyon walls rise as high as 500 feet and are less than 15 feet apart in places. Large breccias in the Bonanza King Formation form stunning mosaics. The dark, fractured rocks, some several feet across, are cemented together with white calcite and have been polished smooth by floods. All too soon the shadowy gorge ends and you emerge into the brilliant light of Death Valley. A broad alluvial fan spreads out from the mouth of Titus Canyon, extending more than 3 miles toward the valley floor. It's a two-way road down the fan; this allows people to drive from the valley floor to the mouth of Titus Canyon, where they can park and then walk into the narrows.

If you would like to add a moderate hike to your Titus Canyon tour or want to explore one of Death Valley's most spectacular gorges, then Fall Canyon is a good choice. The unmarked trailhead for Fall Canyon is located behind the restrooms at the mouth of Titus Canyon (where the two-way and one-way road sections meet). The trail begins by heading north along the base of the Grapevine Mountains for 0.5 mile before entering the wash near the mouth of Fall Canyon. Your route then swings northeast into the canyon, which is soon enclosed by sheer, colorful walls that soar straight up hundreds of feet. At about 2.5 miles from the canyon

Titus Canyon Road offers a spectacular passage across the Grapevine Mountains. JOHN DITTLI

mouth you reach the base of a dry fall. With caution you can climb around the fall on a bypass route that begins on the south side of the canyon, about 300 feet below the fall. After scrambling up the bypass, you enter the tightest narrows in this scenic canyon. The hike to the narrows is 3.5 miles (one-way) with an elevation gain of about 1,400 feet. Many hikers, however, are satisfied with the shorter trip into the canyon's impressive section below the fall.

Directions: *Nearly 27 miles long, Titus Canyon Road is one-way (east to west) for most of its length. It begins on the north side of Highway 374 (Daylight Pass Road) 6.1 miles west of Beatty, or 13.2 miles east of the junction of Daylight Pass Road and Daylight Pass Cutoff Road at Hell's Gate. Although Titus Canyon Road has some tight, steep curves, rocky washboard surfaces, and sandy washes, it is usually passable to most high-clearance, 2-wheel-drive vehicles. Occasionally after washouts, high-clearance, 4-wheel drive will be necessary. Always check on road conditions before starting your trip. The lower, two-way stretch turns off from Scotty's Castle Road about 14 miles north of the junction with Highway 190, or 18.3 miles south of the Grapevine Ranger Station.*

Scotty's Castle

One of Death Valley's most remarkable sights has little to do with natural scenery. It is Scotty's Castle, a palatial residence built during the 1920s when the Northern Mojave was better known for its rough-hewn miner's shacks. This ornate mansion is decorated with turrets, tile roofs, and porticos; a Moorish-style clock tower, topped with intricate orange, blue, and yellow mosaics, presides over the western side of the property. The buildings are surrounded by opulent grounds that include a running stream, tall palms and cottonwoods, grassy lawns, and a huge, unfinished swimming pool. Had this estate been built in Los Angeles, it would hardly have raised an eyebrow. But set against the barren slopes of Grapevine Canyon, the castle—like its flamboyant occupant—became a legend of the desert.

Many books tell the story of Death Valley Scotty (a.k.a. Walter Scott) and his lavish dwelling. Scotty was a complex character who led the colorful life of a prospector. Although he was unlucky when it came to finding gold, he had few problems wrangling it from other people's pockets. His tall tales convinced many wealthy men to invest in what turned out to be a fictitious gold mine in Death Valley.

Everything changed when Scotty met Albert Johnson. The allure of the Wild West captivated the Chicago

Scotty's Castle was built as a vacation retreat by a wealthy Chicago couple and takes its name from their flamboyant friend and long-time occupant of the estate, Death Valley Scotty. JEFF GNASS

millionaire, who proved an easy target for Scotty's tales of adventure and gold. Not only did Johnson invest in the mine, but much to Scotty's chagrin, he came out to see it for himself. The cagey prospector had not counted on an investor that craved adventure more than gold. Johnson eventually realized the mine was a hoax, but he so thoroughly enjoyed his gold-seeking travels with Scotty that he decided to build a vacation retreat in Death Valley. (Scotty's photo is on page 77.)

With Scotty's help, Johnson and his wife, Bessie, purchased property in Grapevine Canyon and began creating the Death Valley Ranch in 1922. Although the so-called castle was built entirely with the Johnson's money, they encouraged Scotty's tall tale about building it with treasure from his gold mine. That way, Scotty received all the public attention, which he craved, and the Johnsons enjoyed privacy at their retreat. Johnson often said of Scotty, "He repays me with laughs."

The National Park Service now owns the castle and its grounds, where you will find a museum, gift shop, snack bar, gas station, and restrooms. Living history tours of the castle are offered daily by Park Service interpreters dressed in period costumes from the 1920s. (Admission is charged for tours.) Beautiful original furnishings still decorate the rooms: Native American baskets, leather couches, Tiffany lamps, Scotty's hats and ties, and even a pipe organ that plays melodies from the day. The living room boasts a waterfall at one end (for summer cooling) and a two-story fireplace at the other (for winter heating). The tour also visits the guest quarters, which housed such notables as John Barrymore, Norman Rockwell, Betty Davis, Will Rogers, and Betty Grable.

Visitors are welcome to roam the grounds of Scotty's Castle and enjoy its stream and picnic area. Look for petroglyphs on the rocks where the stream runs down from the stable, and notice the fanciful handmade hinges on the stable gate. Then imagine talking your way into a set-up like this, one tall tale at a time.

Directions: *To reach Scotty's Castle from the Furnace Creek Visitor Center, drive 17 miles north on Highway 190 to the well-marked turnoff for Scotty's Castle Road. Continue 33.4 miles up the valley on Scotty's Castle Road and bear right at Grapevine Canyon Road, a half-mile past the Grapevine Canyon entrance station. The castle is 2.9 miles up Grapevine Canyon Road. If you are coming from the west on Highway 190, the turnoff for Scotty's Castle Road is 7.4 miles east of Stovepipe Wells Village. If you are coming from the north on Highway 95, turn at Scotty's Junction onto Highway 267 (Bonnie Claire Road) and drive 25.8 miles west to Scotty's Castle.*

Top: Joshua trees frame an entry gate of the castle's Moorish-style complex. JIM STIMSON
Bottom: The mansion's interior can be viewed on Park Service-led tours. FRED HIRSCHMANN

Nearly 700 feet deep, Ubehebe Crater (upper side of photo) is the largest of several adjoining craters, known as explosion pits, that were formed about 2,000 years ago. STEPHEN INGRAM

Ubehebe Crater

Death Valley is justifiably famous for its dunes, badlands, and desert playas, but the park also contains some fine examples of volcanism. Among the best and most accessible volcanic sites is Ubehebe Crater, located less than 10 miles from Scotty's Castle.

Geologists classify Ubehebe Crater and its small neighboring craters as explosion pits. They were formed more than 2,000 years ago when molten rock, or magma, flowed toward the earth's surface and encountered shallow groundwater. The magma instantly superheated the water to steam, which then blasted up through the earth's surface. Ubehebe's eruption spewed ash and cinders over 6 square miles and left a hole nearly 700 feet deep and a half-mile across. It ripped through an overlaying cap of fanglomerates (ancient alluvial fan deposits) visible as white, orange, and beige horizontal bands on Ubehebe's east wall. A gray layer on the top is material from the blast. Sediments from eroding volcanic rock have washed down from the rim, leaving vertical streaks across the crater walls. Ubehebe's bowl shape and colorful patterns may have been the reason for its Timbisha name, Tempin-Ha-Wo'sah, which some have translated as meaning "basket in the rock."

Several trails allow you to explore Ubehebe and its neighboring craters. One trail leads from the parking area and descends into the bottom of Ubehebe. Be prepared for the steep climb back to the rim. Another trail starts to the right side of the parking area and offers a moderate, 1-mile round-trip hike to Little Hebe Crater. Along this route you first pass a small, unnamed crater on your right; a path loops around it and provides a good view of the plants growing on its black inner slopes. Buckwheat, desert holly, creosote, and other shrubs dot the dark soil with a subtle palette of colors. Erosion-cut gullies on the crater's outer west side reveal alternating light and dark layers of ash deposits.

Just beyond this first unnamed crater, the main trail forks. Go straight at this junction to continue

Above: The dark, volcanic soils near Ubehebe Crater can support early-season displays of wildflowers, including this species, Bigelow monkeyflower. FRED HIRSCHMANN
Left: Sediments from Ubehebe's erosion-carved walls accumulate on the crater's floor, accessible via a steep trail. JIM STIMSON

on to Little Hebe (the other fork swings back east to Ubehebe's rim). From here, it is a short distance to Little Hebe's distinctive, well-formed cone. As you explore the area, notice how the dark volcanic soil absorbs heat. This extra warmth encourages flowers to bloom earlier than else-where; you may spot wildflowers along the trails even in the middle of winter.

Directions: *From Highway 190, drive 32.8 miles north on Scotty's Castle Road to Grapevine Ranger Station. Continue 6 miles north on the well-marked paved road to reach the parking area for Ubehebe Crater.*

The entire Racetrack playa and its rock outcrop known as the Grandstand are visible here from Ubehebe Peak. JOHN DITTLI

The Racetrack

California desert lore abounds with tales of lost mines and hidden treasures. Geologic mysteries, however, are far more rare. The "moving rocks" of the Racetrack playa are the Northern Mojave's most famous geologic puzzle, and their presence attracts the interest of tourists as well as researchers. A remote basin between the Cottonwood and Last Chance ranges contains the lakebed known as the Racetrack. What makes this playa so unusual is the presence of tire-sized tracks etched into its surface by skidding boulders that can weigh up to several hundred pounds. This curiosity alone makes Racetrack Valley worth a visit, although the scenery here can hold its own without the help of geologic enigmas.

An outcrop of granitic boulders, known as the Grandstand, erupts from the middle of the Racetrack playa. This island of rock is actually the tip of the valley's bedrock, most of which is buried beneath 1,000 feet of alluvium. The surrounding clay pan stretches off in all directions, cracked into a neat parquet of two- to three-inch-wide polygons. Fern-like impressions left by winter ice crystals decorate the mud. As you look across the playa, the usually bone-dry surface has an enticing sheen.

Part of the allure of the Racetrack is its isolation. A rough dirt road that begins near Ubehebe Crater provides the primary access. The route first climbs up through acres of cactus gardens, and after 20 bone-rattling miles it reaches Teakettle Junction. This desert crossroads is marked by a signpost decorated with just about every kind of teapot, from well-worn silver plate to dented enamel. Head right at Teakettle Junction and continue another 5.7 miles on Racetrack Valley Road to the parking area for the Grandstand. A half-mile hike takes you to the Grandstand's rocky pinnacles of quart monzonite.

The west side of the Grandstand parking area is also the trailhead for climbing 5,678-foot-high Ubehebe Peak. This 2.8-mile-long (one-way) hike follows an old miners' route up the ridge. The trail begins with a moderate ascent up an alluvial fan, and then it climbs steeply up a series of switchbacks. Breathtaking views of Racetrack Valley and Saline Valley unfold when the trail gains the ridge. Another mile of climbing and some rock-scrambling is required to reach the summit of Ubehebe Peak.

The moving rocks, of course, are the center of interest at the Racetrack. To reach the most active "skid" area, drive 2 miles (south) beyond the Grandstand. Park near the interpretive sign and walk toward the dark cliffs, which are the source of the traveling dolomitic rocks. The tracks are easiest to see when backlit by the sun. They are reminiscent of skating tracks on a frozen lake. Some parallel depressions give the appearance of rocks having raced each other across the slippery surface; hence the playa's name. Most of the rocks have traveled northeast, and some have been transported as far as 660 feet. Pick a strong track and follow alongside it. (Although there are many tracks, try not to walk on them. Footprints gradually wear them away.) Some rocks have scribed graceful arcs; others have zigzagged their way across the playa. Some have looped back on themselves in nearly complete circles, recrossing their own tracks several times.

How do the rocks move? Most researchers favor the theory that strong winds push some of the rocks

across a moisture-slickened lakebed. Another theory suggests that the rocks travel across the lakebed after heavy winter rains inundate the playa to a depth of about one foot; low temperatures then freeze the upper six or eight inches of the water, forming an ice sheet that surrounds any rocks laying on the playa. Strong winds then break the ice sheet into pieces that float free on the water's surface, carrying the rocks with them at the whim of the wind. The undersides of the rocks drag on the bottom of the temporary lake, leaving tracks in the mud that remain after the water evaporates. Although scientists have studied the movements of the rocks, the Racetrack phenomenon still remains somewhat mysterious: no one has ever caught the racers in the act.

Directions: *The unpaved 27-mile-long road to the Racetrack begins at the end of the paved loop by Ubehebe Crater. Although 4-wheel drive is recommended, the route is usually passable for high-clearance, 2-wheel-drive vehicles. Patience, however, is always required, as the road is rough.*

Some scientists theorize that rocks move across the Racetrack, leaving tracks like this, when the right combination of shallow flooding, ice, and high winds are present. DENNIS FLAHERTY

Southern Death Valley Region

S o they hitched up and rolled down the cañon, and out into the valley and then turned due south. We had not gone long on this course before we saw that we must cross the valley and get over to the other side. To do this we must cross through some water, and for fear the ground might be miry, I went to a sand hill near by and got a mesquite stick about three feet long with which to sound out our way. I rolled up my pants, pulled off my moccasins and waded in, having the teams stand still till I could find out whether it was safe for them to fol-low or not by ascertaining the depth of the water and the character of the bottom.

The water was very clear and the bottom seemed uneven, there being some deep holes. Striking my stick on the bottom it seemed solid as a rock, and breaking off a small projecting point I found it to be solid rock salt. As the teams rolled along they scarcely roiled the water. It looked to me as if the whole valley, which might be a hundred miles long, might have been a solid bed of rock salt. Before we reached this water there were many solid blocks of salt lying around covered with a little dirt on the top.

—William Manly Lewis,
Death Valley in '49, 1894

The salt polygons, or saucers, on Death Valley's playa are sometimes flooded and partially dissolved during years of above-average rainfall. JIM STIMSON

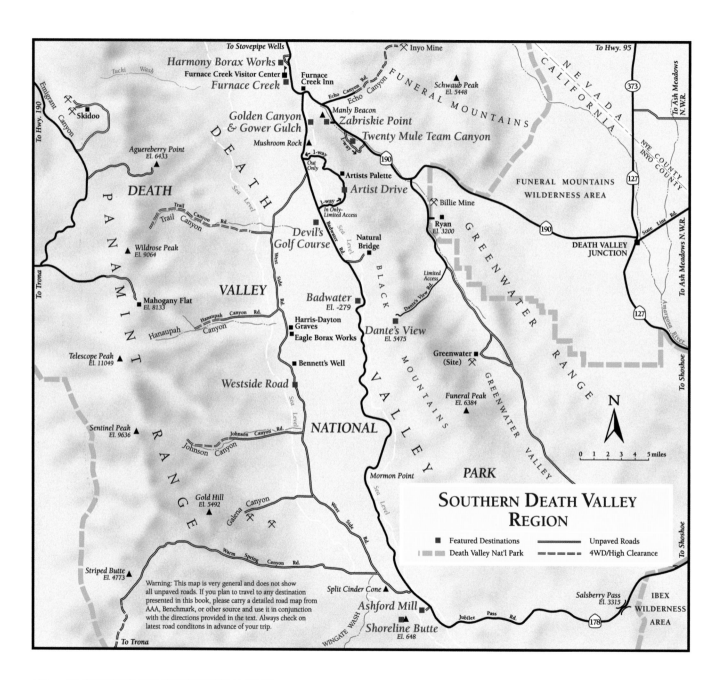

To Stovepipe Wells

Harmony Borax Works ■

Furnace Creek Visitor Center ■

Furnace Creek

Furnace Creek Inn

Echo Canyon Rd.

Echo Canyon

✕ Inyo Mine

To Hwy. 95

FUNERAL MOUNTAINS

Schwaub Peak
El. 5448 ▲

NEVADA

CALIFORNIA

To Ash Meadows N.W.R.

(373)

Tucki Wash

✕ Skidoo

Emigrant Canyon

To Hwy. 190

Aguereberry Point
El. 6433

DEATH

DEATH

Golden Canyon & Gower Gulch

Mushroom Rock ▲

Manly Beacon ▲

Zabriskie Point

Twenty Mule Team Canyon

190

1-way
Out Only

■ **Artists Palette**

■ **Artist Drive**

1-way
In Only–
Limited Access

FUNERAL MOUNTAINS
WILDERNESS AREA

NYE COUNTY
INYO COUNTY

127

190

DEATH VALLEY
JUNCTION ■

To Ash Meadows N.W.R.

State Line Rd.

Trail
Canyon

Trail Canyon Rd.

Sea Level

DEATH

Wildrose Peak ▲
El. 9064

VALLEY

Devil's Golf Course

■ **Natural Bridge**

Badwater Rd.

West Side Rd.

Sea Level

✕ Billie Mine

Ryan ✕
El. 3200

GREENWATER

Limited Access

Dante's View Rd.

BLACK

Mahogany Flat
El. 8133

Hanaupah Canyon Rd.

Hanaupah Canyon

Badwater
El. -279

■ **Harris-Dayton Graves**

■ **Eagle Borax Works**

Dante's View
El. 5475 ■

Telescope Peak ▲
El. 11049

PANAMINT

■ Bennett's Well

Westside Road

VALLEY

RANGE

GREENWATER

Greenwater
(Site) ✕

RANGE

Sentinel Peak ▲
El. 9636

Johnson Canyon Rd.

Johnson Canyon

NATIONAL

MOUNTAINS

Funeral Peak
El. 6384 ▲

GREENWATER VALLEY

N

Sea Level

To Trona

Gold Hill
El. 5492 ▲

Galena Canyon

✕

West Side Rd.

Sea Level

Mormon Point

PARK

0 1 2 3 4 5 miles

To Shoshone

Warm Spring Canyon Rd.

Striped Butte ▲
El. 4773

**SOUTHERN DEATH VALLEY
REGION**

■ Featured Destinations —— Unpaved Roads
▮ ▮ ▮ Death Valley Nat'l Park - - - 4WD/High Clearance

Warning: This map is very general and does not show all unpaved roads. If you plan to travel to any destination presented in this book, please carry a detailed road map from AAA, Benchmark, or other source and use it in conjunction with the directions provided in the text. Always check on latest road conditons in advance of your trip.

Split Cinder Cone ▲

Ashford Mill ■

Shoreline Butte
El. 648

WINGATE WASH

Jubilee Pass Rd.

Salsberry Pass
El. 3315 ✕

178

IBEX
WILDERNESS
AREA

To Shoshone

To Trona

Amargosa River

To Trona

Harmony Borax Works

Of all the images associated with Death Valley, none is more enduring than the 20-mule-team wagons hauling borax across the burning Mojave. The massive wagons only operated from about 1884 to 1888, but they have become the icon of a place and an era. It all began at the Harmony Borax Works.

Little remains today of the famed borax works; a few crumbling adobe walls of the processing plant, a pair of haul wagons, and acres of worked-over salt pan are all that is left. This part of the Death Valley salt pan became known as Cottonball Basin because of the high concentration of fibrous borate nodules, dubbed "cottonballs," found on the playa. William Tell Coleman furnished the capital to open the operation in 1882. Chinese men provided most of the labor. They gathered up the cottonballs with shovels, loaded them into handcarts or wagons, and brought them to the plant where the borates were then dissolved in solution, boiled, and purified. Every four days, the finished product was transported in immense wagons to the railroad at Mojave, 165 miles away. The Mojave-bound borax wagons were hitched in pairs and towed a 500-gallon water tank—a combined weight exceeding 30 tons—that were pulled by 18 mules and 2 draft horses.

By 1888 the borax market was

Adobe ruins, a massive boiler, and settling tanks are among the remnants at Harmony Borax Works. A borax-hauling wagon and interpretive signs round out the historic site. CHUCK PLACE

glutted and Coleman's far-flung financial empire was reeling from losses in raisin holdings. Coleman tried to sell Harmony Borax Works but uncertainties about the price of borax scared away potential buyers. Coleman's creditors demanded payment, forcing the collapse of his business enterprises. He declared bankruptcy and Harmony Borax Works was shut down, never to operate again. There are still piles of cottonball borates out on the playa, arranged in rows, ready for transport to the processing vats.

Directions: Harmony Borax Works is located on the west side of Highway 190, 1.5 miles north of the Furnace Creek Visitor Center. A short interpretive walk leads to the ruins and one of the haul wagons. A 2.5-mile-long (one-way) cross-country route heads west from the borax works, leading across the salt pan to the abandoned cottonball piles. Carry plenty of water and sun protection, since this can be a long, hot walk.

Furnace Creek

Furnace Creek Wash slices through the Amargosa Range, forming a natural corridor that separates the Black Mountains from the Funeral Mountains. Many of the lost emigrants of 1849 traveled down this wash en route to their fateful rendezvous with Death Valley. Just before reaching the valley floor they rested near the mouth of Furnace Creek, where they found springs and a small creek. This oasis is now known as Travertine Springs, and much of the three million gallons of fresh water it issues each day is piped into the Furnace Creek Ranch complex—the center of human activity in Death Valley National Park.

For more than 125 years, the waters of Travertine Spring and nearby Texas Spring have supplied ranches, farms, and resorts in Death Valley. The valley's first homesteader, Andrew Jackson Laswell, grew alfalfa hay here in 1874-75 and sold it for livestock feed in the mining camps of the Panamint Range. Pacific Borax Company established Greenland Ranch northwest of the mouth of Furnace Creek Wash in 1883 and brought water to the site through a mile-long irrigation ditch. The ranch provided meat, fruits, and vegetables for the crews of Harmony Borax Works.

As mining ebbed and tourism grew, the borax company turned the ranch into a resort. Known today as Furnace Creek Ranch, the facilities in this private inholding include modern motel accommodations, several restaurants, a gift shop, grocery store, full-service gas station, and even the famous below-sea-level 18-hole golf course. Three Park Service campgrounds are located nearby. A historic date grove is maintained on the north

The Furnace Creek Visitor Center, which also includes the Death Valley Museum, is an essential stop for the Death Valley traveler. Visitors can view exhibits in the museum, join ranger-led interpretive talks, get information from park staff, and browse in the excellent bookstore. MARK DOLYAK

The private inholdings at Furnace Creek include lodging, restaurants, a gift shop, a below-sea-level golf course, and a historic date grove. MARK DOLYAK

side of the ranch. With its flowing irrigation ditches and welcome shade, it makes an inviting picnic spot. You'll find delicious date bread for sale at stands and shops at the ranch.

The Borax Museum is located near the entrance to Furnace Creek Ranch. The museum building is a historic structure that was once part of the borax mining operations in nearby Twenty Mule Team Canyon. Exhibits here feature old mining photographs and an amazing mineral collection from the Death Valley region. Antique tools and mining equipment, including several well-preserved wagons and a locomotive, are found on the grounds and in several old barns outside the museum.

The national park's Furnace Creek Visitor Center, located about a quarter mile north of the date grove, is an essential Death Valley stop. Park staff answer questions and provide information; interpretive talks and shows take place on the shady patio and in the auditorium; museum exhibits stimulate curiosity about the area; and a bookstore, run by the Death Valley Natural History Association, carries a fine selection of regional books. The visitor center is open from 8 a.m. to 6 p.m. year-round.

Furnace Creek Inn overlooks Death Valley from a hill about 1 mile southeast of the ranch. This luxury hotel was first opened in 1927 by the Pacific Coast Borax Company as part of its effort to replace diminishing mining revenues with earnings from tourism. Its simple, elegant buildings were constructed from locally acquired materials, such as adobe bricks made by Shoshone and Paiute workers, travertine rock mined from a nearby spring, and wooden beams scavenged from a railroad trestle. Open to the public, the beautiful grounds contain a palm-lined stream that cascades down a grassy terraced hillside into rocky pools. Such verdant gardens seem nothing short of a miracle given their location in one of the driest spots on earth.

The inn was built near the village site of Tumbisha, where Shoshone, Kawaiisu, and Southern Paiute people once lived together and made up the largest, most "cosmopolitan" of all the native settlements in the Death Valley region. Today, a small Timbisha Shoshone community is located adjacent to Furnace Creek Ranch. As a result of landmark legislation approved by the U.S. Congress in November 2000, the National Park Service transferred 300 acres at Furnace Creek to the Timbisha, creating the first officially recognized tribal lands within an existing national park. The tribe, whose members had not been able to own land in Death Valley since the park's establishment in 1933, will now be able to build 50 houses, a government complex, an inn, and a cultural center.

Directions: The Furnace Creek Visitor Center is located on the west side of Highway 190, 1 mile north of its junction with Highway 178 (Badwater Road) or 17.3 miles south of its junction with Scotty's Castle Road. For information, call (760) 786-3200. The Furnace Creek Ranch complex and Borax Museum are 0.3 mile south of the Visitor Center. The entrance to Furnace Creek Inn is 1 mile south of the Visitor Center on the east side of Highway 190 near its junction with Highway 178.

As Pacific Coast Borax started to phase out its mining operations in the region during the 1920s, it also began to develop facilities for tourism, including the Furnace Creek Inn, which has offered luxury accommodations in Death Valley since its opening in 1927.
DENNIS FLAHERTY

The sublime view from Zabriskie Point takes in ancient, tilted lakebed sediments and the distinctive promontory of Manly Beacon (upper right). FRED HIRSCHMANN

Zabriskie Point

Zabriskie Point overlooks one of the most barren and yet beautiful landscapes in Death Valley National Park. A short, steep trail from a parking area leads to this famed viewpoint, which was named in honor of Christian Breevort Zabriskie, longtime employee of Pacific Coast Borax. The vista sweeps over miles of wildly eroded badlands, across the Death Valley salt pan, and up to the sub-alpine crest of the Panamint Range.

The Furnace Creek Formation consists of soft rock layers that were first deposited as volcanic ash, mud, silt, sand, and gravel on the floor of ancient Furnace Creek Lake. The lake-bottom sediments were later uplifted and exposed to the elements. They continue to be sculpted, primarily by flowing water. Runoff from cloudbursts erodes the mudstones and carves winding gullies through the hills. Some of the ridges to the south are capped with a dark layer of basalt from eruptions that occurred about three million years ago; this harder volcanic rock resists the forces of erosion more than the deposits at Zabriskie Point.

Manly Beacon, a distinctive butte that protrudes from the badlands west of Zabriskie Point, is named for pioneer William Lewis Manly, who helped guide a party of starving emigrants out of Death Valley in 1849. Early morning light accentuates the pastel layers of Manly Beacon, which range from mauve and dusty pink to milk-chocolate brown. Bands of sediment seem to flow off the peak and roll across adjacent ridges. The colors impart an unexpected softness to the often harsh appearance of the badlands.

Directions: *The turnoff to Zabriskie Point is 4.5 miles southeast of the Furnace Creek Visitor Center on Highway 190. A short gravel road leads to the parking area.*

The broad wash of Gower Gulch cuts through the eroded mudstones below Zabriskie Point and is a popular route for day hikes. JIM STIMSON

Top: Twenty Mule Team Canyon is easily accessible along a graded dirt road that winds through the multi-hued Furnace Creek Formation. STEPHEN INGRAM
Bottom: Rich borate deposits in Twenty Mule Team Canyon were never fully exploited, especially after Pacific Coast Borax developed more accessible mining sites. JOHN DITTLI

Twenty Mule Team Canyon

Death Valley promoters developed the drive through the mudstone badlands of Twenty Mule Team Canyon in the late 1920s. They also came up with its imaginative name. Although this was the site of limited borax mining activity between 1910 and 1920, the famous 20-mule teams probably never set foot here. The canyon's authentic claim to fame, however, should be Monte Blanco, a hill of almost pure borate.

Monte Blanco comes into view after you have driven about 1 mile into Twenty Mule Team Canyon. This golden hill contains about three million tons of ore. Although some mining occurred here, this rich borate deposit was never fully exploited because of its remote location. At one

time a small settlement existed in the canyon. Located about 2 miles from the start of the road, just before it leaves the wash and turns into the hills, is the site of the mining camp of Monte Blanco. From here you can continue up the canyon on foot, following an old road that takes you toward Monte Blanco Hill and into an area of colorful badlands.

The Furnace Creek Formation exposed in Twenty Mule Team Canyon contains at least 26 different borate minerals. With a strong flashlight, you can peer into old prospect holes and see sparkling examples of these minerals. Do not enter the tunnels, however, because their roofs are extremely soft and unstable. A good time to visit the canyon is during the late afternoon, when the low-angle light brings out the warm yellow tones of the mudstone hills.

Directions: The one-way, 2.7-mile-long road through Twenty Mule Team Canyon begins 5.5 miles southeast of the Furnace Creek Visitor Center on Highway 190 and reenters the highway 1.6 miles to the east. The dirt road is fine for 2-wheel-drive vehicles, but trailers and large motor homes are not permitted due to narrow passages, tight turns, and steep hills.

Dante's View

In the 1920s, when Death Valley's boosters wanted to find a scenic viewpoint that would attract tourists, they asked old-timer Charles Brown of Shoshone if he knew of a good spot. "I don't pay much attention to scenery," he said, "but I know one view that made me stop and look." He took them to a cliff that rose over a mile directly above Badwater. Across the valley, Telescope Peak jutted two vertical miles above the salt pan. Snow-capped peaks of the Sierra Nevada peered over the shoulder of the Panamints. To the north, east, and south, range after range of mountains crested like breaking waves as far as the eye could see. Sufficiently impressed, the promoters rounded up the funding and had Brown build a road to the spot. In keeping with Death Valley's devilish theme for place names, the point was christened Dante's View.

To a first-time desert visitor, Dante's View presents an overwhelming spectacle. It is hard to know what to make of such an austere landscape. Others certainly have faced this challenge; among them were Edna Brush Perkins and Charlotte Hannahs Jordan, who may have been Death Valley's first tourists. Wanting to visit the emptiest spot on the map, the two Easterners convinced a local sheriff to take them into the valley by wagon in 1921. Upon seeing the salt pan, Brush wrote, "The strange can only be made comprehensible by comparison to the familiar, and perhaps the best comparison is to a frozen mountain-lake. . . . Death Valley is level like a lake, it is bare like a lake, cloud-shadows drift over it as over a lake, the precipitous mountains seem to jut into it as mountains jut into a lake, but there the comparison ends and its own unfamiliar beauties begin."

The "unfamiliar beauties" of Dante's View are best appreciated in

Dante's View is perched atop the steep western escarpment of the Black Mountains and offers an incomparable vista of the Death Valley basin and its many adjacent ranges. FRANK BALTHIS

early morning or late afternoon light and are especially wonderful on partly overcast days when sun rays peek through the clouds to highlight the rugged topography in luminous strips. Cars traveling below on Badwater Road seem surprisingly tiny, dwarfed by the immensity of the valley's alluvial fans. A footpath heads up the ridge to the right of the parking area, leading to a spot where clear days offer a sweeping panorama of basin and range country. On the western horizon is the Sierra Nevada crest near 14,495-foot-high Mt. Whitney, highest peak in the contiguous 48 states; the salt pan west of Badwater below is the lowest place in the nation; to the southeast are Nevada's Spring Mountains and 11,918-foot Charleston Peak.

Easy access, a gentle grade for walking, and colorful narrows attract many hikers to scenic Golden Canyon. MARC SOLOMON

Directions: The 13.2-mile-long paved road to Dante's View turns off Highway 190 nearly 12 miles east of the Furnace Creek Visitor Center. Due to extremely steep, tight turns near the top, vehicles of 25 feet or longer are prohibited from driving on this road beyond a parking area located 7.4 miles from Highway 190. If you are pulling a trailer, you must drop it at this parking lot before proceeding to the end of the road at Dante's View.

Golden Canyon and Gower Gulch

The adjacent drainages of Golden Canyon and Gower Gulch cut through the multicolored mudstones and volcanic ash deposits of the Furnace Creek Formation. Although neighbors, the two canyons are quite different in character. Golden Canyon once contained a paved road, but now features a popular interpretive nature trail. Gower Gulch is less visited and shows the effects of more frequent scouring by flash floods. A five-mile-long loop trail covers sections of each canyon, allowing you to investigate both in one trip. Most hikers begin the loop by climbing up Golden Canyon and returning down Gower Gulch. The trip can also be made in reverse, or shortened to a hike into the lower reaches of Golden Canyon.

Interpretive pamphlets are usually available at the start of the hike and

lend interest to the first mile of the trail, but this lower part of the canyon is not the most scenic. The route splits just beyond the last trail marker. The left fork is a side trail that leads to the base of Red Cathedral, a butte with deeply fluted cliffs that contrast dramatically with the surrounding yellow mudstone hills. The right fork is the main trail; it passes Manly Beacon's vertical south wall and then winds through the badlands before entering the drainage of Gower Gulch.

Gower Gulch has an open aspect at its upper end, but as you descend, the mudstone walls begin to close in. Evidence of past borax mining activity begins to show up. Pieces of weathered lumber lie scattered about, and inky black tunnels, each with a flattened terrace of tailings in front, stare out from the powdery white slopes. Below the borax workings the canyon narrows even more. Some easy scrambling is required to negotiate several small, dry waterfalls. These falls reveal beautiful polished stone mosaics, or breccias. The canyon ends at a 30-foot-high dry waterfall, but the trail bypasses it on the right and continues back to the Golden Canyon parking area.

An 8- to 10-foot-deep gully slices through the alluvial fan at the mouth of the canyon. This erosion has occurred since the early 1940s when Furnace Creek Wash was artificially diverted into Gower Gulch. With this diversion, Furnace Creek Inn has been spared extensive damage. On the way back to the parking area, look for a reddish outcrop; Native Americans made pigments from this rock for body paint and probably used it to create pictographs.

Directions: *The parking area and trailhead for Golden Canyon and Gower Gulch is 2.1 miles south of Highway 190 on Highway 178 (Badwater Road). A trail guide for Golden Canyon is usually available in the rack by the parking area. The path to Gower Gulch heads south from the parking area along the base of the hills and reaches the canyon mouth in under a mile. The trail system in the Golden Canyon area can be confusing because of the many side routes.*

Devil's Golf Course

Salt pans are usually flat, dry surfaces, but Devil's Golf Course is different. Here, near the lowest point in Death Valley, saline groundwater continually seeps to the surface, where it evaporates and deposits salt crystals. The result is the "golf course from hell," an ankle-twisting jumble of jagged, toothy ridges that sprawls across hundreds of acres.

Devil's Golf Course is thicker and a few feet higher than the rest of the surrounding salt pan. Its surface is always changing. As the salty ground-

In dry periods, this salt pan at Devil's Golf Course develops polygonal fractures; salty water seeps up through these cracks to evaporate and form ridges on the polygons' edges. FRED HIRSCHMANN

water percolates to the top, salt crystals continually build upon each other; this exerts upward pressure on the surface, causing it to buckle and fracture. Rain and wind erosion further shape this convoluted landscape, often carving the salts into sharp blades and spires. On occasion, flooding of the salt pan dissolves the sharp edges, and gives these formations the appearance of lumpy cauliflowers.

Beneath the uppermost salt crust at Devil's Golf Course are alternating layers of old lakebed sediments and salt that continue down at least another 1,500 feet. Mineral-rich waters flowed into Death Valley during several glacial periods, forming a

series of ice-age lakes, including the 600-foot-deep Lake Manly. Each of these ancient lakes eventually evaporated, leaving behind surface deposits of almost pure table salt, three to five feet thick. Today's uppermost salt pan is the product of a more recent lake, about 30 feet deep, that covered the valley floor several thousand years ago.

To get a close-up view of the salt formations, walk out about 200 feet from the parking area and sit down. All around you are craggy tongues of salt sticking up into the air or forming small natural bridges. Large cracks caused by the constant expansion of the growing salt meander in every direction. Peer inside one of the

Above: The winding, dipping loop of Artist Drive climbs a steep alluvial fan of the Black Mountains and crests at the foot of Death Valley's most vibrantly colored slopes. MARK DOLYAK
Opposite: The shallow pool at Badwater is 279 feet below sea level. MARK DOLYAK

miniature grottos formed by the salt, and you can usually see tiny, inch-long hairs of salt sticking out all over. If it is very quiet, you may even hear the movement of the salt, a tiny chorus of plinks and clunks.

Directions: *To reach Devil's Golf Course, head south from the Furnace Creek Visitor Center on Highway 190. Turn right onto Highway 178 (Badwater Road) and continue south 12 miles to the marked turnoff for Devil's Golf Course. A graded dirt road leads a short distance down the alluvial fan to the parking area.*

Artist Drive

The Artist Drive loop takes you through a multicolored landscape that continually changes with the light. The area's beautiful sedimentary rocks are most dramatic in late afternoon, when warm light imparts a glow to the western face of the Black Mountains.

Artist Drive begins at the bottom of a very steep alluvial fan. About 1.5 miles up the fan, look for a large pull-out on the right with a trail leading up a ridge. This is a good place to study the face of the Black Mountains

and appreciate the immense volume of sand, gravel, and rock that have washed down to create the alluvial fans. From this angle, it seems like as much material has come off the mountains as still remains.

Another half-mile up, the road swings north and follows the base of a steep, rocky fault scarp. Along the upper side of this scarp the Black Mountains are rising, while on the lower side Death Valley and the alluvial fan beneath you are dropping. Like most faults, the rate of movement is slow or almost imperceptible; over a 15-year period beginning in 1970, the vertical displacement here measured only one-tenth of an inch. Cataclysmic earthquakes along a fault can speed displacement considerably, however. About 2,000 years ago, an earthquake on a nearby fault created a 20-foot-high scarp in a matter of minutes.

At the same time the Black Mountains are inching slowly upwards, erosion is tearing them down. Beyond the fault scarp, the road passes through two deep water-carved chutes that reveal the cutting power of desert flash floods. You can look upstream from one of these gullies and imagine the water thundering down, bringing with it tons of rock, silt, and debris to be deposited on the alluvial fan.

About 4 miles from the start of the drive, look for the vibrant hues of

Artist's Palette. The rocks forming this "palette" are part of the 7- to 14-million-year-old Artist Drive Formation. As these rocks weather and erode, their sediments splash the hillside with an unusual array of colors, including green, purple, mustard, and orange-tan. The striking colors result from the mixing of red and yellow iron oxides with minerals found in volcanic ash.

Beyond Artist's Palette the road drops into a deep wash, whose walls provide a good cross section view of an ancient alluvial fan. Here, the layers of sand, gravel, and boulders have become cemented together over time into what geologists call a fanglomerate. As you emerge from the wash, the road climbs again to wind through an area of ancient, weathered lava flows. The drive then descends the alluvial fan, offering a fine vista of the long, rugged crest of the Panamint Range pressed against the western sky. Many desert artists have been inspired by just such a view. Their work reveals the simple beauty of this arid landscape and brings to mind the words of author Mary Austin: "The spirit of the land shapes the art that is produced there."

Directions: *The 9-mile-long Artist Drive loop begins and ends on Highway 178 (Badwater Road); trailers, motor homes, and buses are prohibited due to steep grades and tight turns. The narrow drive is one-way, with the entrance at the southern end of the loop. It begins 8.7 miles south of the junction of Highways 178 and 190. About 4.5 miles from the start of the drive, a short side road leads to the parking area for Artist's Palette; from there, a trail heads up to the wildly colored slopes.*

Badwater

At 279 feet below sea level, Badwater is nearly the lowest spot in the Western Hemisphere. Two locations on the salt pan a few miles to the west are actually about three feet lower. Still, Badwater seems low enough, especially after you notice the sign that reads "Sea Level" high on the cliff above the parking area. Even though it is below sea level, Badwater is far above the bedrock; it sits atop Death Valley's 9,000-foot-deep accumulation of sands, silts, and gravels.

Badwater also claims the distinction of being, perhaps, the hottest place in the world. A weather station endured only one year at Badwater, but during that time it recorded consistently higher temperatures than the station at nearby Furnace Creek. On the July day in 1913 that Furnace Creek recorded the western hemisphere's record of 134°F, it is believed that Badwater may have reached 140°F. Had it been official, Badwater's high would have beat the world record of 136°F established at Al Aziziyah, Libya in 1922.

The small, spring-fed pool that gives the place its name emerges along the fault zone at the base of the Black Mountains. The water, although very saline, is not poisonous. The

Directions: *Highway 178 (Badwater Road) turns off Highway 190 1.2 miles south of the Furnace Creek Visitor Center. From this junction it is 17.6 miles to the parking area at Badwater.*

West Side Road

West Side Road runs along the base of the Panamint Range, where it follows part of the historic path of the Bennett-Arcan party of lost '49ers. Later, during the 1880s, the route was traveled by the 20-mule teams of Harmony Borax Works. Although no longer used as a thoroughfare, this dirt road on the western side of Death Valley's salt pan provides access to several rugged canyons and a smattering of historic sites. Watery mirages often waver where the route crosses the salt flats—as if the land is trying to remember a wetter time. The silence can be so deep that a person may be startled to hear himself swallow.

From the west side of the valley, especially in afternoon light, the dramatic geology of the Black Mountains comes into relief. The north end of West Side Road offers good views toward the colorful rocks of the Artist Drive Formation. The Black Mountain "turtlebacks" (which derive their name from their resemblance to a turtle's carapace) are clearly visible from the middle and south stretches of the drive. These domed formations dip to the northwest near Badwater, Copper

From Badwater, paths head west toward the shimmering salt pan and provide hikers with opportunities for quiet contemplation of this immense landscape. JIM STIMSON

pool supports a surprising variety of life, including the tiny Badwater snail, which lives only here and at a few other springs in Death Valley. During wet winters, a very shallow lake that floods much of the salt pan extends to the pool. The water evaporates by summer, leaving only the Badwater pool and miles of gleaming salt pan.

Walk out on the salt pan and you are likely to see a variety of interesting textures. In some places the playa cracks into large polygons edged with salt crystals, while elsewhere it remains smooth and firm. In areas of high groundwater, thick mud may coat the surface. As you return to the parking area, look north along the steep base of the Black Mountains; the metamorphic rocks in this area are the oldest in Death Valley, dating back 1.8 billion years.

Canyon, and Mormon Point. Geologists believe the turtlebacks are hard surfaces along which softer rock has slid off as earthquake faults pull the valley apart.

As you drive south, you may want to stop at the graves of Jim Dayton and Frank "Shorty" Harris, located about 12 miles from the north end of the road. Look for the stone grave marker in a mesquite thicket on the east side of the road. In July of 1898 or 1899, Dayton, then caretaker of the Furnace Creek Ranch, started a journey to Daggett (near modern-day Barstow) for supplies. Battling illness, he made it to this spot before he perished in the heat. At his burial, his friend Frank Tilton proclaimed, "Well, Jimmie, you lived in the heat and you died in the heat, and after what you been through, I guess you ought to be comfortable in hell."

Shorty Harris, one of Death Valley's colorful prospectors, asked to be buried alongside his friend Jim. His wish was granted in 1934. Although Shorty is credited with discovering several successful ore bodies, his weakness for whiskey often got the better of him. The old desert rat never seemed to prosper much from any of his finds. When writer Mary Austin reflected on the lives of Mojave miners, she could have been describing Harris: "The sensible thing for a man to do who has found a good pocket is to buy himself into

business and keep away from the hills. The logical thing is to set out looking for another one." Shorty did just that, setting out over and over again—loving the hills more than he ever loved the gold.

About a half mile beyond the prospectors' graves are the ruins of Eagle Borax Works. Built in 1882, this poorly managed mining enterprise did not last long. All that remains is a mound of borax behind the interpretive sign. Nearby, thick rushes enclose a few spring-fed pools. About 3 miles farther south, a stone

Top: Death Valley's West Side Road follows a route used by some of the '49ers, 20-mule-team borax wagons, and local prospectors, including Shorty Harris, who was buried here. STEPHEN INGRAM
Bottom: The dark volcanic hill of Split Cinder Cone is adjacent to the West Side Road. STEPHEN INGRAM

monument marks the site of Bennett's Well. The actual well, which was only a hole dug in the sand, has disappeared. The Bennett-Arcan party of '49ers camped either here or at the springs near Eagle Borax Works while waiting to be rescued (For more information, see pages 58-59.) Imagine being one of the stranded argonauts, stuck here for 26 days with nothing much to do but listen to the lonesome sound of the wind.

The far southern end of the road—about 2 miles from its intersection with Highway 178—passes Split Cinder Cone (shown as Cinder Hill on some maps). Here, along the Death Valley fault zone, a volcanic eruption less than 300,000 years ago spewed molten basalt and gas hundreds of feet into the air. The blobs of superheated lava cooled and solidified as they fell back to the ground, turning to cinders. Most of them piled up in a cone around the erupting vent. The cone has subsequently split into two sections due to lateral movement along the fault zone. A short walk west from the road (no developed trail) takes you to the cone summit and offers a nice view of the Black Mountains, especially in late afternoon.

Directions: The 36-mile-long West Side Road is unpaved and occasionally rough, but accessible to all 2-wheel-drive vehicles. (There are also several 4-wheel-drive routes that enter canyons in the Panamint Range from the West Side Road, but they are not covered in this book.) The north end of West Side Road begins 6.1 miles south of the junction of Highways 190 and 178; the south end begins 42.2 miles south of the junction, or 30 miles northwest from the junction of Highways 178 and 127 near Shoshone. Many drivers prefer to enter from the north end, drive as far as Bennett's Well, and then return north to Highway 178 (Badwater Road) by the same route.

Ashford Mill and Shoreline Butte

Ashford Mill sits on a bluff overlooking the Amargosa River wash in the southern part of Death Valley. Concrete walls and foundations are the only remains of the building that once housed a 40-ton roller mill. For a short while in the 1910s, more than 50 men worked here and at the nearby Golden Treasure Mine, day and night. The thundering sound of the mill must have echoed off the slope of Shoreline Butte on the other side of the river—hardly the peaceful place it is today.

The Ashford brothers began developing the Golden Treasure Mine in a canyon east of the mill in about 1910 after bringing suit against the Key Gold Mining Company for defaulting on their annual assessment work. They exposed enough good-looking ore to option the mine to a self-styled Hungarian nobleman, Count Kramer, for $60,000. He in turn optioned it to an oil man from Los Angeles, Benjamin McCausland, for $105,000.

McCausland and his son further developed the mine, built the mill, and started production in February 1915. Seven months later they quit and defaulted on their purchase. The Ashford brothers again headed for court and eventually regained title to the mine and mill. Although the McCauslands had taken nearly all the high-grade ore out of the mine, the Ashford brothers persisted for another 25 years. They located a few pockets of good ore, repeatedly came close to selling the mine, and ended up back in court several more times. The whole episode was later summed up by Greenwater newspaperman Carl Glasscock, who wrote that the brothers

had managed to get "just enough gold to keep them in groceries and lawsuits for more than a third of a century."

Shoreline Butte is a volcanic hill that rises across the wash to the west of the mill. The butte was formed about 1.5 million years ago during an eruption along the Death Valley fault zone. Its tough basaltic surface is etched with ancient wave-cut terraces that formed along the shorelines of Pleistocene Lake Manly. The upper-most wave-cut bench near the top of Shoreline Butte records the lake's high point, when it was about 600 feet deep. This occurred about 10,000 to 12,000 years ago as melting glaciers in the Sierra Nevada flooded Death Valley and other low-lying basins of the Mojave. As the flooding ended and the lake dropped, wind-whipped waves cut new terraces at each descending water level. The terraces on Shoreline Butte are most visible in late afternoon.

Directions: *The signed turnout for Ashford Mill is on the west side of Highway 178, just north of Ashford Junction where the highway turns east to head over Jubilee Pass to Shoshone. It is located almost exactly half way (27 miles) between Badwater and Shoshone. The interpretive sign and viewing area for Shoreline Butte is 1.3 miles north of Ashford Mill, also on the west side of Highway 178.*

Above: Desert gold blooms in bajadas of the Black Mountains. SCOTT T. SMITH
Opposite: The bluff-top site of Ashford Mill provides a good view west to Shoreline Butte, which is etched with wave-cut terraces from ancient Lake Manly. JOHN EVARTS

Amargosa Valley and Shoshone Region

The railroad runs along the east side of Death Valley, separated from it by a range of mountains. It follows the course of the Amargosa River as it flows south through the desert. In some places the riverbed was full of water, in others it was a dry wash. Where the water is certain large mesquites and cottonwood trees grow and the mining stations, consisting of a store and one or two houses, are nearby. The mountains along the route are scarred with mines and prospect holes. At Death Valley Junction a branch road goes to the large borax mine at Ryan on the edge of the valley.

The country is very desolate. Soon after leaving Silver Lake we passed a group of big sand dunes with summits blown by the wind into beautiful sharp edges. . . . Now we passed near enough to see their impressive size and how the wind makes their beautiful outlines. When the sand is deep and fine, the wind is forever at work upon it, blowing it into dunes, changing their shapes, piling them up and tearing them down. It gradually moves them along in its prevailing direction by rolling their tops down the lee side and pushing up the windward side for a new summit. The dunes literally roll over.

—Edna Brush Perkins,
The White Heart of the Mojave, 1922

Opposite: Dune primrose and sand verbena grow at the base of the Dumont Dunes, a popular weekend destination for off-highway vehicle recreation. JOHN DITTLI

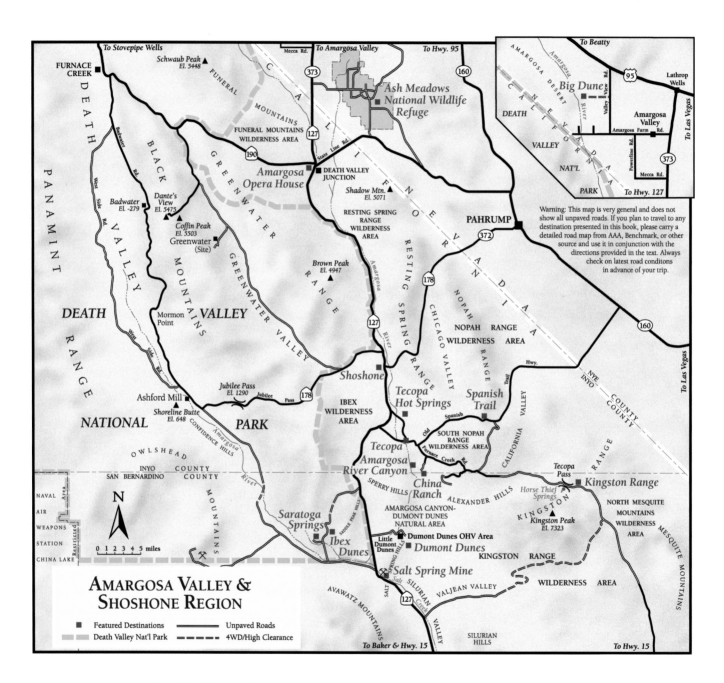

AMARGOSA VALLEY & SHOSHONE REGION

Warning: This map is very general and does not show all unpaved roads. If you plan to travel to any destination presented in this book, please carry a detailed road map from AAA, Benchmark, or other source and use it in conjunction with the directions provided in the text. Always check on latest road conditons in advance of your trip.

To Stovepipe Wells
FURNACE CREEK
Schwaub Peak El. 5448
Mecca Rd.
To Amargosa Valley
To Hwy. 95
160
373
FUNERAL MOUNTAINS
Ash Meadows National Wildlife Refuge
DEATH
FUNERAL MOUNTAINS WILDERNESS AREA
190
127
Static Line Rd.
Amargosa Opera House
DEATH VALLEY JUNCTION
Shadow Mtn. El. 5071
PAHRUMP
VALLEY
Badwater Rd.
West Side Rd.
BLACK
Dante's View El. 5475
Coffin Peak El. 5503
Greenwater (Site)
RESTING SPRING RANGE WILDERNESS AREA
372
Badwater El. -279
MOUNTAINS
GREENWATER
Brown Peak El. 4947
Amargosa River
RESTING SPRING RANGE
178
NOPAH
178
160
CALIFORNIA
NEVADA
Mormon Point
VALLEY
VALLEY
GREENWATER
NOPAH RANGE WILDERNESS AREA
RANGE
127
CHICAGO VALLEY
Hwy.
NYE COUNTY INYO
To Las Vegas
PANAMINT
West Side Rd.
Jubilee Pass El. 1290
Shoshone
Tecopa Hot Springs
Spanish Trail
Trail
DEATH
Ashford Mill
Jubilee Pass
IBEX WILDERNESS AREA
Spanish
CALIFORNIA VALLEY
RANGE
Shoreline Butte El. 648
178
Old Furnace Creek Rd.
SOUTH NOPAH RANGE WILDERNESS AREA
Tecopa Pass
Kingston Range
NATIONAL
Amargosa River
Tecopa
Horse Thief Springs
NORTH MESQUITE MOUNTAINS WILDERNESS AREA
PARK
CONFIDENCE HILLS
Amargosa River Canyon
Amargosa River
OWLSHEAD
INYO COUNTY
SAN BERNARDINO COUNTY
China Ranch
ALEXANDER HILLS
KINGSTON
Kingston Peak El. 7323
MESQUITE
SPERRY HILLS
AMARGOSA CANYON–DUMONT DUNES NATURAL AREA
KINGSTON RANGE
NAVAL
MOUNTAINS
Restricted Area
N
Saratoga Springs
SADDLE PEAK HILLS
Little Dumont Dunes
Dumont Dunes OHV Area
VALJEAN VALLEY
WILDERNESS AREA
AIR WEAPONS STATION
0 1 2 3 4 5 miles
Ibex Dunes
Dumont Dunes
SALT SPRING HILLS
Salt Creek
Salt Spring Mine
RANGE
MOUNTAINS
CHINA LAKE

AMARGOSA VALLEY & SHOSHONE REGION

■ Featured Destinations — Unpaved Roads
Death Valley Nat'l Park - - - 4WD/High Clearance

AVAWATZ MOUNTAINS
127
SILURIAN HILLS
SILURIAN VALLEY
To Baker & Hwy. 15
To Hwy. 15

Inset (upper right):
To Beatty
AMARGOSA DESERT
Amargosa River
95
Big Dune
Valley View Rd.
Lathrop Wells
DEATH
Amargosa Farm Rd.
Amargosa Valley
Powerline Rd.
Mecca Rd.
VALLEY NAT'L PARK
373
To Las Vegas
To Hwy. 127

Death Valley Junction and the Amargosa Opera House

In 1907 Pacific Coast Borax Company completed a narrow-gauge branch line that connected its Lila C. Mine and the company town of Ryan with the Tonopah & Tidewater Railroad, about seven miles to the northeast. Although the two railroads met in the Amargosa Desert, the spot was named Death Valley Junction. Most of the men working at the Lila C. lived in Ryan, but on their days off, they often visited Death Valley Junction's combination store, saloon, and brothel.

The Lila C. was played out by 1915, but the discovery of rich borax ore deposits at the head of Furnace Creek breathed new life into Death Valley Junction. The mill at Ryan was relocated to Death Valley Junction, and from 1914 until 1927 a 20-mile-long standard gauge line, the Death Valley Railroad, steadily hauled ore from the Furnace Creek mines to the junction. Although Pacific Coast Borax prospered, Death Valley Junction amounted to little more than a smattering of shacks around the mill and train depot during the early 1920s. Western writer Zane Grey's derogatory comments about the run-down town, first published in *Harper's Magazine,* spurred the borax company to build a modern Spanish-style Civic Center in 1924, complete with a movie theater called Corkill Hall. The U-shaped adobe building

also housed sleeping quarters for a crew of 200, along with a gymnasium, swimming pool, kitchen, dining hall, billiard parlor, library, barbershop, butcher shop, bakery, ice cream parlor, store, post office, company offices, and hospital—a veritable town under one roof. The new Civic Center fell into disuse just a few years later when Pacific Coast Borax shifted its mining operations from Furnace Creek to Boron. The site subsequently functioned as a hotel for Death Valley-bound visitors arriving by train. Its role as a tourist hub was short-lived, however, since the Death Valley Railroad ceased operations in 1930 as automobiles became the favored means of transportation.

The facility collected dust until 1967, when New York ballerina Marta Becket and her husband came to Death Valley Junction to have a flat tire repaired. Becket had a break in her West Coast touring schedule, so the couple decided to vacation in Death Valley. While waiting for the tire, Becket wandered across the street to the old Corkill Hall and peered through a hole in the door. In the dim light she could make out a stage and realized the building had been a theater. Suddenly the idea dawned on her that she was looking through a hole into her future. Later she wrote of the moment, "The building seemed to be saying, 'Take me. . . do something with me. . . I offer you life.'"

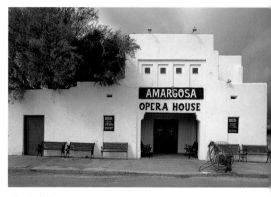

The hall housing the Amargosa Opera House was originally part of a civic center built by Pacific Coast Borax in 1924. DENNIS FLAHERTY

She and her husband answered the call just a few months later when they returned to lease the building for $45 a month.

Becket began the slow process of restoring Corkill Hall and renamed it Amargosa Opera House. She started giving dance lessons to local children and presenting concerts herself on the creaky stage. Each evening a performance was scheduled, she would dance, audience or not. One day, while cleaning out the theater after a flash flood, she got the idea of painting herself an audience. For the next four years she covered the walls with opulent gentlemen and ladies from the Renaissance. She even painted the ceiling.

These days the Opera House is rarely empty on performance nights. Becket has become internationally

Left: Bulrushes rim the waters of aptly named Crystal Reservoir at the spring-fed wetlands complex of Ash Meadows National Wildlife Refuge. STEPHEN INGRAM
Above: The refuge is home to an usually high concentration of endemic species, including the endangered Ash Meadows speckled dace.
U.S. FISH AND WILDLIFE SERVICE

known from articles in such magazines as *National Geographic* and *Life*. Although age has required her to perform fewer strenuous ballet pieces, she has augmented her program with original mime and melodramas based on local characters. The landscape beyond the walls of the theater also permeates her performance; for her closing number she dances as a dust devil whirling across the desert.

Directions: *Death Valley Junction is located at the intersection of Highways 127 and 190, about 30 miles east of the Furnace Creek Visitor Center. For information about the Amargosa Opera House and Amargosa Hotel, call (760) 852-4441.*

Ash Meadows National Wildlife Refuge

Ash Meadows has a mythical quality. Cool, sweet water seems to flow out of the very stones. At one section of the refuge, known as Point of Rocks Springs, water issues from a small cave. Listen carefully and you can hear it gurgling into the sunlight for the first time in thousands of years. This is "fossil" water that entered the groundwater system long ago, rising here and at adjacent springs in Ash Meadows to sustain a natural oasis.

More than 30 seeps and springs emerge across Ash Meadows, including 15 major springs that collectively discharge more than 15,000 gallons

per minute. The water, thought to be 2,000 to 5,000 years old, flows from vast underground reservoirs north of Las Vegas and surfaces at Ash Meadows where a fault forms a barrier, forcing it upward. It fills several pools, reservoirs, and marshes, each with its own character.

The wetlands of Ash Meadows are unusual because they are a haven for so many endangered and rare species. The wildlife refuge harbors at least 24 plants and animals that are found nowhere else in the world. This concentration of endemics is the highest for any similarly sized area in the United States; of these, four fish and one plant are currently listed as endangered. (The animals are the

Devil's Hole, Ash Meadows, and Warm Springs pupfishes, and the Ash Meadows speckled dace; the plant is the Amargosa niterwort.)

Ash Meadows has a long history of human use. The Anasazi came to the area between 850 and 1,500 years ago. In more recent times, the Ash Meadows Paiute cultivated corn, squash, beans, and sunflowers along the streams to augment their harvest of wild foods. The transition of these native people to the ways of the early white settlers was eased somewhat by intermarriage. Around 1889, Fannie Black, an Ash Meadows Paiute, married Jack Longstreet, a retired gunman, cattle rustler, and general frontiersman. Together, they homesteaded near the spring that now bears his surname. Other settlers came and continued the Paiute's tradition of farming in the area. Over the years Ash Meadows also became the site of peat and clay mining and a cattle-ranching enterprise. Ash Meadows may take its name from the white, ash-colored soils; others say its name honors the velvet ash trees that flourish near its watercourses and pools.

To a large extent, Ash Meadows owes its current protected status to the Devil's Hole pupfish. This one-inch-long fish inhabited a large inland lake here that began drying up thousands of years ago. Eventually, the only remnants of this species' habitat were the top few feet of a flooded limestone cavern whose ceiling had collapsed, exposing a narrow pool to sunlight. Known as Devil's Hole, the pool is located near the edge of the refuge in a 40-acre parcel that was added to Death Valley National Monument in 1952. Although Devil's Hole was protected as part of the national monument, it and the other spring-fed pools remained vulnerable to human impacts to the surrounding environment. Carson Slough, on the west side of the refuge, was the largest marsh in southern Nevada until it was drained and mined for peat in the 1960s. Groundwater pumping and diversion of surface water for agriculture in the 1960s and 1970s further threatened not only Devil's Hole, but the entire Ash Meadows ecosystem and its assemblage of endemic species of fish, snails, insects, and plants. There were even plans for a resort community at Ash Meadows.

A lawsuit filed by conservationists eventually resulted in a 1976 U.S. Supreme Court decision that halted excessive groundwater pumping in the area. In 1984 The Nature Conservancy purchased 12,613 acres and then sold them to the U.S. Fish and Wildlife Service to establish the Ash Meadows National Wildlife Refuge. The U.S. Fish and Wildlife Service continues to administer Ash Meadows and is working to restore damaged habitats within the refuge, which now encompasses 23,447 acres. Devil's Hole is fenced off from public entry to help protect the declining population of pupfish, but you can view Ash Meadows' pupfish at Crystal, Point of Rocks, and other springs within the refuge.

Directions: *Drive 8.7 miles north of Death Valley Junction on Highway 127 (this becomes Highway 373 in Nevada) or 14.4 miles south of Lathrop Wells on Highway 373. Turn east onto a paved road that becomes a gravel road and continue about 5.5 miles to reach the refuge's headquarters. A visitor information kiosk, restrooms, picnic ramada, and .25-mile-long boardwalk to Crystal Spring are located here. An alternate route is from State Line Road, which begins across from the Amargosa Opera House at Death Valley Junction. Head northeast on this road for about 7 miles and watch for a sign marking the refuge boundary.*

"Fossil" water that has been underground for 2,000 to 5,000 years emerges at the refuge's Point of Rocks Springs. STEPHEN INGRAM

Big Dune and Carrara

A massive mountain of sand has accumulated in the middle of the Amargosa Desert east of Death Valley. Early settlers gave the 500-foot-high mound a straightforward name: Big Dune. The dune's undulating slopes develop interesting formations known as Chinese walls because their shape resembles the Great Wall of China. Big Dune is also a "singing" dune, one of about 30 dunes around the world that emit sound when sand is pushed down the slip face. Researchers believe that cascading avalanches of sand sometimes generate an acoustical vibration, which then becomes amplified. The sound has been variously described as a booming, roaring, squeaking, singing, or rumbling noise.

Big Dune has played a varied role in the human history of the Northern Mojave. In the old days, Paiute women harvested seeds from sand bunchgrass that grows around the dune. In 1985 Big Dune was used as a backdrop for the futuristic movie *Cherry 2000,* in which convincing models of Las Vegas casinos were buried in the sand. Today it is the site of occasional off-highway vehicle use, mostly on weekends.

About a dozen miles north of Big Dune are the ruins of Carrara, a mining community that was named after the famous marble mines of Italy. The townsite of Carrara was laid out near the Tonopah & Tidewater Railroad

Big Dune in the Amargosa Desert rises nearly 500 feet and its windward side displays a classic pattern of ridges and troughs known as wind ripples. DAVID LANNER

tracks in 1913 when two marble quarries began operating on the slopes of nearby Bare Mountain. The pride of short-lived Carrara was its marble fountain, said to be the only one in Nevada. This town centerpiece—18 feet across and 3 feet deep—shot up a 6-foot-high column of water. Nothing remains of Carrara today except foundations. Boulders of raw marble are scattered in the brush; some still show their grooved quarry lines. Although the marble was beautiful, it turned out to be too fractured for use in anything larger than tombstones. The town went the way of so many mining camps, deserted for good soon after the quarries closed in 1917.

Directions: To reach Big Dune from the north, turn off Highway 95 onto Valley View Road, which intersects the highway 8.3 miles northwest of Lathrop Wells, or 21 miles south of Beatty. Proceed 2.1 miles south on Valley View Road to an unsigned dirt road on the right and follow it west 1.3 miles to an off-highway vehicle staging area; beyond this point it is too sandy for 2-wheel-drive vehicles. From here it is a short walk to the base of Big Dune through dense stands of creosote bush. From the south, drive about 18.2 miles north of Death Valley Junction along Highway 127/373 and turn left (west) onto Amargosa Farm Road. Proceed 7 miles to Valley View Road, turn right (north), and continue 5.4 miles to the unsigned dune access described above.

The townsite of Carrara is located just east of Highway 95 on a dirt road that turns off the highway about 20.7 miles northwest of Lathrop Wells, or 8.3 miles south of the center of Beatty.

Shoshone

The little town of Shoshone began its life in 1907 as a stop for the Tonopah & Tidewater Railroad. Mining and tourism have been its mainstay ever since. Early residents—mostly miners—had to be resourceful about housing because of a shortage of lumber. In several places near Shoshone miners built dugouts into the area's soft sedimentary hills. Others created housing by salvaging buildings from nearby mining camps that had gone bust. One of the salvagers, old-timer "Dad" Fairbanks, moved what was left of the copper town of Greenwater to Shoshone in 1909. In 1925-26, he and his son-in-law, Charlie Brown, enlarged their growing hotel business with scavenged buildings. Tourism was beginning to pick up in nearby Death Valley, and Shoshone was located along one of the main routes into the area.

The quaint old gas station that now serves as the Shoshone Museum was moved to the site in 1919. It was built in Greenwater about 1906, and when that short-lived mining camp faded, the structure was transported to Zabriskie, a stop on the Tonopah & Tidewater. After several years it

was brought to its present home. The Shoshone Museum sits on the east side of the highway in the center of town. In the evening, pretty twinkling lights decorate its unusual architecture and the old gas pumps out front. The museum grounds are crowded with mining and farming equipment. The

Top: Some of Shoshone's first miners and settlers made homes by excavating dugouts in nearby cliffs. STEPHEN INGRAM
Bottom: The Shoshone Museum features regional-interest exhibits, books, and travel information. JOHN EVARTS

Grimshaw Lake Natural Area near Tecopa is an important wetland used by a variety of waterfowl. STEPHEN INGRAM

gas station building houses interesting exhibits, a book nook, and a gift shop with local goods. Out the back door, beyond the Amargosa River, is a beautiful view of the brightly banded Resting Spring Range—a place inhabited by bighorn sheep, wild horses and burros, golden eagles, and prairie falcons.

Directions: *Shoshone is located 27 miles south of Death Valley Junction on Highway 127 near its junction with Highway 178. It has a motel, restaurant, post office, market, and gas station—often the only such services available for miles. You can ask for directions to the miners' dugouts and other points of interest at the Shoshone Museum and Chamber of Commerce. Call (760) 852-4524.*

Ancient Lake Tecopa and Tecopa Hot Springs

The Amargosa River empties into Death Valley, but this is a fairly recent development in geologic time. Beginning more than two million years ago, the terminus for the Amargosa River was ancient Lake Tecopa. At times the water covered about 85 square miles and reached depths of 400 feet. About 160,000 years ago, or possibly earlier, the Tecopa basin was breached, perhaps in a catastrophic event that carved Amargosa Canyon. With the water drained, the soft lake-floor deposits were exposed and eroded, resulting in the badlands we see today. These largely mudstone lakebeds have been mined for nitrates and other minerals and have yielded some fossil remains of mammals. The site has also attracted geologists, who have dated the age of the lake by examining distinct ash layers in the deposits and matching them to known

volcanic eruptions from the past.

Near the lakebed's center is a surprising cluster of salt marshes and spring-fed pools. Flocks of shorebirds swirl and glide above the water surface. Ducks seem to magically appear, flying over cracked mud hills and then dropping to the pools, splashing silvery trails. These wetlands, known today as Grimshaw Lake Natural Area, are home to a number of endangered and rare species including the Amargosa vole, least Bell's vireo, and two fish: the Nevada speckled dace and Amargosa River pupfish.

Archeological records show that human settlement of the Tecopa area reaches back at least 8,000 years. When New Mexican horse traders passed through in 1830, they encountered the Southern Paiute village of Yaga near the hot springs at Tecopa. Yaga, with 70 residents, was the largest Native American village in the Death Valley region. Its farmers cultivated melons, squash, grapes, sunflowers, corn, and beans to augment their wild food harvests. Tecopa is probably derived from *Tuku-pida,* the name of the informal leader of the area's Paiutes. He lived in nearby Pahrump and became an influential negotiator with pioneer traders, settlers, and miners who made their way into the Northern Mojave.

The Resting Spring Mining District attracted more people to the Tecopa region beginning about 1875. The district's mines were largely unprofitable until 1907 when the Tonopah & Tidewater Railroad was completed and alleviated the high cost of shipping ore from this remote area. By 1928 the district's lead and silver mines had produced $4 million. Another early-day development near Tecopa was the Amargosa Borax Works, which was operated by William Coleman in 1884-88 to process borate during the summer months when it was too hot for the laborers at his Harmony Borax Works in Death Valley.

The village of Yaga, the Tecopa mines, and the Tonopah & Tidewater Railroad have all faded into the past, but Tecopa Hot Springs continues as a gathering place. The hot springs form the hub of a community of "snowbirds" who have traveled from colder climates to spend all or part of the winter at the park's campground enjoying the warm weather, the beauty

of the surrounding desert, and each other's company.

The Paiutes believed the springs had healing powers and brought their infirm to soak in the mineral-rich waters. According to some accounts, the Paiutes also wanted the healing waters to remain free and accessible to anyone who needed them. The springs are located on BLM property and have been leased to Inyo County as a public park since 1969. There are bathhouses that offer separate men's and women's wings, each with showers, changing rooms, and outdoor and indoor pools. Bathing in the hot springs is still free to all.

Directions: *Tecopa Hot Springs and the town of Tecopa are located less than 2 miles apart on Tecopa Hot Springs Road. From the north drive 5.2 miles south from Shoshone on Highway 127 to reach Tecopa Hot Springs Road; from that junction drive 2.7 miles to the county park or continue south to Tecopa. From the south, take Highway 127 to Ibex Pass and continue about 7 miles to the turnoff (right) for Old Spanish Trail Highway. Proceed 3.9 miles east to Tecopa and the junction with Tecopa Hot Springs Road. The county park is less than 2 miles north of town. Crumbling adobe walls of the Amargosa Borax Works are located on both sides of Highway 127 about 0.8 mile south of its junction with Tecopa Hot Springs Road.*

Grimshaw Lake Natural Area has

These mud hills are formed of sediments that accumulated beneath the deep waters of ancient Lake Tecopa. STEPHEN INGRAM

three main access points. 1) Drive north from the center of Tecopa on Tecopa Hot Springs Road. After 0.7 mile turn left at a BLM sign and follow the main dirt road southwest 0.1 mile to a parking area. 2) A trail leads down to the wetlands from the bottom of the campground at Tecopa Hot Springs. 3) Heading north from the county park, Tecopa Hot Springs Road drops down a hill to the bottom of the lakebed. Wetlands can be seen on either side of the highway. The Tonopah & Tidewater Railroad grade crosses the road in this section and makes a good trail for hiking south into the wetlands.

The Spanish Trail

Sun-bleached bones and the hoof prints of thousands of horses and mules once marked the Spanish Trail. Today, a solitary white monument at Emigrant Pass in the Nopah Range commemorates a segment of this largely forgotten trade route. A faint trail still winds up the rocky, black slope, curving between clumps of red-tinged barrel cactus. From the crest, the route descends down a ridge into the vast Basin and Range country to the east.

The Spanish Trail was a circuitous overland route that linked the Mexican settlements of Santa Fe and Los Angeles. The traders who established this trail headed clear up into

An obelisk marks the route of the historic Spanish Trail in the Nopah Range. STEPHEN INGRAM

Utah to avoid the warring Apache of Arizona, then turned south and west, cutting diagonally across the Mojave Desert. In 1830, when the trade route was forged, New Mexicans had a surplus of woolen goods and a dearth of livestock. Their land was fine for raising sheep, but horse and mule breeding was less successful. The coastal ranchos of Alta California, on the other hand, had the opposite problem. Horses and mules were abundant, but stocks of sheep were low. It was a trade situation made in heaven, if only the arduous four-month round trip could be made successfully.

For two decades the trail experienced regular use and was frequented by traders, thieves, and adventurers. One of the trail's most difficult and feared sections began a few miles southwest of the Nopah Range at Resting Spring (now a private ranch). From this oasis it was 80 miles to the next plentiful source of water—the Mojave River near present-day Barstow. Horse rustlers who raided California ranchos sometimes lost half their stolen herd to thirst and exhaustion along this stretch as they pushed the stock hard to escape their pursuers.

Trade along the Spanish Trail began to decline in the late 1840s. With the advent of the Mexican-American War and, later, the gold rush, the importance of this route faded. Most of the '49ers who traveled overland followed more northern

trails, and California's mushrooming population created a greater demand for locally bred livestock. Some western sections of the Spanish Trail later became part of a wagon road between Salt Lake City and San Bernardino, known as the Mormon Road. One of the last, large emigrant wagon trains to use the Spanish Trail was the Hunt party of 1849, which included the Jayhawkers who split off in search of a shortcut and became lost in the unmapped country near Death Valley.

Much of the Spanish Trail has evolved into present-day highways. The 1,200-mile-long route can still be followed across six states. Occasional monuments mark the general course, although many of the life-sustaining water holes remain in wild areas and can only be reached on foot or horseback. From these peaceful oases you can still imagine the evening camp of a Mexican caravan—the smell of coffee and *cigarritos* in the air, the tired shuffling of the horses as they rest after the long *jornada*.

Directions: *The Old Spanish Trail Monument is located on Emigrant Pass in the Nopah Range. Take Spanish Trail Highway out of Tecopa, pass the turnoff to Furnace Creek Road, and continue about 9 miles to the summit of the pass. From there, a short dirt road leads north along the ridge to a viewpoint. Walking the ridge line, you first cross the Old Mormon Road, which parallels the*

Spanish Trail. The Spanish Trail lies at the extreme north end of the ridge at the base of a steep slope and is marked by a white column. (Another stop on the Spanish Trail was located at the base of the Salt Spring Hills; see pages 188-189.)

Amargosa River Canyon

For most of its length, the Amargosa is an underground river. You could wander along its 180-mile-long drainage for days and rarely see flowing water. Originating north of Beatty, Nevada, the Amargosa flows south to a point near the Salt Spring Hills before turning northwest into Death Valley. The river ends its J-shaped course near Badwater. Only in the gorge south of Tecopa does the Amargosa run permanently on the surface. Here it has cut an 800-foot-deep canyon through the colorful Sperry Hills, creating one of the most scenic and verdant riparian corridors in the Northern Mojave.

The name Amargosa is from the Spanish word for "bitter." Although early explorers were disappointed that its waters were so mineralized, the Spanish Trail from Santa Fe to Los Angeles followed this watercourse through Amargosa River Canyon, where there was grazing for animals and a few shade trees for the travelers. The canyon later became the route of the Tonopah & Tidewater Railroad. Landslides and washouts slowed its construction, but the rail

The Northern Mojave's only desert river is the Amargosa, and where it flows through scenic Amargosa River Canyon it supports a dense cover of riparian vegetation. JIM STIMSON

line finally emerged from the canyon near present-day Tecopa in May 1907.

Although sections have been washed away, the old railroad grade offers one of the best hiking routes through Amargosa River Canyon. Near the north entrance to the canyon, beautiful red cliffs rise above a tangle of riparian growth. Thickets of willows and mesquites shelter migrating and nesting birds. A ribbon of water meanders over the flats, then cascades in a series of little falls. In some places, where the river is joined by tributary washes, it has undercut

tall bluffs at the edge of the canyon. Mesquite grows right to the edge of these crumbling terraces, forming "hanging gardens" where 15- to 20-foot-long branches dangle over the cliffs' vertical faces.

Directions: *The easiest access point to Amargosa River Canyon is located at the north end near Tecopa. Begin at the dirt road that leads south from the wide parking area between Tecopa's post office and general store. Keep to the left on this road until you reach a small parking area at 0.5 mile where you'll see the BLM sign*

Built of volcanic tuff, this 1903 assay house is near China Ranch. STEPHEN INGRAM

marking the boundary of the Amargosa River Canyon Area of Critical Environmental Concern. A trail enters the brush near the sign, climbs a low hill that offers a view of the riparian woodland, and then continues into the canyon. For a shuttle trip, you can follow this well-marked trail for about 5 miles to reach China Ranch.

Amargosa River Canyon is also accessible from the south via Dumont Dunes Road. Upon reaching the dunes, keep to the left forks until coming to the edge of the Area of Critical Environmental Concern, where the route is closed to motorized traffic. This access requires 4-wheel drive, but does enable an ambitious hiker to walk through the entire gorge if a shuttle vehicle can be arranged. The hike is about 6 to 7 miles long (one way). The middle section of the canyon is also accessible from China Ranch via guided nature walks or by special arrangement. (See pages 185-186 for more information.)

China Ranch and Willow Creek Canyon

The road to China Ranch begins on the flat, dry mesa above Tecopa and then drops abruptly into a chalky white ravine riddled with prospect holes. After a few miles, the arroyo suddenly opens into a broad canyon where a small creek threads among thick groves of willow and cottonwood. Gleaming fronds of date palms shimmer above the layers of native green, lending an exotic air to this riparian setting. The oasis is rimmed by colorful, eroded cliffs formed from ancient lakebed sediments tipped on edge.

Human history in the China Ranch area extends back about 8,000 years. The good water flowing from Willow Spring attracted Native Americans, who used the canyon as a seasonal camp. Sometime during the 1890s, the canyon was settled by a Chinese immigrant named Ah Foo (sometimes called Quon Sing) who had been employed at the nearby Amargosa Borax Works. Ah Foo developed the water source and began a small farming operation to serve local mines. His homestead was known as Chinaman's Ranch. Local legend has it that a scoundrel named R. D. Morrison ran Ah Foo off at gunpoint and filed claim to the ranch himself on April 16, 1900. Although Morrison "owned" the farm for years, people still called it China Ranch in memory of its founder.

Between 1915 and 1918 a railroad spur ran from the Tonopah & Tidewater Railroad in Amargosa River Canyon to the Gypsy Queen mine located in the ravine along the ranch entrance road. The gypsum operation experienced two tragedies during its short tenure. First, a loaded train derailed on the steep mile-long spur, killing the fireman and badly injuring the engineer. Not long after this accident, a cave-in killed two men and shut down the mine.

Sometime in the early 1920s, Alex Modine and his wife Vonola, daughter of local pioneer settlers Mr. "Dad" and

Date palms were first planted at secluded China Ranch in the 1920s. DENNIS FLAHERTY

Mrs. R. J. Fairbanks, planted the original date grove at China Ranch. The young bride wanted a tree-lined drive up to the ranch house, so they ordered date seeds through the mail. As it turned out, about half the trees she planted were pollen-producing males and half date-producing females. The Modines had grand plans for the ranch, but after their five-year-old son was burned to death in a storage shed fire, a distraught Vonola insisted that they move. Alex disagreed, but one day while he was working at the local mines, Vonola carried their furniture outside and burned down their house, settling the argument. The Modines left the ranch, but Vonola's date palms survived and the female palms eventually bore fruit.

During the ensuing years, a series of owners farmed at China Ranch, raising crops as varied as figs and alfalfa. In 1970 the ranch was purchased by the Modine's nephew and niece, Charles Brown, Jr. and Bernice Sorrells. The 218-acre ranch has remained in the family and is now run as a working date farm by Brian and Bonnie Brown. In addition to the Modine's original palms, the Browns have planted a new date grove and expanded the operation to include a gift shop that features date products, local crafts, and a cactus nursery. This place may seem like heaven on earth for date lovers, who can sit on the

Willow Creek is a tributary of the Amargosa River, and upstream from China Ranch it has cut an impressive gorge through the sedimentary mesas of the Tecopa basin. STEPHEN INGRAM

patio beneath the palms, sipping a fresh date shake and listening to the canyon wrens sing.

Between October and April, the Brown's offer guided nature walks on weekend mornings or by special arrangement. The tour follows Willow Creek to its confluence with the Amargosa River in the remote mid-section of Amargosa River Canyon. The 3-mile round-trip hike passes interesting historic sites and provides an opportunity to observe some of the 225 species of birds that visit this area. The Browns have also developed

a variety of self-guiding hikes on the ranch, ranging from easy interpretive strolls to challenging 5-mile-long trails for rock climbers.

Visitors to China Ranch may want to include a side trip to visit a nearby gorge dubbed the "Grand Canyon of the Amargosa." It is located about 3 miles upstream from China Ranch where sheer, 500-foot-high cliffs flank Willow Creek as it cuts through Bon Mesa. The remnants of a Depression-era homestead, Canyon Ranch, are located amid this highly eroded landscape dissected by slot

Isolation, rugged terrain, and unusual plants—such as this Parry's nolina in the foreground—are some of the hallmarks of the 7,000-foot-high Kingston Range. STEPHEN INGRAM

canyons. You can walk to the gorge by hiking up-canyon from China Ranch, or you can drive to a spectacular overlook on cliffs above the chasm. There is no warning sign or barrier at the edge of the cliffs, so you must use extreme caution when approaching the overlook by vehicle. Near the road-end parking and viewpoint, a steep, challenging trail—marked by a cairn—descends to the canyon. An easier route to the bottom follows an abandoned jeep road that begins on the bluff tops about

0.5 mile upstream (to your left as you face the canyon).

Directions: *To reach China Ranch from Tecopa, head east on Old Spanish Trail Highway. In about 1.5 miles turn right onto Furnace Creek Road and after 1.8 miles turn right again onto China Ranch Road. Take this road 2 miles to the hidden oasis, then follow the signs to the gift shop. Advance reservations are requested for the guided walks; call (760) 852-4415. To reach the Willow Creek canyon overlook, return to Furnace Creek Road*

and turn right. Drive 2.4 miles east on Furnace Creek Road and turn right onto the unpaved power-line road. This road heads southeast under the pole lines for about 0.4 mile before it reaches an abrupt end at the cliffs.

Kingston Range

The rugged Kingston Range emerges out of the surrounding desert basins like an island. Its main ridgeline rises above 6,000 feet in elevation for 17 miles. Kingston Peak, the highest point at 7,300 feet, even supports a small stand of white fir. Bighorn sheep frequent the Kingston's upland areas, coming down to springs along the base of the mountains to drink.

A drive over the northern end of the Kingston Range reveals a veritable botanic garden. More than 500 plant species crowd onto the steep slopes of this range, making it one of the most diverse habitats in the California desert. Three-foot-tall barrel cactus mingle with blooming rabbitbrush. Willows and cottonwoods grow near springs, while pinyon pines climb sheer slopes toward the rocky summits. On the east and south side of the range, long bajadas support Joshua tree woodlands. In addition, a number of species that are endemic to limestone and dolomitic soils—and which are unusual elsewhere in California—are fairly abundant in the Kingstons.

One of the range's most spectacular botanical offerings is Parry's nolina.

Indeed, the Kingston Range might well have been named the Nolina Range after its outstanding specimens of this showy, yucca-like plant. Edmund Jaeger, in his book *Desert Wild Flowers*, writes that the nolina "differs radically from the yucca in its narrow, more pliant, grass-like leaves, much smaller flowers, and papery, dry-winged fruits containing small, round, hard seeds. . . . Some extraordinarily fine specimens . . . are found in the Kingston Mountains . . . . The plants have very long leaves and make a spread of 12 feet. The flower stalks are a foot in diameter at the base and fully 12 feet high. What magnificent plants and what a sight by moonlight!"

The Kingston's natural diversity helped support a Southern Paiute village, Moqua, at what is now called Horse Thief Spring. Unfortunately the residents of Moqua and other villages along the Spanish Trail were heavily impacted by the traders and pioneers who traveled this route. Misunderstandings and aggressive behavior on both sides caused strife. One such episode in 1844, during John C. Frémont's second expedition through the west, gave the springs at Moqua their current name.

A small group of New Mexican horse traders was returning from Los Angeles when a group of Paiute from Moqua raided their camp at Resting Spring. The Paiutes stole many of the horses and killed all but two of the party. The survivors backtracked on the trail, encountering Frémont's expedition. After hearing their story, Frémont sent Kit Carson and Alex Godey to investigate the crime. The famous scout and his companion tracked the raiders to Moqua, where the people had already butchered several of the horses and were preparing for a feast. Carson and Godey entered the village, killed and scalped two men in retaliation, and returned victorious to the American's camp. Frémont so praised the daring deed that one member of the expedition, Charles Preuss, suspected the commander was envious. Preuss himself thought the "butchery disgusting."

Frémont's expedition apparently named the Kingston Range after the town of Kingston, New York. Perhaps the range reminded some of the group of the topography at Kingston, where Storm King Mountain juts out of the Hudson River Valley. Whatever the connection between the two locations, the name remains on one of the most remote and wild ranges in the Northern Mojave.

Directions: From Tecopa, take Old Spanish Trail Highway east 1.5 miles and turn right onto Furnace Creek Road. Follow Furnace Creek Road about 7.3 miles to where it merges with Mesquite Valley Road. Continue another 1.3 miles on Mesquite Valley Road and turn right onto Smith Talc Road, which begins on pavement and turns to gravel, finally becoming a rough, graded dirt road as it climbs 5,100-foot-high Tecopa Pass. Smith Talc Road rounds the north end of the range and swings south where it becomes Excelsior Mine Road and returns to pavement. The Kingston Range is also accessible from the southeast by taking the Cima Road exit off Interstate 15, located about 26 miles east of Baker. On the north side of the freeway Cima Road is called Kingston Road. Drive 12.3 miles north on Kingston Road to where you continue straight onto Excelsior Mine Road. (Kingston Road veers right, to the northeast.) Excelsior Mine Road continues through the Kingston Range and meets up with Smith Talc Road near Tecopa Pass. Check on road conditions in advance and remember that routes in this area are not well-signed.

Buckhorn cholla and other cacti grow on the Kingston's south-facing slopes. STEPHEN INGRAM

Dumont Dunes

A series of low sand hills, known as Little Dumont Dunes, spreads beneath the striated western face of the Salt Spring Hills. But these hummocks only hint at the stunning sight just around the corner—the enormous Dumont Dunes. Rising 500 feet above the Amargosa River, the Dumont Dunes exhibit sheer white slopes composed mostly of quartz grains that have been swept by wind from the riverbed to accumulate in a "mountain" of sand.

Edna Brush Perkins, an early tourist to the Death Valley region, described the dunes in 1921: "Soon after leaving Silver Lake we passed a group of big sand dunes with summits blown by the wind into beautiful, sharp edges. . . . The wind is forever at work upon [the sand], blowing it into dunes, changing their shapes, piling them up and tearing them down. It gradually moves them along in its prevailing direction by rolling their tops down the lee side and pushing up the windward side for a new summit. The dunes literally roll over. The artist . . . at Silver Lake called them the 'marching sands'."

Since the "marching sands" are unstable, they support little plant and animal life—one reason the BLM decided to designate the Dumont Dunes as an off-highway vehicle area. This is one of the few Northern Mojave dune systems open to this type of recreation, and it is an extremely popular site despite its remote location.

Directions: The dirt road to the Dumont Dunes begins on the east side of Highway 127, about 22 miles south of Shoshone or 4 miles north of the Harry Wade Exit Route Monument. It reaches the dunes in just over 4 miles and is subject to blowing sand drifts and occasional washouts where it crosses the bed of the Amargosa River. At times, 4-wheel drive may be needed at the river crossing.

Salt Spring Mine

The Salt Spring Hills edge the Amargosa River drainage where it makes a sweeping U-turn and drains north toward its Death Valley terminus. It was here, near the southwestern tip of the hills, that gold was first discovered in the Northern Mojave.

The Salt Spring Mine began with a serendipitous discovery of gold-bearing quartz by James S. Brown and

The towering sand hills of the Dumont Dunes represent an immense accumulation of windborne sand that was scoured from nearby deposits along the Amargosa River. JEFF GNASS

Addison Pratt, two young Mormons bound for a mission in Tahiti. Pratt and Brown had already been to the California goldfields. Brown, in fact, had been helping with the construction of Sutter's Mill in the Sierra Nevada foothills when James Marshall found the first flake of the Mother Lode in 1848. In December 1849 the two missionaries were traveling with the Hunt party following the Spanish Trail to California. Along with a few others, they rode ahead to check the condition of Salt Spring, where the wagon train planned to camp. Taking a shortcut through a saddle in the Salt Spring Hills, Pratt noticed bits of loose quartz and suggested they check it for gold. A few minutes later they found several pea-sized grains and excitedly gathered up samples of ore to show around when they reached Los Angeles. Brown and Pratt had to sail to the South Pacific, but others returned to Salt Spring with plans to develop a gold mine.

During the next 50 years, a number of individuals attempted to profitably operate the Salt Spring Mine, but none succeeded. The site's remote location, lack of fuel for boilers, and a salt-laden water supply all conspired to frustrate a series of hard-luck owners. The biggest excitement came in 1882 when mine speculators Caesar A. Luckhardt and James Madison Seymour orchestrated a stock scam. Perhaps in reference to the mine's

original Tahiti-bound discoverers, they called it the South Pacific Mining Company. Over the course of a few months, the schemers made well over a million dollars by manipulating their stock in an essentially fictitious mining venture. When the charade was over, the unprofitable mine was awarded to the superintendent and crew in place of unpaid wages.

Over the decades, miners have terraced the area with roads and dotted the slopes with tailing piles. Deep, dark vertical shafts plunge into the ground, which often has an unnerving hollow sound underfoot. Mine entrances yawn above the ruins, their gaping mouths tenuously propped open by cock-eyed timbers. Relics of the mining era litter the landscape and include remnants of an 1880s stamp mill. The stone walls of a three-room office and house constructed in 1850-52 may be the oldest standing building in the Mojave Desert. The ruins overlook an arroyo filled with rusting metal castoffs. The gentle calls of birds come from the brush that is slowly encroaching on this wreckage.

The riparian corridor of Salt Creek lies a short distance southwest of the mine and is part of the BLM's Salt Creek Hills Area of Critical Environmental Concern (ACEC). A parking area and trailhead located alongside Highway 127 provide access for hikers. An interpretive trail

begins here and leads into this mesquite-shaded drainage that was once a haven for weary travelers along the Spanish Trail. From the creek you can continue up the gentle ascent to the mine.

Directions: Drive about 28.5 miles north of Baker or 27 miles south of Shoshone to reach the Salt Creek Hills ACEC parking area. It is about 3 miles round trip from the highway to Salt Spring Mine. For those with 4-wheel drive, an alternate entrance to the area is via a dirt road that connects with Highway 127 0.3 mile north of the Harry Wade Exit Route Monument. You can follow this 4-wheel-drive road 1 mile to the base of the mine.

The oldest building in the Northern Mojave may be this stone structure at Salt Creek Mine, site of an early gold discovery on the Spanish Trail. STEPHEN INGRAM

Above: The ponds at Saratoga Springs are visited by at least 150 species of birds and are also the only home of the Saratoga Springs pupfish. STEPHEN INGRAM
Opposite: Evening light brings out the rich tones in the sands of lovely Ibex Dunes. MARC SOLOMON

Saratoga Springs

The sounds of Saratoga Springs emerge from the ear-ringing silence that often envelops southern Death Valley. Reeds and bulrushes rustle in the breeze. Flowing water gurgles in spring-fed pools. Tiny bubbles rise from the springs to burst at the surface, sounding like the patter of raindrops. Frogs call from hidden perches among the rushes. Wrens and fly-catchers bustle in thickets rimming the waters, while coots carry on staccato conversations on open ponds. Clouds of insects buzz so loudly their collective hum can be heard from yards away. Water gives this desert a chorus of voices.

The springs issue from near the base of the Ibex Hills. They sustain more than 15 acres of wetlands, including pools that are the only home of the Saratoga Springs pupfish.

The cerulean blue male and olive-brown female pupfish feed in the pools' thick pondweed; their mouths form tiny bubbles on the cool green surface. The two-inch-long pupfish are most visible during their spring breeding season, when the males aggressively court the females and defend their tiny territories. Like other species of desert pupfish in the Northern Mojave, the Saratoga Springs pupfish were relatively abundant during wetter Pleistocene times but are now confined to small, relictual habitats. The Saratoga Springs wetlands shelters many other animals, including five rare invertebrates. At least 150 species of birds visit the area, including waterfowl that rest here during long-distance spring and fall migrations.

This oasis has long been a magnet for humans. Native Americans made seasonal hunting camps near the wetlands, and some artifacts recovered from the site date back 1,500 years. During the California gold rush, the springs were a critical watering hole on the Walker Cut-Off, which ran from the Spanish Trail to Walker Pass in the southern Sierra Nevada. Between 1883 and 1888, 20-mule-team wagons of the Amargosa Borax Works would stop here on their way to the railroad at Mojave; the stone ruins of a crude store remain from this time. In 1909 nitrate miners enlarged the ponds in anticipation of a processing plant that was never built. The Saratoga Water Company operated a bottling plant and health resort at the springs during the 1930s. Swimming was the big draw, and tourists flocked to this remote spot until gasoline rationing during World War II restricted auto travel; some rock foundations are the only remnants of the resort. Since that time, not much has happened at Saratoga Springs except for an ambitious and seemingly successful Park Service effort to eradicate tamarisk, a thirsty non-native tree that was out-competing the native marsh plants.

Directions: *Take Highway 127 to Harry Wade Exit Route Monument, which marks the turnoff for Harry Wade Road, (also shown on some maps as Saratoga Springs Road), located about 26 miles south of Shoshone, or 29.4 miles north of*

Baker. Head west on Harry Wade Road and after 5.8 miles turn north on Saratoga Springs Road. At 0.3 mile farther, you reach the boundary for Death Valley National Park and the first deep wash of the Amargosa River; you'll cross another big wash in about 2 miles. (Following rain, you may need 4-wheel drive to cross these washes). After crossing the second wash, turn left at the junction with Ibex Valley Road and continue 1.2 miles to Saratoga Springs' parking area. This last section of road can become impassable after heavy rainstorms. A hiking trail heads over a small hill to the ponds. By keeping the ponds on your left, you can walk to a good overlook near an abandoned talc mine, then complete a loop around the north and west sides of the wetlands.

Ibex Dunes

In 1901 desert naturalist John Van Dyke wrote, "The landscape that is the simplest in form and the finest in color is by all odds the most beautiful." He could well have been describing the Ibex Dunes at the base of the Saddle Peak Range. Although this dune field may be the smallest in Death Valley National Park, it is also among the loveliest.

The dunes share their unusual name with nearby hills, a valley, a mine, a spring, and two mountain passes. Early miners sometimes referred to desert bighorn sheep as "ibexes," naming them after the mountain goat native to their European homelands. Desert bighorn do not occupy the Ibex Dunes, but fringe-toed lizards, other reptiles, and insects are common.

The Ibex Dunes cover about 2 square miles and rise more than 160 feet above the desert floor. Rocks and shrubs are scattered among the lower dunes, creating abstract still-life arrangements against the rippled sand. In the late-afternoon sun, the upper dunes often take on a beautiful coral glow, which makes them appear to float above their rocky surroundings. Since no roads approach these dunes, they retain a quiet, remote atmosphere where even the sound of a scurrying lizard stands out against the prevailing silence.

Directions: *To reach the Ibex Dunes, begin by following the directions for Saratoga Springs (page 190). After crossing the Amargosa River wash, bear right at the first junction (left goes to Saratoga Springs) and head north on Ibex Valley Road for about 1 mile. Park along the road and hike about 1.5 miles east to the dunes, which are visible. A 2-wheel-drive vehicle can travel to this dune parking area, but if you plan to travel more than a mile farther north on Ibex Valley Road, 4-wheel drive is necessary.*

Visitor Resources in the Northern Mojave

PUBLIC AGENCIES

BLM/Barstow Field Office
2601 Barstow Road
Barstow, CA 92311
(760) 252-6000
www.ca.blm.gov

BLM/Bishop Field Office
351 Pacu Lane, Suite 100
Bishop, CA 93514
(760) 872-4881
www.ca.blm.gov

BLM/Ridgecrest Resource Area
300 South Richmond Road
Ridgecrest, CA 93555
(760) 384-5400
www.ca.blm.gov

BLM/Tonopah Field Station
1553 South Main Street
P.O. Box 911
Tonopah, CA 89049-0911
(775) 482-7800
www.nv.blm.gov

Death Valley National Park
P.O. Box 579
Death Valley, CA 92328
(760) 786-3200
www.nps.gov/deva/

Death Valley National Park Beatty Information Center
307 Main Street
Beatty, NV 89003
(775) 553-2200

California State Parks—Mojave Sector
43779 15th Street West
Lancaster, CA 93534
(661) 942-0662
www.calparksmojave.com

U.S. Fish and Wildlife Service Ash Meadows National Wildlife Refuge
HCR 70, Box 610Z
610 Spring Meadows Drive
Amargosa Valley, NV 89020
(775) 372-5435
http://desertcomplex.fws.gov/
ashmeadows

MUSEUMS AND VISITORS CENTERS

Borax Museum
Located on the grounds of
The Furnace Creek Ranch
Highway 190 South
Death Valley, CA 92328

Eastern California Museum
155 North Grant Street
P.O. Box 206
Independence, CA 93526
(760) 878-0258

Eastern Sierra InterAgency Visitors Center
Highways 136 & 395
Lone Pine, CA 93545
(760) 876-6222

Furnace Creek Visitor Center
Highway 190
Death Valley National Park
Death Valley, CA 92328
(760) 786-3200

Jawbone Station (BLM)
28111 Jawbone Canyon Road
P.O. Box 1902
Cantil, CA 93519
(760) 373-1146
www.jawbone.info

Maturango Museum
100 E. Las Flores Avenue
Ridgecrest, CA 93555
(760) 375-6900
www.maturango.org

Old Guest House Museum
13193 Main Street
Trona, CA 93592
(760) 372-4800

Randsburg Desert Museum
P.O. Box 307
Randsburg, CA 93544
(760) 374-2111

Red Rock Canyon State Park Visitor Center
Abbot Drive and Highway 14
Cantil, CA 93519

Scotty's Castle & Gas House Museum
(760) 786-2392

Shoshone Museum
Highway 127
P.O. Box 38
Shoshone, CA 92384
(760) 852-4414

REGIONAL HISTORICAL AND INTERPRETIVE ASSOCIATIONS

Death Valley Natural History Association
P.O. Box 188
Death Valley, CA 92328
(760) 786-2146

Death Valley 49ers Inc.
P.O. Box 338
Death Valley, CA 92328
www.deathvalley49ers.org

Desert Tortoise Natural Area
c/o Desert Tortoise Preserve Committee
4067 Mission Inn Avenue
Riverside, CA 92501
(909) 683-3872
www.tortoise-tracks.org

Eastern Sierra Interpretive Association
190 East Yaney Street
Bishop, CA 93514
(760) 873-2411

Historical Society of the Upper Mojave Desert
P.O. Box 2001
Ridgecrest, CA 93556-2001
(760) 375-8456
www.maturango.org/hist.html

Red Rock Canyon Interpretive Association
P.O. Box 848
Ridgecrest, CA 93556

Searles Valley Historical Society
P.O. Box 630
Trona, CA 93592-0630
(760) 372-4800
www1.iwvisp.com/svhs

NORTHERN MOJAVE LODGING INFORMATION

Beatty Chamber of Commerce
P.O. Box 956
119 E. Main
Beatty, NV 89003
(775) 553-2424
www.governet.net/nv/as/bea

Death Valley Chamber of Commerce
Highway 127
Shosone, CA 92384
(760) 852-4524
www.deathvalleychamber.org

Furnace Creek Inn/Furnace Creek Ranch
Highway 190 South
P.O. Box 1
Death Valley, CA 92328
(760) 786-2345
www.furnacecreekresort.com

Panamint Springs Resort
40440 Highway 190
P.O. Box 395
Ridgecrest, CA 93556
(775) 482-7680
www.deathvalley.com

Ridgecrest Area Visitors Bureau
139 Balsam Street
Ridgecrest, CA 93555
(800) 847-4830
www.visitdeserts.com

Stove Pipe Wells Village
Highway 190
Death Valley, CA 92328
(760) 786-2387

DEATH VALLEY NATIONAL PARK CAMPGROUNDS

Furnace Creek Campground reservations: (800) 365-2267

All others available on a first come, first served basis.

Selected References

Austin, Mary. *The Land of Little Rain.* Albuquerque: University of New Mexico Press, 1976. (Reprint of 1903 edition.)

Baldwin, Bruce G, et al, editors. *The Jepson Desert Manual, Vascular Plants of Southeastern California.* Berkeley: University of California Press, 2002.

Barbour, Michael, Bruce M. Pavlik, Frank Drysdale, and Susan Lindstrom. *California's Changing Landscapes: Diversity and Conservation of California Vegetation.* Sacramento: California Native Plant Society, 1993.

Barras, Judy. *Their Places Shall Know Them No More.* Tehachapi, CA: Judy and Bud Barras, 1984.

Becket, Marta. *Marta Becket: A Theatrical Portrait Before The Amargosa Opera House.* Death Valley Junction, CA: Marta Becket, date n/a.

Bessken, Donna. *Sand Dunes Story.* Death Valley, CA: Death Valley Natural History Association, date n/a.

Bowers, Janice E. *Flowers and Shrubs of the Mojave Desert.* Tuscon, AZ: Southwest Parks and Monuments Association, 1999.

Brandt, Roger G. *Titus Canyon Road Guide: A Tour Through Time.* Death Valley, CA: Death Valley Natural History Association, 1992.

Brown, Brian. *China Ranch: A Brief History.* Tecopa, CA: Brian Brown, date n/a.

Bryan, T. Scott, and Betty Tucker-Bryan. *The Explorer's Guide to Death Valley National Park.* Niwot, CO: University Press of Colorado, 1995.

Bureau of Land Management. *BLM Wilderness Areas: National Parks and Preserve.* Washington D.C.: U.S. Department of the Interior, 1994.

Burley, Virginia. *Salt Creek Nature Trail.* Death Valley, CA: Death Valley Natural History Association, 1978.

Chalfant, W. A., *The Story of Inyo.* Bishop, CA: Chalfant Press, 1922.

Cohenn, Michael P. *A Garden of Bristlecones: Tales of Change in the Great Basin.* Reno: University of Nevada Press, 1998.

Collier, Michael. *An Introduction to the Geology of Death Valley.* Death Valley, CA: Death Valley Natural History Association, 1990.

Cornett, James W. *The Joshua Tree. Palm Springs Desert Museum Natural Science Publication 1-91.* Palm Springs, CA: Palm Springs Desert Museum, date n/a.

Cornett, James W. *Wildlife of the North American Deserts.* Palm Springs, CA: Nature Trails Press, 1987.

Dawson, E. Yale. *Cacti of California.* Berkeley: University of California Press, 1982.

Death Valley Natural History Association. *Badwater: Self-Guiding Auto Tour.* Death Valley, CA: Death Valley Natural History Association, 1968.

Decker, Barbara, and Robert Decker. *Road Guide to Death Valley.* Mariposa, CA: Double Decker Press, 1989.

DeDecker, Mary. *Flora of the Northern Mojave Desert, California.* Sacramento: California Native Plant Society, 1984.

DeDecker, Mary. *White Smith's Fabulous Salt Tram.* Death Valley, CA: The Death Valley '49ers, Inc., 1993.

Digonnet, Michel. *Hiking Death Valley: A Guide to its Natural Wonders and Mining Past.* Palo Alto, CA: Michel Digonnet, 1997.

Dyke, John C. *The Desert.* Salt Lake City: Peregrine Smith, 1980. (Reprint of 1901 edition.)

Eriksen, Clyde and Denton Belk. *Fairy Shrimps of California's Puddles, Pools, and Playas.* Eureka, CA: Mad River Press, Inc., 1999.

Farquhar, Francis P. *History of the Sierra Nevada.* Berkeley: University of California Press, 1965.

Faull, Mark R., and Margaret Hangan. "The Evolution of the Bullion Road: Prosperity for Emergent Los Angeles and Connectivity to the Northern Mojave and Eastern Sierra Provinces." In proceedings of *The Millennium Conference: The Human Journey and Ancient Life in California's Deserts.* Barstow, CA: Barstow Community College, (In press).

Ferris, Roxana S. *Death Valley Wildflowers.* Death Valley, CA: Death Valley Natural History Association, 1974.

Fiero, Bill. *Geology of the Great Basin.* Reno: University of Nevada Press, 1986.

Foster, Lynne. *Adventuring in the California Desert.* San Francisco: Sierra Club Books, 1987.

Gebhardt, Chuck. *Backpacking Death Valley: A Hiker's Guide.* San Jose, CA: Chuck Gebhardt, 1985.

Graves, Kate. *Rhyolite Tour Guide: A Walking Tour of Rhyolite, Nevada.* Amargosa Valley, NV: Friends of Rhyolite, 1992.

Grayson, Donald K. *The Desert's Past: A Natural Prehistory of the Great Basin.* Washington, D.C.: Smithsonian, 1993.

Greene, Linda W., and John A. Latschar. *Historic Resource Study: A History of Mining in Death Valley National Monument.* Denver: National Park Service, 1981.

Gregory, Jennifer L., and E. Joan Baldwin, editors. *Geology of the Death Valley Region.* Santa Ana, CA: South Coast Geological Society, 1988.

Hafen, Leroy R., and Ann W. Hafen. *Old Spanish Trail: Santa Fe to Los Angeles.* Lincoln: University of Nebraska Press, 1993.

Hall, Clarence A. *Natural History of the White-Inyo Range, Eastern California.* Berkeley: University of California Press, 1991.

Hickman, James C., Editor. *The Jepson Manual: Higher Plants of California.* Berkeley: University of California, 1993.

Hildreth, Wes. *Death Valley Geology: Rocks and Faults, Fans and Salts.* Death Valley, CA: Death Valley Natural History Association, 1976.

Houghton, Samuel G. *A Trace of Desert Waters: The Great Basin Story.* Salt Lake City & Chicago: Howe Brothers, 1986.

Hubbard, Paul B. *Garlock Memories: A Tribute to East Kern County's Pioneer Citizens.* Ridgecrest, CA: Hubbard Printing, Inc., 1960.

Hunt, Charles B. *Death Valley: Geology, Ecology, Archaeology.* Berkeley: University of California Press, 1975.

Jaeger, Edmund C. *A Naturalist's Death Valley.* Death Valley, CA: The

Selected References

Death Valley '49ers, Inc., 1979.

Jaeger, Edmund C. *Desert Wild Flowers*. Stanford, CA: Stanford University Press, 1979.

Jaeger, Edmund C. *Desert Wildlife*. Stanford, CA: Stanford University Press, 1961.

Kirk, Ruth. *Exploring Death Valley*. Stanford, CA: Stanford University Press, 1956.

Lanner, Ronald M. *Trees of the Great Basin: A Natural History*. Reno: University of Nevada Press, 1987.

Larson, Peggy. *The Deserts of the Southwest*. San Francisco: Sierra Club Books, 1977.

Lawson, Cliff. *Death Valley: A Survival Guide*. Ridgecrest, CA: unpublished manuscript, 1993.

Lawson, Cliff. *Getting There Is Half The Fun!: Driving From Ridgecrest to Death Valley National Park*. Ridgecrest, CA: Maturango Museum brochure

Lawson, Cliff. *A Traveler's Guide To Death Valley National Park*. Death Valley, CA: Death Valley Natural History Association, 1996.

Leadabrand, Russ. *A Guidebook to the Mojave Desert*. Los Angeles: The Ward Richie Press, 1970.

Lingenfelter, Richard E. *Death Valley and the Amargosa: A Land of Illusion*. Berkeley: University of California Press, 1986.

McCracken, Robert D. *The Modern Pioneers of the Amargosa Valley*. Tonopah, NV: Nye County Press, 1992.

McPhee, John. *Basin and Range*. New York: Farrar-Straus-Giroux, 1981.

Mitchell, Roger. *Death Valley Jeep Trails*. Glendale, CA: La Siesta Press, 1969.

Mitchell, Roger. *Inyo Mono Jeep Trails*. Glendale, CA: La Siesta Press, 1969.

Mozingo, Hugh. *Shrubs of the Great Basin*. Reno: University of Nevada Press, 1987.

Moritsch, Barbara, and Mark Savoca. *Trail Guide to Golden Canyon*. Death Valley, CA: Death Valley Natural History Association, 1989.

Munz, Philip A. *California Desert Wildflowers*. Berkeley: University of California Press, 1962.

Murphy, Robert. *Wildrose Charcoal Kilns*. Death Valley, CA: The Death Valley '49ers, Inc., 1972.

Myrick, David. *Railroads of Nevada & Eastern California, Vol. II.* Reno: University of Nevada Press, 1991.

Newhall, Nancy, Ansel Adams, and Ruth Kirk. *Death Valley*. San Francisco: 5 Associates, 1954.

Norris, Robert M., and Robert W. Webb. *Geology of California*. New York: John Wiley & Sons, 1976.

Pendleton, Elsa and Betty Gross, editors. *Indian Wells Valley and Northern Mojave Desert Handbook*. Ridgecrest, CA: China Lake-Ridgecrest Branch of the American Association of University Women, 1996.

Perkins, Edna Brush. *The White Heart of the Mojave*. New York: Boni and Liveright, 1922.

Pracchia, Lou. *Indian Wells Stage and Freight Stops 1874 -1906*. Ridgecrest, CA: Historical Society of the Upper Mojave Desert, 1994.

Reynolds, Robert E. and Jennifer Reynolds, editors. *Death Valley, The Amargosa Route: The 1997 Mojave Desert Quaternary Research Center Field Trip*. Redlands, CA: San Bernardino County Museum Association, 1997.

Ryser, Fred A., Jr. *Birds of the Great Basin*. Reno: University of Nevada Press, 1985.

Sanborn, Sherburn R. *The Lizard-Watching Guide*. Glen Ellen, CA: Sherby Sanborn Nature Photography, 1994.

Schoenherr, Allan A. *A Natural History of California*. Berkeley: University of California Press, 1992.

Sharp, Robert P. *Geology Field Guide to Southern California*. Dubuque, IA: Kendall/Hunt Publishing Company, 1976.

Sharp, Robert P. and Allen F. Glazner. *Geology Underfoot in Death Valley and Owens Valley*. Missoula, MT: Mountain Press Publishing Company, 1997.

Starry, Roberta Martin. *Exploring the Ghost Town Desert*. Pasadena, CA: The Ward Richie Press, 1973.

Stewart, Jon M. *Mojave Desert Wildflowers: A Field Guide to High Desert Wildflowers of California, Nevada, and Arizona*. Albuquerque: Jon Mark Stewart, 1998.

Sturtevant, William C. *Handbook of North American Indians: Great Basin, Vol. 11.* Washington D.C.: Smithsonian Institution, 1986.

Trimble, Steven. *The Sagebrush Ocean: A Natural History of the Great Basin*. Reno: University of Nevada Press, 1989.

Unrau, Harlan D. *A History of the Lands Added to Death Valley National Monument by the California Desert Protection Act of 1994: Special History Study*. Death Valley, CA: United States Department of the Interior, National Park Service, 1997.

Weight, Harold, and Lucile Weight. *Rhyolite: The Ghost City of Golden Dreams*. Twentynine Palms, CA: The Calico Press, 1959.

Weight, Harold. *Greenwater: Death Valley's "Greatest Copper Camp on Earth."* Twentynine Palms, CA: The Calico Press, 1969.

Westbrook, Janet. *Day Adventures From Ridgecrest: Exploring in the Northern Mojave Desert, Death Valley, Antelope Valley, Owens Valley, and the Southern Sierra*. Ridgecrest, CA: Janet Westbrook, 1997.

Wheelock, Walt. *Gentlewomen Adventures in Death Valley*. Death Valley, CA: The Death Valley '49ers, Inc., 1986.

Winslow, Sylvia. *The Trail of a Desert Artist*. Ridgecrest, CA: Maturango Museum, 1972.

Wuerthner, George. *California's Wilderness Areas: The Complete Guide. Volume 2. The Deserts*. Engelwood, CO: Westcliffe Publishers, 1998.

Younkin, Elva, editor. *Coso Rock Art: A New Perspective*. Ridgecrest, CA: Maturango Press, 1998.

Index

Index